# Introduction

This book is specifically designed to meet the needs of those who are studying the maths of computing on the NCC Threshold and Diploma courses. It is equally suited to any students on other introductory courses who have to understand the important ways in which mathematics and data processing interrelate.

There exists a tradition that it is necessary to be "good" at maths in order to be "good" at computing. This is quite untrue (though many of the characteristics of skilled mathematicians, eg logical and analytical ability, are also of value for programmers and systems analysts).

With this book, you'll learn what you need to know and how to apply techniques – rather than mathematical theory. In an ideal world, theory and practice should go together – but for us it is more important to work on practicalities for the benefit of all, rather than on both theory and practice for the few who can cope with both.

The many worked and unworked examples I give are, in most cases, set in a computing context, since it is in such a context that you need to apply them. If you work through questions which relate to file sizes, computer word-length and down-time analysis, you have the best opportunity to see the value of what you are learning. So, don't just read! Think about what you read and try to understand the techniques.

To help you, there is an appendix at the end of the book. This gives answers to the questions and problems that appear throughout the chapters; sometimes there's an extra note or two to explain a tricky technique.

I hope very much that you like this book and find it helpful. Please respond with any comments you may have.

# Contents

# 1 Simple arithmetic

**OBJECTIVES**

When you've worked through this Chapter, you should be able to:

— add, subtract, multiply and divide
  whole numbers (integers) with signs
  fractions
  numbers with decimal fractions
  expressions that include brackets

— understand and use ratios.

**INTRODUCTION**

For success in any career, a good grasp of basic arithmetic is needed – computing is no exception. You must be able to work fast and accurately, and have confidence in your answers.

There is no need to feel under pressure to perform mental calculations – though it's a very valuable skill if you can. Being able to use a calculator is all that is required plus a feel for the accuracy of your answers.

This chapter on basic arithmetic is important, therefore; you should give some time to it, even if you feel you're good at arithmetic.

## 1.1 WORKING WITH SIGNED WHOLE NUMBERS

First, let's check how to work with whole numbers (called integers), and with their signs (+ or −).

(i) *Multiplying* When you multiply two numbers, the answer is their product. If the two numbers have the same sign, the sign of the product is +; if they differ, the product is −. (Note that + 6 and 6 are exactly the same in this context).

eg $\qquad 6 \times +3 = + 18$

$\qquad\qquad -5 \times -7 = + 35$

but $\qquad -3 \times +8 = - 24$

and $\qquad +7 \times -6 = - 42$

1

(ii) *Dividing* If you divide one number by a second, the rules are just the same as for multiplication.

eg $\qquad +36 \div 4 = + 9$

$\qquad\qquad -45 \div -3 = + 15$

$\qquad\qquad +30 \div -5 = - 6$

$\qquad\qquad -28 \div +7 = - 4$

(iii) *Adding* To add a negative number (such as $-5$) it's easier to subtract the value (ie subtract 5).

eg $\qquad 12 + -3 = 12 - 3 = 9$

$\qquad\qquad 23 + -7 = 23 - 7 = 16$

$\qquad\qquad -18 + (-5) = -18 - 5 = -23$

Note the (occasional) use of brackets to hold the $-$ (minus) and the 5 together.

(iv) *Subtracting* To subtract a negative number (eg $-4$) it's easier to add the value (ie add 4).

eg $\qquad 17 - -3 = 17 + 3 = 20$

$\qquad\qquad -26 - -4 = -26 + 4 = -22$

$\qquad\qquad 19 - -12 = 19 + 12 = 31$

$\qquad\qquad 63 - (-32) = 63 + 32 = 95$

**NOW TRY THESE...**

Work out each of the following. Note that if brackets enclose an expression which can be calculated itself, you must first work out the expression.

| | | | |
|---|---|---|---|
| (a) | $8 \times 15$ | (n) | $27 + (-6)$ |
| (b) | $-7 \times -3$ | (o) | $59 + (-32)$ |
| (c) | $-8 \times +13$ | (p) | $28 - +8$ |
| (d) | $+6 \times -17$ | (q) | $19 - +13$ |
| (e) | $18 \times (-11)$ | (r) | $22 - +17$ |
| (f) | $48 \div 4$ | (s) | $34 - (+11)$ |
| (g) | $-55 \div -11$ | (t) | $14 - (+9)$ |
| (h) | $-27 \div +3$ | (u) | $3 \times -4 \times -2$ |
| (i) | $56 \div -7$ | (v) | $-6 \times -3 \times -7$ |
| (j) | $+15 \div (-3)$ | (w) | $29 + (-3 \times -2)$ |

| | |
|---|---|
| (k)  14 + −4 | (x)  +13 − (−3 × 2) |
| (l)  23 + −11 | (y)  18 − +3 −7 |
| (m)  18 + −9 | (z)  25 + −6 + −8 |

## 1.2   CALCULATIONS IN COMPUTING

The next set of questions are to test the same skills, but arise from situations in a data processing environment.

1. A full box of printer paper contains 2000 sheets. How many sheets are there in 37 boxes?

2. A disk pack has 203 cylinders for data storage. Of these, four are for control and system information; the disk already holds three files – these take up 23, 39 and 16 cylinders respectively. How many cylinders are available for other purposes?

3. A processor operates at 8 mips (million instructions per second); how long would it take to carry out 144 million instructions?

4. A print buffer can hold 132 characters. Four fields of data occupy columns 12 to 29, 37 to 53, 68 to 80, and 93 to 108. How many columns are empty?

5. A programmer produces, on average, 156 lines of tested code a day. How many lines does he produce in six weeks, working five days a week (except for two days when he was away on a course)?

6. A file holds 12,500 records. Each record consists of seven fields; these contain respectively 23, 16, 29, 14, 6, 12 and 9 characters.

(a)  How many characters are there in the whole file?

(b)  You are to store the file on a disk with 2 megabytes −2MB− free. (1MB = 1,000,000 bytes, and 1 byte holds one character of information). How many bytes are left over? (Ignore inter-block gaps, header labels, etc).

(c)  The file header and trailer occupy a total of 178 bytes and there are 251 inter-block gaps, each of which occupies 900 bytes. How much space is left free on the disk?

## 1.3   WORKING WITH FRACTIONS

Here are a number of rules for dealing with fractional values.

(i)  When you add or subtract fractions express both with the same denominator (bottom part) before you simplify it. For instance:

$\frac{2}{3} + \frac{5}{6} = \frac{4}{6} + \frac{5}{6} = \frac{9}{6} = \frac{3}{2}$ or $1\frac{1}{2}$

Don't be tempted to write:

$\frac{2}{3} + \frac{5}{6} = \frac{7}{9}$

Both $\frac{2}{3}$ and $\frac{5}{6}$ are well over $\frac{1}{2}$, so the sum *must* be greater than 1. First, therefore, convert the fractions to have the same (common) *denominator* (bottom part). Find the smallest number into which you can divide the denominators; in the case of 3 and 6 that is 6. To convert the denominator 3 into 6 you have to double it. You must do the same to the *numerator* (the top part of a fraction): hence you double the 2, to get 4. When the denominators are the same, you can add the two numerators, 4 and 5, to get the 9. Then you divide both the numerator, 9, and the denominator, 6, by the common factor, 3, to simplify the value to $\frac{3}{2}$, the same as $1\frac{1}{2}$.

Here are some more:

$$\frac{3}{8} - \frac{5}{16} = \frac{6}{16} - \frac{5}{16} = \frac{1}{16}$$

$$\frac{7}{10} - \frac{1}{3} = \frac{21}{30} - \frac{10}{30} = \frac{11}{30}$$

$$\frac{2}{7} + \frac{1}{4} = \frac{8}{28} + \frac{7}{28} = \frac{15}{28}$$

$$\frac{1}{2} + \frac{1}{3} = \frac{3}{6} + \frac{2}{6} = \frac{5}{6}$$

$$\frac{4}{9} + \frac{1}{2} = \frac{8}{18} + \frac{9}{18} = \frac{17}{18}$$

If one or more of the fractions is a mixed number eg $2\frac{1}{2}$, $3\frac{1}{8}$, $7\frac{2}{9}$ turn it or them into *improper fractions*. (An improper fraction has a larger numerator than denominator). Thus turn $2\frac{1}{2}$ into $\frac{5}{2}$; $3\frac{1}{3}$ becomes $\frac{10}{3}$. Now, try these:

$$2\frac{1}{2} + 3\frac{1}{3} = \frac{5}{2} + \frac{10}{3} = \frac{15}{6} + \frac{20}{6}$$

$$= \frac{35}{6} = 5\frac{5}{6}$$

$$3\frac{1}{3} - 2\frac{1}{2} = \frac{10}{3} - \frac{5}{2} = \frac{20}{6} - \frac{15}{6} = \frac{5}{6}$$

(ii) When you multiply two fractions together, first divide tops and bottoms by common factors, where possible; then multiply the numerators together, and then the denominators. For instance:

$$\frac{7}{8} \times \frac{2}{21} = \frac{1}{8} \times \frac{2}{3} \text{ (dividing by 7)}$$

$$= \frac{1}{4} \times \frac{1}{3} \text{ (dividing by 2)} = \frac{1}{12}$$

$$\frac{15}{24} \times \frac{36}{55} = \frac{3}{24} \times \frac{36}{11} \text{ (dividing by 5)}$$

$$= \frac{1}{8} \times \frac{36}{11} \text{ (dividing by 3)}$$

$$= \frac{1}{2} \times \frac{9}{11} \text{ (dividing by 4)} = \frac{9}{22}$$

You *must* first express mixed numbers as improper fractions. For instance:

$$1\frac{1}{2} \times 2\frac{2}{3} = \frac{3}{2} \times \frac{8}{3}$$

$$= \frac{1}{2} \times \frac{8}{1} \text{ (dividing by 3)}$$

$$= \frac{1}{1} \times \frac{4}{1} \text{ (dividing by 2)} = 4$$

$4\frac{2}{7} \times 5\frac{1}{3} = \frac{30}{7} \times \frac{16}{3}$

$= \frac{10}{7} \times \frac{16}{1}$ (dividing by 3) $= \frac{160}{7}$

or $22\frac{6}{7}$

Do note that you *can't* calculate the product of mixed numbers correctly by multiplying the integer and fractional parts separately. $4\frac{2}{7} \times 5\frac{1}{3}$ is *not* $20\frac{2}{21}$!

(iii) When you divide one fraction by a second, leave the first fraction alone, change the division sign to a multiplication sign and invert the second fraction − then proceed as for multiplication.

eg  $\frac{8}{9} \div \frac{2}{3} = \frac{8}{9} \times \frac{3}{2}$

$= \frac{4}{9} \times \frac{3}{1}$ (dividing by 2)

$= \frac{4}{3} \times \frac{1}{1}$ (dividing by 3) $= \frac{4}{3}$ or $1\frac{1}{3}$

$2\frac{3}{4} \div 1\frac{1}{3} = \frac{11}{4} \div \frac{4}{3} = \frac{11}{4} \times \frac{3}{4}$

$= \frac{33}{16}$ or $2\frac{1}{16}$

## NOW TRY THESE ...

1. Work out each of the following: simplify each answer where you can.

(a) $\frac{3}{10} + \frac{1}{2}$  (g) $\frac{4}{9} \times \frac{3}{16}$

(b) $\frac{2}{7} \times 1\frac{1}{4}$  (h) $\frac{12}{25} \times \frac{15}{16}$

(c) $2\frac{1}{8} + 3\frac{1}{9}$  (i) $1\frac{1}{4} \times 1\frac{1}{15}$

(d) $\frac{7}{8} - \frac{1}{2}$  (j) $\frac{3}{4} \div \frac{1}{2}$

(e) $4\frac{1}{3} - 1\frac{1}{6}$  (k) $\frac{7}{10} \div 1\frac{4}{5}$

(f) $3\frac{1}{7} - 2\frac{3}{4}$  (l) $2\frac{3}{4} \div 2\frac{1}{16}$

2. A magnetic tape library contains 480 tapes; of these four-fifths are 9-track tapes and the rest are 7-track tapes. How many 7-track tapes are there?

3. Half of the 72 staff in a computer department are female and one third of the rest are single. How many married men are in the department?

4. Over a 24-hour period the main processor was down for one third of the time. Routine test jobs occupied a quarter of the time that was left, and one third of the balance involved the systems testing of a new stock control system. How many hours were left for other work?

5. An exchangeable disk pack has 11 disks, with 400 tracks on each surface. There are 13,500 characters per track. The data transfer rate is 806,000 cps (characters per second):

(i)   How many characters can the pack store? (Bear in mind that the two outermost surfaces aren't used to record data). Give your answer in MB.

ii)   One third of the pack holds data on company product lines. How many MBytes remain for other purposes?

(iii) How long will it take to transfer 4,191,200 characters?

6. Three people in a data preparation section have keyboard speeds of 8500, 9200 and 9800 characters per hour respectively. If they work together on a job which involves 123,750 characters, how long will it take them to complete it? How many characters will each person have input?

## 1.4   DECIMAL FRACTIONS

Working with decimals is just the same as when working with integers – except for placing the decimal point. When you're adding and taking away decimal numbers, line up the values so the points are in a column, like this:

write $31.76 + 2.754 + 197.2$ as:

$$
\begin{array}{r}
31.76 \\
2.754 \\
+ \quad 197.2 \\
\hline
231.714 \\
\hline
\end{array}
$$

write $51.82 - 24.975$ as:

$$
\begin{array}{r}
51.82 \\
- \quad 24.975 \\
\hline
26.845 \\
\hline
\end{array}
$$

When multiplying, count how many figures there are after the decimal point in each of the numbers and add these together; this gives the number of figures after the decimal point in the product. Then multiply the numbers together, paying no attention at all to the decimal points. After that, put the decimal point into the result. For instance: multiply 3.75 by 16.207. There will be $2 + 3 = 5$ figures after the decimal point in the answer. Multiply 375 by 16207 to get 6077625; then put in the decimal point five positions from the right-hand end – to get the answer, 60.77625.

As for division, suppose you have to divide number $A$ by a second number $B$. Move the decimal point in $B$ to the right until it becomes an integer, counting up how many places you moved it; now move the decimal point in $A$ by the same number of places to the right. Divide the new $A$ by the new $B$ in the usual way. For instance – divide 37.6 by 0.47. Move both decimal points two places to the right – now we divide 3760 by 47, to give 80, the correct answer.

**NOW TRY THESE . . .**

1. Add together 27.65, 1964.3 and 11.217.

2. Subtract 59.73 from 107.3.

3. Multiply 21.34 by 2.1.

4. Divide 3.87 by 0.3.

5. A consultant charges $53.50 an hour. What will she charge for 3.5 hours?

6. Three files require, respectively, 2.3 MB, 1.74 MB and 3.165 MB of storage space.

    (i)   What is their total requirement?

    (ii)  How much space remains on a 10 MB disk after storing these files?

7. A program has to multiply two numeric fields. Field $A$ has four digits before and two after the decimal point; field $B$ has three digits before and three after the point. How many digits will there be in the product $AB$

    (i)   Before the decimal point?

    (ii)  After the decimal point?

## 1.5 RATIOS

If we were to divide a computer department into operational and development sections, we might find seven people on the operational side and eight on the development side. We could then speak of dividing the 15 staff in the ratio 7:8. If, however, there were 14 operational and 16 development staff, the ratio remains exactly the same – though this time we might speak of dividing up a staff of 30 in the ratio 7:8. See Figure 1.1. The ratio provides a comparison between the respective sizes of the operational and development teams and, as such, (like a fraction) it ignores absolute values. (Half an apple means the same whether the apple is large or small).

We can make two fractions from the ratio above. Since $7 + 8 = 15$, we can view the '7' as holding seven shares of a total of 15. $\frac{7}{15}$ represents the operational staff as a fraction of the total. Again, the fraction would be the same whether considering seven people in 15 or 14 in 30. In the same way, $\frac{8}{15}$ can express the number of people in the development

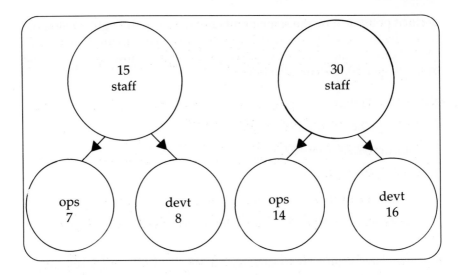

**Figure 1.1    Ratios**

team as a fraction of the total staff. Ratios therefore relate very closely to fractions.

Perhaps of the 15 staff, five are female and ten are male. The ratio of females to males is 5:10 or 1:2 (since we can divide both sides by 5); it also means that the ratio of males to females is 2:1. If 12 of the 15 staff are non-graduates and three are graduates, the ratio of graduates to non-graduates is 3:12 or 1:4.

The task of generating 500 lines of code is shared between two programmers, Farooq and Alex in the ratio 2:3. Then Farooq has to handle two "shares" out of the five (2+3) available – so contributes ⅖ of the work: ⅖ × 500 = 200 lines, against the ⅗ × 500 = 300 for Alex. Note that, as a check, 200:300 = 2:3.

Sometimes, we may refer to increasing the size of main store as in the ratio 2:1; this means a comparison between the "new" size, represented by two "shares", and the old size, represented by one "share". Hence the "new" store is twice as large as the "old". If the old were 8MB, the new will be 16MB. Likewise, increasing in the ratio 5:4 an 8MB store means the new one holds 10MB – each "share" of which the old store had four, will be worth ⁸⁄₄ or 2MB, so the new store has 5 × 2MB, 10MB.

You may meet a statement such as "The profits of the three divisions P, Q and R of a company were in the ratio 3:2:7, and totalled $24,000". Clearly this is a way of comparing three values, the profits of P, Q and R, in a single statement. Adding up the 3, the 2 and the 7 gives a total of 12 "shares" – each must be worth $²⁴,⁰⁰⁰⁄₁₂ or $2,000. Since division P gets 3 shares of the 12 its profit is 3 × $2,000, or $6,000; likewise Q gets 2 shares: 2 × $2,000 = $4,000, and R 7 × $2,000 = $14,000. Check that the three figures – $6,000, $4,000 and $14,000 – total $24,000.

**NOW TRY THESE . . .**

1. Production and Maintenance share computer time in the ratio 5:1. How many hours do Maintenance get over the course of a 5-day week of 12 hours a day?

2. Of the 120 people employed in a computer bureau, 84 are aged 21 or above. What is the ratio of those to the rest?

3. The cost of printer paper is shared between the DP department and a user department in the ratio 4:3. How much does the user department pay of a total bill of $476?

4. If the size of the programming section is increased in the ratio 5:3 from its present size of 15 staff, how many staff will it employ in the future?

5. In a large civil engineering computer department the processor time splits between commercial applications, engineering applications and system software activities in the ratio 8:6:1. How many hours are used for engineering applications in a 90-hour week?

6. If the space housing the machine room area is reduced in the ratio 5:4 because of the use of a smaller system, how big will it be if it was 95 square metres before?

# 2 Percentages and powers

## OBJECTIVES

When you've worked through this Chapter, you should be able to:

— understand percentages and their use

— understand and use positive and negative integer and fractional powers

— explain and use the concept of proportion.

## INTRODUCTION

In the last chapter we had some practice using the four rules of arithmetic, ie adding, subtracting, multiplying and dividing. We worked with whole numbers and with proper and decimal fractions. We also checked out the special form of proper fraction called ratio.

In this chapter, we look at percentages – a second special form of fraction. Then we'll turn to what should be called the fifth rule of arithmetic, raising a numer to a power, eg squaring it (Exponentiation). Lastly, we'll discuss the concept of proportion.

## 2.1   WHAT IS A PERCENTAGE?

A percentage is a special kind of fraction. Thus 7% of a number is just the same as $\frac{7}{100}$ of it. So 7% of \$500 is $\frac{7}{100} \times \$500 = \$35$, after simplifying. In general, x% of a number is the same as $\frac{x}{100}$ of it.

A common context where people meet percentages is the interest rates offered by banks, etc on their savings. If I have \$150 in a savings account that pays 8% per year interest, I will get an extra $\frac{8}{100} \times \$150 - \$12$ interest after one year, so the amount I have there goes up to \$150 + \$12, or \$162. When I leave that \$162 for a second year at the same rate of interest, I will get $\frac{8}{100} \times \$162 - \$12.96$ – interest this time; there will then be \$162 + \$12.96 or \$174.96 in my savings account. Where interest goes up each year like that, we call it *compound interest*, this is indeed how most accounts work.

However, the interest rate may be more awkward, eg 8¾% per year. You can easily deal with this by calling the rate 8.75% – using a decimal value instead of the fraction. Then 8¾% of $260 is $^{8.75}\!/_{100}$ × $260, which comes to $22.75.

Sometimes you have to give one number as a percentage of a second. In this case, first express the two as a fraction, then multiply by 100 – this gives the percentage at once. For instance, to express 12 as a percentage of 300, work out the fraction, $^{12}\!/_{300}$, and multiply by 100 – to give $^{12}\!/_{300}$ × 100, or 4%. In the same way, 60 as a percentage of 800 is $^{60}\!/_{800}$ × 100 = 7½%.

Quite often, people talk of computer hardware as an asset which depreciates; in other words, its value falls with time. Perhaps a system may depreciate at 15% per year. Thus, if the initial cost was $80,000 the depreciation in the first year will be $^{15}\!/_{100}$ × $80,000 = $12,000 – so the value of the system has fallen to $68,000.

In the documentation of a computer system you may find statements like "Growth rate such and such %". This is how the designer states by what percentage he or she expects the volume of data processed by the system to grow each year. Maybe the file size is 8,500 records at first, and is expected to grow by 4% per year. It will therefore increase by $^{4}\!/_{100}$ × 8,500, or 340 records, in the first year – to a size of 8,840 records; in the second year, it may grow by $^{4}\!/_{100}$ × 8,840 = 353.6 (354 records to the nearest whole number), making the file 9,194 records in size.

## 2.2   PERCENTAGE CHANGE

If a value changes, say, from 25 to 28, what is the percentage change?

In this case, first find the actual change, which is 28 – 25 or 3; then express this as a percentage of the original figure, 25. Thus the percentage change is $^{3}\!/_{25}$ × 100 – a 12% increase (since the value has gone up).

In just the same way, people talk about a percentage profit. In this case, express the actual profit as a percentage of what the goods cost in the first place (the cost price) – so, if you buy something for $20 and sell it for $23.50, actual profit is $3.50, and the percentage profit is $^{3.50}\!/_{20}$ × 100 = 17½%.

Problems on percentage profit are harder when the cost and selling prices relate to different quantities of goods. Here is an example:

> Floppy disks cost $6.50 for ten and retail at $0.95 each: what is the percentage profit made? It doesn't matter whether you work with the prices per disk or that of ten, as long as you are consistent; here I think it's easier to quote the price for ten in each case. So the selling price is $9.50 for ten, so the profit is $3 for ten. The percentage profit is $^{3}\!/_{6.50}$ × 100 = $^{6}\!/_{13}$ × 100 = $^{600}\!/_{13}$ = 46.2% (correct to one place of decimals).

**NOW TRY THESE...**

1. Find 12% of $750.

2. A departmental budget rises from $5,500 by 8%. What is its new value?

3. A microcomputer sells at $1,700. Then there is a price cut of 7%. What is its new selling price?

4. I invest $500 in a savings account which pays 6% per year interest. If the interest is added to the account at the end of each year with nothing drawn out from the account at any stage, how much would be in the account at the end of:

  (i)  the first year?

  (ii) the second year?

  (iii) the third year?

5. If you have $2,000 in an account which pays 9 ¼% per year interest, how much interest will you earn in the first year?

6. The price of a software package is $350 and the microcomputer costs $1,800. Give the price of the package as a percentage of the price of the micro.

7. The hardware in a large computer installation is valued at $1,300,000 and depreciates at the rate of 12% per year, based on its value at the start of the year. What is its value after:

  (i)  one year?

  (ii) two years?

8. A file takes up 65KB of disk space and is assumed to grow at 5% per year (based on its size at the start of the year). How much storage will it require after:

  (i)  one year?

  (ii) two years?

9. A programmer on $400 a week gets a rise to $430. What is the percentage rise?

10. The cost of a box of printer ribbons goes down from $16 to $13. What is the percentage decrease in price?

11. I buy floppy disks at $12 for a box of ten, and I sell them at $1.25 each. What is my percentage profit?

12. The usual price for some public domain software is $36 for any five titles. A special promotion offers them at $39 for any seven. What is the percentage reduction in price?

## 2.3  POWERFUL NUMBERS

Powers (also called indices or exponents) are quite useful as a short way to write numbers. Using powers, 7 times 7 becomes $7^2$ (read as 7 squared, or 7 to the power of 2). In this case we call 2 the index (plural "indices"); it shows how many of the 7s to multiply together.

So we can write $5 \times 5 \times 5$ as $5^3$ (read as 5 cubed, or as 5 to the power of 3); both have the same value, 125. The index in this case is 3, since there are three 5s multiplied together. Here are some more examples,

$4 \times 4 \times 4 \times 4 \times 4 = 4^5 = 1024$

$7 \times 7 \times 7 \times 7 = 7^4 = 2401$

$2 \times 2 \times 2 \times 2 \times 2 \times 2 \times 2 = 2^7 = 128$

So far, the powers have been positive whole numbers. However, a power can be zero, negative, or fractional. These are harder to understand – but here is what you need to know.

— Any value with a zero power is *always* equal to 1. So $8° = 1$, just as are $3°$ and $5°$ and $12°$.

— For a negative power, ignore the negative sign and make the expression the denominator of a fraction whose numerator is 1. Work through these examples.

$8^{-1} = \frac{1}{8}$

$4^{-3} = \frac{1}{4^3} = \frac{1}{64}$

$5^{-2} = \frac{1}{5^2} = \frac{1}{25}$

$2^{-5} = \frac{1}{2^5} = \frac{1}{32}$

— A fractional power represents a "root" –

$4^{1/2} = $ square root of 4 (which is 2) since $2^2 = 4$

$27^{1/3} = $ cube root of 27 (which is 3) since $3^3 = 27$

$32^{1/5} = $ fifth root of 32 (which is 2) since $2^5 = 32$

## NOW TRY THESE . . .

1. Rewrite each of the following using powers. In each case also work out the value.

(a)  $4 \times 4 \times 4 \times 4 \times 4$

(b)  $2 \times 2 \times 2 \times 2 \times 2 \times 2 \times 2 \times 2$

(c)  $5 \times 5 \times 5 \times 5$

(d)  $3 \times 3 \times 3 \times 3 \times 3 \times 3 \times 3$

2. What is the value of each of the following?

   (a) $6^0$

   (b) $3^{-2}$

   (c) $4^{-1}$

   (d) $8^{1/3}$

   (e) $25^{1/2}$

   (f) $1024^{1/10}$

## 2.4   GETTING THINGS IN PROPORTION

The idea of proportion follows on from ratios.

"The space taken up by data on a disk is proportional to the number of characters stored." What does that mean? It means if you double the number of characters, the data takes up twice as much room; if you have only a tenth of the characters, you need just a tenth of the space. In other words, if two measures are in proportion, any change in one gives a change of the other in the same ratio. Or, if you like, the ratio of the two measures is constant.

Another example using figures is "The electric power a micro uses is proportional to the time it's switched on." In fact, the micro being used consumes one unit of power every four hours. How much will it use in eight hours? Twice the time, twice the power – so the answer is two units. What about two hours? – half the time, half the power, giving half a unit. Here the two measures, time and power, are in proportion, so their ratio is constant.

   (i)   1 unit in 4 hours – ratio $\frac{1}{4}$

   (ii)  2 units in 8 hours – ratio $\frac{1}{4}$

   (iii) $\frac{1}{2}$ unit in 2 hours – ratio $\frac{1}{4}$

A modem transfers data at the rate of 72 KB per minute. Do you agree that data transfer is proportional to time? In other words, does it make sense to say that the modem will transfer four times as much data in four minutes? How much is that? It is $4 \times 72$ KB, or 288 KB. Work through the following:

   (i)   72 KB in 60 seconds – ratio $72/60 = 1.2$KB/sec

   (ii)  How long for 6 KB?

   $$\frac{6}{1.2} = 5$$

   So time needed is 5 s

(iii) How long for a book chapter, 30 KB?

$$\frac{30}{1.2} = 25$$

So time needed is 25 sec

(iv) How much data in 15 minutes?

15 minutes = 15 × 60 sec

So volume of data is 15 × 60 × 1.2KB = 1080KB

(just over a megabyte)

So we call two measures proportional if, for instance, doubling one doubles the other. Strictly, they are "directly" proportional.

There are, however, cases where doubling one measure causes the other to halve. We can still use modems to show this.

The modem transfers data, at 1200 B/s (bytes, or characters, per second). In fact, that's its top rate. If the phone line is poor quality, it can drop the rate to 600 B/s, or even to 300 B/s – halving each time. If the data transfer rate halves from 1200 B/s to 600 B/s, will it take twice as long to transfer a certain file?

For example, the file might be that book chapter – 30 KB. We have just seen that at 1200 B/s, the modem could transfer the chapter in 25 seconds. At half the rate, 600 B/s, the transfer would take twice as long, ie 50 sec. How long would the chapter take to go through at 300 B/s? That's half the rate again – so the time doubles again, to 100 sec (1 minute 40 seconds).

We call these two measures "inversely" proportional, rather than directly proportional. (Inverse means upside down.)

Another example is the current in a mains powered printer which is inversely proportional to the printer's resistance. One printer, with a resistance of 50 ohms, passes a current of 5 A (A is short for ampere.) How much current will a 75 ohm printer pass?

Follow my working. This time, the product is constant not the ratio.

5 A at 50 ohms – product: 5 × 50 = 250

(i) Current at 75 ohms – product: current × 75 = 250

So current is $^{250}/_{75}$ A = 3 ⅓ A (3.333. . . .A)

(ii) What about a 125 ohm printer?

Product: current × 125 = 250

So current is $^{250}/_{125}$ A = 2 A

(iii) What resistance for 1 A?

Product: resistance × 1 = 250

So resistance is $^{250}/_1$ ohm = 250 ohm

## NOW TRY THESE

1 In each case, state whether you think the measures noted are directly or inversely proportional.

   (i)   the current in a simple circuit; the voltage applied

   (ii)  disk rotation speed; rate of transfer of data to/from disk

   (iii) speed of mouse movement; speed of cursor movement

   (iv) printer speed; time to print a page

   (v)  length of printer ribbon; time before you need a new ribbon

2 My printer can produce a 66-line page of text in 22 seconds. Work out the average time it will take to output:

   (i)   one line

   (ii)  ten pages

3 Find how much the same printer will output in:

   (i)   11 minutes

   (ii)  11 minutes using double spacing

   (iii) 11 minutes using single spacing and double density (bold) type

   (iv) 1 second – in characters, assuming an average of 60 characters a line

# 3 Base numbers

**OBJECTIVES**

When you've worked through this Chapter, you should be able to:

- understand the concept of a number base
- work with place values in different bases, for integers and fractions
- convert values between decimal (denary), binary, octal and hex (adecimal) bases
- add and subtract binary integers.

**INTRODUCTION**

So far, this book has mainly concentrated on manual arithmetic. We base this arithmetic on the denary (here called "decimal") system; in this case the number base is 10. However, computers carry out operations using arithmetic based on binary numbers, ie numbers with base 2.

It is not necessary to have a previous knowledge of computer arithmetic to use a computer. On the other hand, to program and work closely with a computer, it helps to have some understanding of binary arithmetic.

## 3.1   COMMON BASES

We're all used to working with numbers in what's called the decimal (or denary) number system. This system follows our having ten fingers – indeed "digit" (which means number) comes from an ancient word for finger. People have, in the past, used systems based on other numbers – such as 60 (in ancient Mesopotamia; we all still use this number base when working with angles and time) and 20 (as with the old English way of counting in "scores" – twenties – and in France, where the word for 80 is "quatre-vingts", four twenties).

"Digital" computers, however, don't have ten "fingers". They are "two-state" devices – with a voltage or current being low (0, zero) or high (1, one), a gate being closed (0) or open (1), a photo cell with a current output (1) or not (0).

The number system of these two-state devices is called binary; two other systems closely relate to it – octal and hexadecimal ("hex" for short).

Each number system has what we call a base; this is the number of different symbols used for digits. In the case of the decimal (or denary) system, the base is ten – there are ten different symbols, the digits 0, 1, 2, etc, up to 9). To represent a value less than ten involves only one digit; larger values need two or more digits. From what I've already said about the binary system, the base must be two, with only the digits 0 and 1 available. Thus to show values of two or over requires two or more binary digits. This makes the system appear quite clumsy at first.

The octal system has eight as its base; it uses the symbols 0, 1, 2 up to 7 only. In this case we need two or more digits for values of eight and above. The hexadecimal (hex) number system has sixteen as its base; we use A, B, C, D, E, F to stand for the "digits" ten, eleven, twelve, thirteen, fourteen and fifteen. This appears rather strange at first, but is a logical way of providing the 16 "digits" needed. See Figure 3.1.

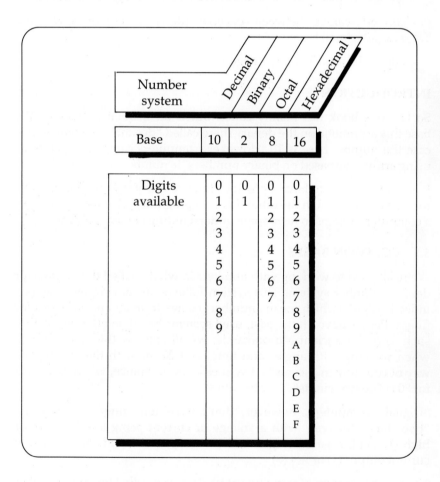

**Figure 3.1　Number base representations**

## 3.2  PLACE VALUES

So far we haven't related the bases and the digits used to the values of any particular quantities.

### 3.2.1  Decimal

What does the decimal number 258 mean? The 8 represents the number of units; since the 5 is one place left of the units column it stands for the number of tens. With ten as the base, each place further left has a value ten times greater. Thus the 2 gives the number of "ten times ten" or hundreds: so 258 has a value of 2 hundreds plus 5 tens plus 8 units.

In other words, the place values in a decimal whole number are (moving from right to left) units, tens, hundreds, thousands, tens of thousands, and so on. For this reason, the 2 in the example does not have a value one quarter of the 8 – it stands for 200 not 2 units.

Place value depends on the base used. Therefore the second place from the right stands for tens only because ten is the base; and the third place from the right stands for hundreds only because "the base times the base" is a hundred.

In the case of the four values 5, 57, 513 and 5728, the 5 has a different value each time – in the first it represents 5 units, in the second 5 tens (50), in the third 5 hundreds (500), and in the fourth 5 thousands (5000).

### 3.2.2  Binary

The base of the binary system is two. Therefore, starting from the units column (the least significant position in a whole number) and working to the left, each place value is two times greater than the one to its right. So the place values are 1, 2, 4, 8, 16, 32, 64, etc – they increase far more slowly than with decimal values which reach the order of millions at the seventh place.

Study the example shown in Figure 3.2. This shows that the binary value 110101 is the same as decimal 53. If, therefore, a micro has to store 53 in numeric form, it would be as 110101. 53 and 110101 are different ways to show the same value – one is suited to people, and the other is a form a computer can handle.

In the same way, the decimal value of 101010 would be $1 \times 32$ plus $0 \times 16$ plus $1 \times 8$ plus $0 \times 4$ plus $1 \times 2$ plus $0 \times 1$, $-32 + 8 + 2$, or 42. Check this with care, please, perhaps as in Figure 3.2. (There are more for you to try in a couple of pages.)

### 3.2.3  Octal

The octal number system uses eight as its base. So the place values moving left from the right end are 1, 8, 64, 512, 4096, and so on. These values increase far more rapidly than in binary, but not so quickly as

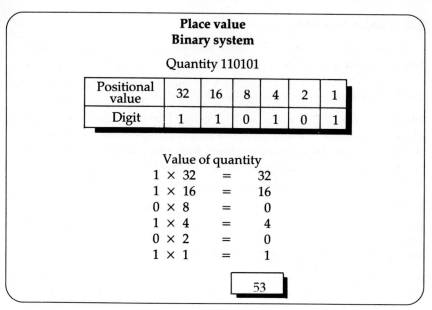

**Place value**
**Binary system**

Quantity 110101

| Positional value | 32 | 16 | 8 | 4 | 2 | 1 |
|---|---|---|---|---|---|---|
| Digit | 1 | 1 | 0 | 1 | 0 | 1 |

Value of quantity

| | | | |
|---|---|---|---|
| 1 × 32 | = | 32 |
| 1 × 16 | = | 16 |
| 0 × 8 | = | 0 |
| 1 × 4 | = | 4 |
| 0 × 2 | = | 0 |
| 1 × 1 | = | 1 |

53

**Figure 3.2   The value of a binary number**

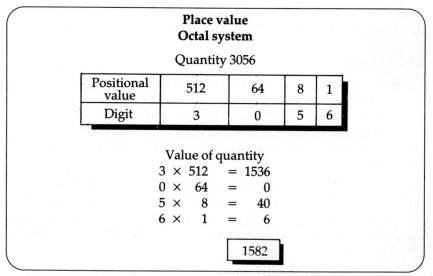

**Place value**
**Octal system**

Quantity 3056

| Positional value | 512 | 64 | 8 | 1 |
|---|---|---|---|---|
| Digit | 3 | 0 | 5 | 6 |

Value of quantity

| | | | |
|---|---|---|---|
| 3 × 512 | = | 1536 |
| 0 × 64 | = | 0 |
| 5 × 8 | = | 40 |
| 6 × 1 | = | 6 |

1582

**Figure 3.3   The value of an octal number**

with decimal. Figure 3.3 shows that the value of the octal quantity 3056 is 1582 decimal – again, these two are simply alternative forms of showing the same value.

Thus the decimal value of octal 47023 is 4 × 4096 plus 7 × 512 plus 0 × 64 plus 2 × 8 plus × 1 – or 16384 + 3584 + 16 + 3, or 19987.

### 3.2.4   Hex(adecimal)

Really there's no difference in the way we deal with hex numbers. However, because hex uses the digits A to F after 0 to 9, it's not so easy. The place values are, from the right, 1, 16, 256, 4096, 65536, and so on. These increase at a greater rate than in decimal. Figure 3.4 shows how to convert the hex number 2FA6 to decimal, giving a value of 12198.

Using the same method, ABC in hex becomes, in decimal, $10 \times 256$ plus $11 \times 16$ plus $12 \times 1$, $-2560 + 176 + 12$, or 2748.

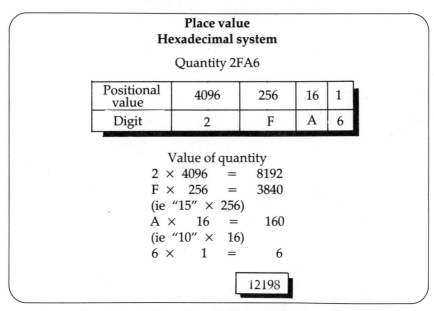

**Place value**
**Hexadecimal system**

Quantity 2FA6

| Positional value | 4096 | 256 | 16 | 1 |
|---|---|---|---|---|
| Digit | 2 | F | A | 6 |

Value of quantity
$2 \times 4096 = 8192$
$F \times 256 = 3840$
(ie "15" × 256)
$A \times 16 = 160$
(ie "10" × 16)
$6 \times 1 = 6$

12198

**Figure 3.4   The value of a hexadecimal number**

It is now obvious that, unless the context makes it absolutely clear, you should state the base used when giving a value – octal 73, decimal 73 and hex 73 may all look the same, yet they have totally different values (59, 73 and 115 in decimal respectively). Generally we assume values to be decimal. Always take care, though – it's all too easy to overlook the base used.

### 3.2.5   Fractions

So far we've dealt only with integers – but the approach is easy to extend to fractions. In the case of decimal numbers, place values moving right from the decimal point refer to units of 0.1, then 0.01, 0.001, etc – they decrease by a factor equal to the base of the number system with each step. On this basis, decimal 36.528 has a value of $3 \times 10$ plus $6 \times 1$ plus $5 \times 0.1$ plus $2 \times 0.01$ plus $8 \times 0.001$.

In the same way, the binary fraction place values decrease by a factor of two with each step to the right of the binary point, so are 0.5, 0.25, 0.125, etc. Thus binary 101.011 has a decimal value of 1 x 4 plus 0 × 2 plus 1 × 1 plus 0 × 0.5 plus 1 × 0.25 plus 1 × 0.125 – 4 + 1 + 0.25 + 0.125, or 5.375.

With fractions in octal, place values go down by a factor of eight, giving 0.125, 0.015625, etc. The octal quantity 31.27 in decimal is 3 × 8 plus 1 × 1 plus 2 × 0.125 plus 7 × 0.015625 – 24 + 1 + 0.25 + 0.109375, or 25.359375.

Finally, hex fractions involve place values decreasing by a factor of 16, – 0.0625, 0.00390625, etc. So hex 0.CF has a value of 12 × 0.0625 plus 15 × 0.00390625 – that's 0.75 + 0.05859375, or 0.80859375 in decimal.

Now it's time for you to practise. Refer to Figures 3.2–3.4 as much as you need.

**NOW TRY THESE . . .**

1 Convert each of these binary values to decimal:

| | | | |
|---|---|---|---|
| (i) | 110 | (vi) | 110010 |
| (ii) | 1001 | (vii) | 11010 |
| (iii) | 11101 | (viii) | 1110011 |
| (iv) | 1101 | (ix) | 11001101 |
| (v) | 10011 | (x) | 10010110 |

2. Convert each of these octal values to decimal:

| | | | |
|---|---|---|---|
| (i) | 17 | (vi) | 362 |
| (ii) | 25 | (vii) | 407 |
| (iii) | 43 | (viii) | 713 |
| (iv) | 156 | (ix) | 1536 |
| (v) | 204 | (x) | 2715 |

3. Convert each of these hex values to decimal:

| | | | |
|---|---|---|---|
| (i) | 14 | (vi) | A2 |
| (ii) | 23 | (vii) | AB3 |
| (iii) | 1B | (viii) | B05 |
| (iv) | 3C | (ix) | FAD |
| (v) | 7D | (x) | F23E |

4. Convert each of these fractions to decimal

| | | | |
|---|---|---|---|
| (i) | 1.01 binary | (v) | 5.07 octal |
| (ii) | 110.101 binary | (vi) | 10.35 octal |
| (iii) | 0.0011 binary | (vii) | 3.B hex |
| (iv) | 2.23 octal | (viii) | 19.25 hex |

## 3.3   DECIMAL TO OTHER BASES

It is easy to convert a decimal value to any other base. Simply divide the base into the quotient – keep repeating the process until there's a zero quotient (this must always happen sooner or later). Reading off the remainders in the reverse order of how you wrote them down gives the answer.

### 3.3.1  Decimal to binary

Figure 3.5 shows how this works to convert the decimal 117 into binary.

Since the base of binary numbers is the number 2, divide 2 into 117 to get the quotient of 58 and a remainder of 1.

```
2)    117
2)     58     rem  1
2)     29     rem  0
2)     14     rem  1
2)      7     rem  0
2)      3     rem  1
2)      1     rem  1
        0     rem  1
     117 decimal = 1110101 binary
```

**Figure 3.5   Decimal to binary**

Now divide 58 in turn by 2 – giving a quotient of 29 and a remainder of 0. Keep going, until at last you divide 2 into 1 – to give a zero quotient and a remainder of 1. At this point the process ends. Reading off the remainders from the bottom up gives the answer 1110101 as the binary value of decimal 117.

### 3.3.2   Decimal to octal

I've said that the general method for conversion from decimal to any other base involves repeated division by the base value. So, to convert a decimal number into octal, keep on dividing by 8.

Figure 3.6 shows how to convert decimal 236 to octal. Division by 8 first gives a quotient of 29 with a remainder of 4. Dividing 8 into this quotient

```
8)    236
8)     29     rem  4
8)      3     rem  5
        0     rem  3
     236 decimal = 354 octal
```

**Figure 3.6   Decimal to octal**

of 29 yields a new quotient of 3 with a remainder of 5; then the final step is dividing the quotient of 3 by 8 – giving a zero quotient and a remainder of 3. The process ends when you reach a zero quotient – now read the remainders from the bottom upwards, to give the result, so 354 octal is the same as decimal 236.

Dividing by eight can give remainders of only 0 to 7 – the digits 8 and 9 can never appear in an octal quantity.

### 3.3.3   Decimal to hex

Predictably you should divide by 16 this time. Remember that if a remainder is between 10 and 15 (decimal) you need to write it as A, B, C, etc in hex.

Look at Figure 3.7. Division by 16 first gives a quotient of 29 and a remainder of 9. Dividing 16 into the 29 gives 1; the remainder is 13 in decimal, ie D in hex. The next division gives the final zero quotient and a remainder of 1. Reading the remainders, as before, from the bottom gives the value 1D9 hex.

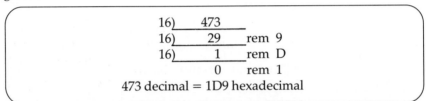

```
16)     473
16)      29     rem  9
16)       1     rem  D
          0     rem  1
473 decimal = 1D9 hexadecimal
```

**Figure 3.7    Decimal to hex**

Dividing by 16 can leave remainders (in decimal terms) up to 15; it's no surprise to see the use of A to F as the hex equivalents of the decimal 10 to 15 appear frequently as remainders.

This conversion is no harder than from decimal into either binary or octal; the use of the digits A to F, however, makes it appear so. Now practise these conversions.

**NOW TRY THESE . . .**

1. Convert each decimal value to binary:

|        |     |         |     |
|--------|-----|---------|-----|
| (i)    | 13  | (vii)   | 103 |
| (ii)   | 25  | (viii)  | 175 |
| (iii)  | 29  | (ix)    | 236 |
| (iv)   | 64  | (x)     | 199 |
| (v)    | 73  | (xi)    | 274 |
| (vi)   | 127 | (xii)   | 493 |

2. Convert each decimal value to octal:

|        |    |         |     |
|--------|----|---------|-----|
| (i)    | 9  | (vii)   | 96  |
| (ii)   | 17 | (viii)  | 100 |
| (iii)  | 23 | (ix)    | 127 |

|        |     |        |     |
|--------|-----|--------|-----|
| (iv)   | 39  | (x)    | 301 |
| (v)    | 47  | (xi)   | 532 |
| (vi)   | 83  | (xii)  | 798 |

3. Convert each decimal value to hex:

|         |     |         |       |
|---------|-----|---------|-------|
| (i)     | 23  | (ix)    | 254   |
| (ii)    | 29  | (x)     | 260   |
| (iii)   | 35  | (xi)    | 509   |
| (iv)    | 42  | (xii)   | 537   |
| (v)     | 59  | (xiii)  | 1295  |
| (vi)    | 79  | (xiv)   | 1998  |
| (vii)   | 97  | (xv)    | 2748  |
| (viii)  | 140 | (xvi)   | 12047 |

## 3.4   CHANGING DECIMAL FRACTIONS TO BINARY

Earlier we looked at the place values of binary, octal and hex fractions, and tried some conversions from these into decimal; in each case an exact conversion was possible.

However, you know that it is not always possible to represent some fractions exactly as decimal fractions. Thus, while ¼ is indeed exactly 0.25, ⅓ is 0.3333 recurring – it has no exact decimal fraction equivalent.

In just the same way, we can't give some decimal fractions exactly as binary fractions (nor as octal or hex) – even if they are exact in decimal.

An obvious example is ¹⁄₁₀ – exactly 0.1 in decimal, but a recurring binary fraction. This is a major cause of errors in computers working with fractional values – they can handle some of these only approximately, so accumulate errors in calculations.

Some decimal fractions do convert exactly, and, where this is not the case, we can control the accuracy of conversions.

Figure 3.8 shows how to convert the decimal fraction 0.743 into binary. The process involves repeatedly multiplying by 2 that part of the decimal fraction to the right of the decimal point, and writing down the

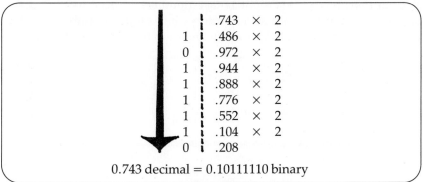

|   |      |   |   |
|---|------|---|---|
|   | .743 | × | 2 |
| 1 | .486 | × | 2 |
| 0 | .972 | × | 2 |
| 1 | .944 | × | 2 |
| 1 | .888 | × | 2 |
| 1 | .776 | × | 2 |
| 1 | .552 | × | 2 |
| 1 | .104 | × | 2 |
| 0 | .208 |   |   |

0.743 decimal = 0.10111110 binary

**Figure 3.8   Converting decimal fractions to binary**

whole number part of the product at each stage (but not involving it in subsequent multiplication). Reading the whole number parts down from the top gives the binary fraction to as many places as you want.

So when you multiply 0.743 by 2 to get 1.486 write down the whole 1, then double only the 0.486 to give 0.972 at the next stage (note you must record the 0). Repeat this process eight times – to produce a value of 0.10111110, cut off after eight places.

Now convert the value obtained back into decimal 0.7421875. You can see that this contains an error at the third decimal place if the binary value is taken to as few as eight places.

To reduce errors of this type, computers need to store such converted values to a large number of binary places – eight, in this case, is clearly not enough.

Converting from decimal fractions to octal or hex involves the same process as with binary, but using multipliers of 8 and 16 respectively. Also, note that to convert a mixed decimal number (eg 13.743), work separately on the whole and fraction parts. Then link the two answers together with a point.

### 3.5 BINARY, OCTAL AND HEX

I'm sure you've noticed that the bases of these three systems – 2, 8 and 16 – are closely related, as $8 = 2^3$ and $16 = 2^4$.

This lets us convert directly between binary and octal and between binary and hex, without needing to use decimal values at all. This is specially useful when writing machine code programs – we give numbers in octal or hex which convert easily into the binary that the computer uses. Dumps (copies on paper) from store are often in octal or hex for ease of use, even though the machine actually stores data in binary.

### 3.5.1 Binary to octal

You must learn the first eight binary numbers in octal (0 to 7) – see Figure 3.9. Then split any binary number into groups of three, from the point outwards – to the left for an integer or to the right for a fraction (or

| Binary | 000 | 001 | 010 | 011 | 100 | 101 | 110 | 111 |
|--------|-----|-----|-----|-----|-----|-----|-----|-----|
| Octal  | 0   | 1   | 2   | 3   | 4   | 5   | 6   | 7   |

Figure 3.9   Binary to octal

both in the case of a mixed number). Now simply replace each group of three binary digits (bits) with the octal value – so 010 gives 2, 101 gives 5, and so on.

Where there isn't a full group of three, add zeroes to make it up, that's why, in the second example in Figure 3.10, the solitary 1 becomes 001 for this purpose. If you need zeroes, add them to the left of integers and to the right of fractional values.

|  | | | | | |
|---|---|---|---|---|---|
| Binary | 101 | 010 | 110 | 001 | |
| equals octal | 5 | 2 | 6 | 1 | |
| Binary | 001 | 011 | 100 | 101 | 111 |
| equals octal | 1 | 3 | 4 | 5 | 7 |

**Figure 3.10    Binary and octal**

### 3.5.2    Octal to binary

This is the exact reverse of the previous case. Replace each octal digit by the appropriate "triple" of binary digits (bits). You can prune any unnecessary zeroes afterwards, as in Figure 3.11.

| Octal | 2   7   4   3 |
|---|---|
| equals binary | 010 111 100 011 |
| ie | 010111100011 |
| | |
| Octal | 7   6   3 · 1   4 |
| equals binary | 111 110 011· 001100 |
| ie | 111110011 · 0011 |

**Figure 3.11    Octal to binary**

| Binary | Hex | Binary | Hex |
|---|---|---|---|
| 0000 | 0 | 1000 | 8 |
| 0001 | 1 | 1001 | 9 |
| 0010 | 2 | 1010 | A |
| 0011 | 3 | 1011 | B |
| 0100 | 4 | 1100 | C |
| 0101 | 5 | 1101 | D |
| 0110 | 6 | 1110 | E |
| 0111 | 7 | 1111 | F |

**Figure 3.12    Binary to hex conversion**

### 3.5.3 Binary to hex

Once again you must learn the conversions between binary and the 16 hex digits 0 to F – see Figure 3.12.

Just as with binary to octal, split the binary value into binary groups – though this time into blocks of four – and read off the hex values directly. Again add zeroes if you need – treat the 110 in the first example Figure 3.13 as though it were 0110.

| | | | | |
|---|---|---|---|---|
| Binary | | 110 | 1011 | 1011 |
| equals hex | | 6 | B | B |
| Binary | | 0101 · | 0110 | 1100 |
| equals hex | | 5 · | 6 | C |

**Figure 3.13    Binary and hex**

### 3.5.3 Hex to binary

Predictably, this reverses the previous case of binary to hex conversion – see the examples in Figure 3.14.

| | |
|---|---|
| Hex | 9AC |
| equals binary | 100110101100 |
| Hex | 70F2 |
| equals binary | 0111000011110010 |
| ie | 111000011110010 |
| Hex | 62·9E |
| equals binary | 01100010·10011110 |
| ie | 1100010·1001111 |

**Figure 3.14    Hex to binary conversion**

### NOW TRY THESE . . .

1. Stopping (truncating) each time after eight binary places, convert these decimal fractions to binary.

      (i)        0.528
      (ii)      0.9074
      (iii)     0.2935

2. Truncating after six octal places, convert 0.392 decimal into octal.

3. Truncating after five hex places, convert 0.203 decimal into hex.

4. Convert each of these binary values into octal.

|        |           |         |           |
|--------|-----------|---------|-----------|
| (i)    | 101101110 | (v)     | 0.110101  |
| (ii)   | 110001100 | (vi)    | 0.1011    |
| (iii)  | 11011     | (vii)   | 11.01     |
| (iv)   | 10110     | (viii)  | 1011.1011 |

5. Convert each of these octal values into binary.

|       |     |       |        |
|-------|-----|-------|--------|
| (i)   | 725 | (iii) | 23.4   |
| (ii)  | 536 | (iv)  | 106.53 |

6. Convert each of these binary values into hex.

|       |          |       |         |
|-------|----------|-------|---------|
| (i)   | 11010011 | (iii) | 0.111   |
| (ii)  | 100101   | (iv)  | 101.01  |

7. Convert each of these hex values into binary.

|       |     |       |        |
|-------|-----|-------|--------|
| (i)   | 2B  | (iii) | 8.C    |
| (ii)  | FC7 | (iv)  | 3D.E2  |

## 3.6  COMPUTER CALCULATIONS

Computers record numbers as binary quantities. To understand how they carry out calculations you need to understand how to handle binary calculations.

There are, in fact, no real differences between handling decimal or binary calculations that are not covered by the differences (and the conversions) between the two number systems – so there's very little by way of new techniques to learn.

There is, however, a warning! A computer stores several different types of data – numeric data, character strings, program instructions; all of these are in binary, and there's no easy way to tell which of the three is represented, for example, 0110 1101. (From now on, by the way, I'm going to group bits in fours in the standard way). Even if you know that 0110 1101 is an item of numeric data, it still might be an integer, a fraction or a mixed number, or it might be in one of a number of other forms we'll meet later. So, take care not to carry out calculations on data which is really, for example, a character string. Though you may be able to do the figure work, the results will be nonsense – and the danger exists that the computer could accept them as valid. However, this problem is less common with high level program languages than with assembly codes.

Another problem is that different computers carry out certain processes differently from each other, though this shouldn't affect your work in this chapter. Addition is generally under hardware control, and the same addition circuits can deal with subtraction if the numbers are stored in the right way. Multiplication often involves addition circuits, plus a technique called shifting. To control these functions requires software which, if permanently embedded in a chip, is called firmware.

One important limitation is, of course, the fact that computer storage units, bytes or words, are fixed in size – there may be problems when storing (and working with) values too large or too small for these units. We'll discuss the whole area of accuracy later, in Chapters 19 and 20.

## 3.7  ADDING BINARY NUMBERS

To add binary numbers you need to know these rules:

$$0 + 0 = 0 \text{ carry } 0 = 00$$
$$0 + 1 = 1 \text{ carry } 0 = 01$$
$$1 + 1 = 0 \text{ carry } 1 = 10$$
$$1 + 1 + 1 = 1 \text{ carry } 1 = 11$$

|  |  |
|---|---|
| | 10 $1010_2$ |
| + | 11 $1001_2$ |
| Carry: | 111 |
| Result | 110 $0011_2$ |
| | 11 $0110_2$ |
| | 10 $1101_2$ |
| + | 111 $1010_2$ |
| Carry: | 1111 1110 |
| Result | 1101 $1101_2$ |

**Figure 3.15    Adding binary numbers**

In Figure 3.15 I add binary numbers using these rules. Note the use of the subscript $_2$ to denote binary numbers.

If you are in any doubt about an answer, one way to check is to convert each of the numbers into decimal (giving, in the first case, 42 and 57 and for the sum 99), then you can confirm by decimal addition. Needless to say, whilst this provides reassurance (as well as more practice at binary to decimal conversions), it would be a great waste of time and effort every time you do a binary addition. Still, one point to note is that in decimal, 42 added to 57 is 99, no matter whether the numbers are given and added in binary (as here) or in octal, or indeed in any other number base.

These two examples show the main features of binary addition. If you have to add a set of binary digits, convert them in your head to decimal and change the total back into binary until you're happy with the result. For instance, $1 + 1 + 1 + 1 + 1 + 1$, gives decimal 6, or binary 110, so the result is 0 with the 'carry' as 11.

### 3.8   SUBTRACTING BINARY NUMBERS

It is not hard to subtract binary numbers, but how we do it is not generally the method used in a computer. (Chapter 4 covers that fully).

The example in Figure 3.16 shows the use of "borrowing" from the next column to the left. This is a standard approach to subtraction, but one you may find awkward when working in binary. Again, you can check in decimal; 108 from 213 is 105.

$$11^101\ {}^10101_2$$
$$-\,{}^{10}11^10\ 1100_2$$
$$\overline{\text{Result } 110\ 1001_2}$$

**Figure 3.16   Subtracting binary numbers**

**NOW TRY THESE . . .**

Using binary arithmetic work out each of these.

1.   $1101 + 1\,0111$
2.   $1\,0110 + 1\,1011$
3.   $1\,0111 + 1\,0101 + 110$
4.   $11\,0011 + 11\,0101$
5.   $1101 + 1011 + 1\,0110$
6.   $1\,0111 + 1\,1101 + 1\,0001$
7.   $101\,1101 + 110\,1011 + 11\,0101$
8.   $10\,1101 - 1\,0110$
9.   $101\,1011 - 11\,0111$
10.  $1010\,1011 - 111\,1101$

# 4 Fixed-length computer calculations

## OBJECTIVES

When you've worked through this Chapter, you should be able to:

— state how a digital computer stores integers, fractions, mixed numbers, and negative numbers

— carry out binary subtraction using twos-complements

— outline how shifting allows multiplication and division

— convert decimal numbers to binary coded decimal (BCD)

— add BCD numbers.

## INTRODUCTION

In Chapter 3 we looked at "pure" binary calculations. However, differences do exist between "pure" calculations and those carried out by a computer.

A computer holds numbers in fixed-length storage cells; in general, it stores one number in each cell; this clearly means there's an upper limit to the size of stored numbers. We call a set of eight bits a byte (B for short). A 16-bit computer has cells able to store 16 bits, or two bytes. We say this computer has a word length of 16 bits – it handles numbers and other data in 2B chunks.

## 4.1 STORING NUMBERS

In much of this chapter, we'll assume a 12-bit computer, a machine whose storage cells hold 12 bits.

### 4.1.1 Integers

Take the decimal number 735 as our first example. In Chapter 3 we saw how to convert this into binary – producing 10 1101 1111, a 10-bit quantity. Since our computer has a word length of 12 bits, it would add two zeroes to the left-hand end of the value in order to store it in a cell.

Actually, in the case of a 12-bit value, the first (left-hand) bit is not part of the value of the number; rather it carries its sign (if 0, the number is positive). Thus we have only 11 bits to hold the value of the number. We shall come back to negative numbers soon, but you can suppose that for these the sign bit is 1.

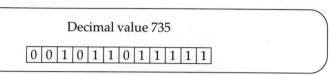

Decimal value 735

| 0 | 0 | 1 | 0 | 1 | 1 | 0 | 1 | 1 | 1 | 1 | 1 |

**Figure 4.1    Example of bit storage**

The second example involves storing the decimal value 174. In "pure" binary this is 1010 1110, taking up only eight bits; to store it in a 12-bit cell requires four extra zeroes at the left-hand end, including the sign bit.

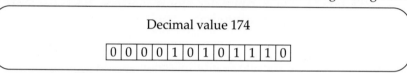

Decimal value 174

| 0 | 0 | 0 | 0 | 1 | 0 | 1 | 0 | 1 | 1 | 1 | 0 |

**Figure 4.2    Storage of 8-bits in a 12-bit cell**

Clearly therefore, a computer uses more space to store a small number than it actually needs. It would hold 9, for instance, as 0000 0000 1001. This may appear a waste of space – but it is actually one of the very necessary facts of computer storage.

There's also an upper limit to the size of a stored number. The largest binary value a 12-bit word can hold is 0111 1111 1111; in decimal terms this is 2047 – a very modest upper limit.

One common way to overcome this problem is to combine two (or more) words together. This apparently gives us 24 bits for storage. In fact, since the first bit is still the sign bit and the 13th bit is the sign bit of the second word (and isn't used), only 22 bits are available to hold the value. Even so, the value of the largest number goes up to 4,194,303 in the double-length word. Figure 4.3 shows 7649 held this way.

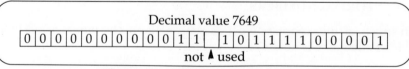

Decimal value 7649

| 0 | 0 | 0 | 0 | 0 | 0 | 0 | 0 | 0 | 0 | 1 | 1 | 1 | 0 | 1 | 1 | 1 | 1 | 0 | 0 | 0 | 0 | 1 |

not ▲ used

**Figure 4.3    Multiple word storage**

A system could combine as many 12-bit words as may be necessary to hold exact integral values of any size. In practice, there's some loss of accuracy because of the use of floating-point representation (see Chapter 5).

With different word lengths, the sizes of numbers the system can store will clearly be different from the example in Figure 4.3, for example, an 8-bit word can hold only up to 127. It is still possible to combine two or more such words to extend the range. Do note, however, that if a system combines three words in this way, there will be two redundant sign bits.

### 4.1.2  Storing fractions

The first bit still serves as the sign bit, but if a "pure" binary fraction is smaller than the storage space available in the 12-bit word, then zeroes are added – as with integers, but at the right-hand end. Notice that the binary point itself isn't stored, but implied; otherwise, the binary pattern could just as easily be that of an integer.

Figure 4.4 shows the storage of decimal 0.4140625. This has the exact binary value of 0.0110 101 – so needs four extra zeroes at the right-hand end.

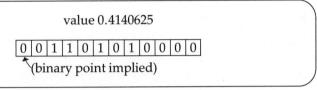

**Figure 4.4    Storage of fractional values**

If, however, the binary value exceeds the number of bits available, we must either round or truncate it to fit the word space. This action has the immediate risk of errors of approximation. (I referred to this in Chapter 3, and we'll come back to it later). This is, in fact, quite common – many decimal fractions have no exact binary value, so it's a major source of potential error.

Figure 4.5, below, shows decimal 0.7328 stored in a single word, truncating the bits that don't fit the space.

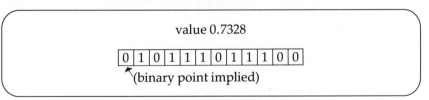

**Figure 4.5    Storage of truncated word**

As with integers, we can combine two words; this increases the precision with which a system can store fractional values. Once again only 22 bits are available to hold the value of the fraction.

In Figure 4.6, below, the storage of decimal 0.7328 can be seen truncated to fit into a double-length space.

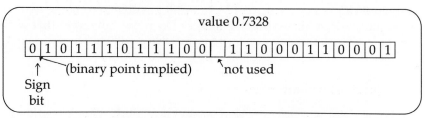

Figure 4.6    **Fractional value stored in double-length word**

In the case of fractions, the range of values a system can store in a 12-bit word is not so restricted as with integers; for all practical purposes the range is from 0 to binary 0.111 1111 1111, which is approximately decimal 0.999 512. The use of double-length working doesn't change this range, it simply provides for more precise storage of the numbers involved, ie less rounding or truncation error.

### 4.1.3    Storing mixed numbers

It is possible to store a mixed number in a single word, as long as there's an agreed number of bits for the integer part (and the balance for the fractional part). The position of the binary point is once again implied.

Clearly, we must hold the whole of the integer part, so the number of bits left for the fractional part may be so small as to lead to relatively large errors. The next example shows the storage of decimal 11.75; there are five bits for the integer part 01011 and six for the fraction 110000.

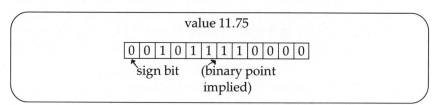

Figure 4.7    **Storing a mixed number**

If we use double-length working to hold mixed numbers, it's usual for one word to hold the integral part and the other the fractional part. This method is capable of as much extension as you want – allowing for three or even four words to be put together, to provide as much precision as may be desired. However, apart from quite exceptional cases, double-length is adequate.

The next illustration in Figure 4.8 shows the storage of decimal 74.890625 in two words, using the first for the integral, 74, and the second for the fractional part.

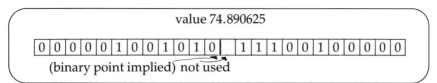

**Figure 4.8   Example of Two-Word Storage**

### 4.1.4   Storing negative values

What's the difference between $+596$ and $-596$? The way we show one is positive and the other is negative is using the $+$ or $-$ sign in front of the value.

It is quite easy and, indeed, most obvious, to extend this approach into computer storage – it's the sign-and-modulus method. The sign bit value for a positive and 1 if it's negative. Figure 4.9 shows the two decimal values $+157$ and $-157$ stored using the sign-and-modulus method.

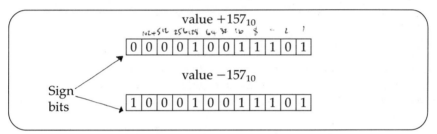

**Figure 4.9   Sign and modulus storage**

This method is simple, but has one major drawback – it's quite unsuitable for calculations. For this reason, we use the twos-complement method of storing negative numbers. This is well suited to calculations.

There are three stages in finding the twos-complement of a negative number – such as decimal $-837$.

(a)  Write $+837$ as a 12-bit binary word. Since this involves a positive quantity the method is as described earlier.

(b)  Invert (flip) all 12 bits – that is, change every 0 to a 1 and every 1 to a 0.

(c)  Add 1 (to the right-hand, less significant, end).

Figure 4.10 shows this in detail.

The twos-complement of $-837$ is 1100 1011 1011. The presence of the 1 in the leading (sign bit) position reminds us that the value is a negative one. This method is more involved than sign-and-modulus method, but does give values a system can use for calculation.

| + 837 | 0011 | 0100 | 0101 |
| (invert) | 1100 | 1011 | 1010 + |
| (add 1) |  |  | 1 |
| − 837 | 1100 | 1011 | 1011 |

**Figure 4.10    Finding the twos-complement**

To convert a 12-bit value in twos-complement form to decimal use the same three steps as before. Given the twos-complement value 1001 1101 0110, proceed as follows.

(a)  Flip the bits, giving 0110 0010 1001

(b)  Add 1 (to the right-hand end) now giving 0110 0010 1010

(c)  Convert to decimal, 1578, and place a minus sign in front, −1578.

Therefore, 1001 1101 0110 is the twos-complement version of −1578.

The range of values available for positive numbers in a 12-bit word is from 0 to +2047. Introducing the twos-complement method to store negative numbers, has no effect on positive values – these remain exactly as before. Now, the "most negative" quantity we can have is 1000 0000 0000, −2048 decimal. Thus the range of integers a 12-bit word can hold is from −2048 up to +2047, a total of 4096 different values. In the same way, an 8-bit word can hold from −128 up to +127, 256 different values.

Double-length working is just as useful for negative values as for positive ones. The process is just as before, again with the second sign bit unused.

**NOW TRY THESE . . .**

1. Store decimal 729 in a 12-bit word.

2. Store decimal 97 in an 8-bit word.

3. Store decimal 0.372 in an 8-bit word (truncate as necessary).

4. Combine two 8-bit words to store decimal 0.372 accurately to 14 binary places (truncate as necessary).

5. Use a 12-bit word with seven bits for the integral part to store the decimal value 18.875 exactly.

6. Store decimal −275 using twos-complement form in a 12-bit word.

7. A 12-bit word, using twos-complement storage format, contains the binary value 1100 1100 1100. What is the decimal value?

8. Store decimal −57 using twos-complement form in an 8-bit word.

9. An 8-bit word, using twos-complement storage format, contains the binary value 1100 0011. What is the decimal value?

10. What range of integral values can a 10-bit word hold?

11. A 12-bit word, using six bits for the integral part, stores a mixed number as 0010 1110 1011. What is its decimal value?

12. Store decimal −271 using twos-complement form in a 10-bit word.

## 4.2 SUBTRACTION USING TWOS-COMPLEMENT

The value of 1382 − 797 is just the same as that of 1382 + (−797). In other words, to take 797 from 1382, you must add the complement of 797 (−797 is the complement of 797) to 1382. In a computer this idea is very convenient – it can carry out subtraction by addition and so can use addition circuitry for both purposes.

Look at the calculation of 1382 − 797 in figure 4.11. First find the twos-complement form of −797; since +797 is 0011 0001 1101, −797 will be 1100 1110 0011. Now carry out the addition. Note that, as we use 12-bit values, there will always be a carry into a 13th place (at the left-hand end). Clearly, a 12-bit word cannot hold such a carry, but this isn't important as you can ignore it, the answer is 0010 0100 1001 – decimal +585, the correct result of the subtraction.

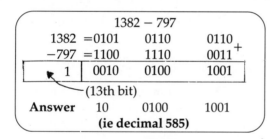

**Figure 4.11   Twos-complement subtraction**

Here's another example – use 8-bit words to work out 93 − 47. The binary value of 93 is 0101 1101; that of 47 is 0010 1111, so −47 is 1101 0001.

Adding gives

$$\begin{array}{r} 0101\ 1101 \\ +\qquad 1101\ 0001 \\ \hline (1)0010\ 1110 \end{array}$$

ignore the excess bit at the left to give 10 1110 – decimal 46, the correct answer.

**NOW TRY THESE . . .**

1. Using 8-bit words, find   (i)   $87 - 53$

                             (ii)  $107 - 28$

2. Using 12-bit words, find (i)   $392 - 135$

                             (ii)  $1826 - 399$

                             (iii) $2217 - 1543$

## 4.3   SHIFT OPERATIONS

Now we've looked at computer addition and subtraction, we can examine the other two basic operations – multiplication and division – these involve processes of repeated addition and subtraction.

In decimal terms, 59 times 4 involves working out $59 + 59 + 59 + 59$; to divide 17 by 3 we count how many times we can take 3 from 17 until a value less than 3 remains.

So multiplication and division are closely related to adding and subtracting; however, one other operation has a place here – that of shifting.

Shifting involves the actual physical movement of bits in a word – moving them left or right. There are a number of different forms of shifting (such as circular, logical and arithmetic, each with its own special function). We look at the arithmetic shift only here, as it's the one most relevant to calculation.

### 4.3.1   Shifting to achieve multiplication

First consider decimal 735; if you move each digit one place left, so each enters a higher place-value (eg the 7 in the hundreds place moves up into the thousands place), the process would leave nothing in the units column, so a 0 would have to go there.

The effect is to change the number to 7350 – multiplying the original value by 10. Doing the same thing to a binary number is like multiplying by 2 (noting the different bases of the two systems).

If you do this leftwards shift twice, you multiply the original number by 2 twice, ie by $2^2$ or 4; three places to the left gives multiplication by $2^3$, or 8. In general, therefore, a shift left of $n$ places is the same as multiplication by $2^n$.

Shifting to the left creates gaps at the right-hand end which you must fill with zeroes. However, in a fixed-length word, there's the risk that, sooner or later, the sign bit may change as other bits move into that place. Clearly, doubling a number again and again can't alter its sign – so one of the rules of arithmetic shifting in fixed-length words is that the sign bit must not change if the result is to be valid.

One way to reduce the risk is to store the number in a double-length word; in practice, a special register (storage cell) flags changes in the sign bit position as and when they occur, so the system can take remedial action.

Figure 4.12, using 12-bit words, shows the effect on 11 0010 (decimal +50) of shifting to the left.

### 4.3.2.   Shifting to achieve division

Just as shifting left gives multiplication by the relevant power of 2, so shifting right gives division by the relevant power of 2. This time, as bits shift right, gaps appear at the left-hand end; the sign bit doesn't change, but copies of the sign bit go into the gaps to ensure the result retains its arithmetic significance. This is slightly more straightforward than when shifting left. However, bits moving beyond the right-hand end of the word are lost – this is a truncated form of division. It's the same as saying that decimal 17 divided by 3 is 5. On the other hand, if you allow the last bit to fall off the right and add it back into the bit now in the units column, the result is a rounded form of division. This is the same as decimal 17 divided by 3 being 6 when rounded to the nearest digit.

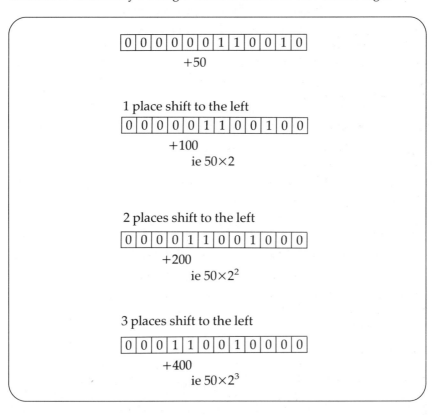

Figure 4.12   Shifting gives multiplication

Figure 4.13 shows the division of decimal 437 by 8 by shifting three places right, with both truncated and rounded results.

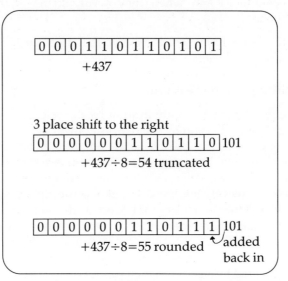

Figure 4.13   Shifting gives division

**NOW TRY THESE ...**

In each case assume 12-bit words.

1. Express decimal 97 in 12-bit binary, and find the decimal result of shifting it four places left.

2. To multiply by 64, how many places must you shift a binary value to the left?

3. Express decimal 537 in binary; find the decimal results of shifting three places right

   (i)  with truncation

   (ii) with rounding

4. Express decimal 1243 in binary; give the decimal results of shifting five places right

   (i)  with truncation

   (ii) with rounding

## 4.4   BINARY CODED DECIMAL

Sometimes systems store decimal numbers, not as the binary values, but by coding each decimal digit separately. This involves giving each digit four binary spaces (half a byte, or one nibble), and giving each its 4-bit code. Thus, we code 6 as 0110, 9 as 1001 and so on).

This method is "binary coded decimal" (BCD), or "packed decimal". It's not such an efficient way of storing numbers as "pure" binary but it is more convenient for storing very long numbers than giving each in character format (when each would take up a whole byte of storage space). Also, BCD isn't the most convenient form for calculation, but it is possible – Figure 4.14 shows how to add decimal 129 and 346 in BCD.

The method involves adding corresponding groups of 4 bits, and keeping the result a valid BCD code (ie if it's the same as a decimal digit in the range 0 to 9). If the result of adding is not a valid BCD code, then add 0110 to produce one which is valid and carry 1 to the column to the left.

Binary coded decimal is most common where (as in many commercial situations) very long numbers may occur – conversion to pure binary would be very time-consuming (even if done automatically by the computer) yet calculation is still needed.

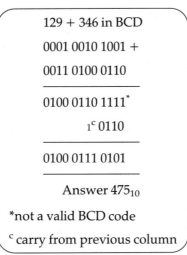

129 + 346 in BCD

0001 0010 1001 +

0011 0100 0110

——————————

0100 0110 1111$^{*}$

$_1{}^c$ 0110

——————————

0100 0111 0101

——————————

Answer $475_{10}$

$^{*}$not a valid BCD code

$^c$ carry from previous column

**Figure 4.14   Adding in binary coded decimal**

**NOW TRY THESE . . .**

1.  Express decimal 1526 in BCD

2.  Express decimal 253 and 426 in BCD. Now add them and convert the BCD result to decimal.

3.  Express decimal 1356 and 267 in BCD, add them, and convert the BCD result into decimal.

**4.5   SOME MORE QUESTIONS . . .**

1.  Store decimal 592 in a 12-bit word.

2.  Store decimal −276 in twos-complement form using a 12-bit word.

3. Use the results of questions 1 and 2 to calculate 592 − 276 in binary. Convert your result back to a decimal value.

4. Store decimal 0.735 in a 12-bit word; truncate as necessary.

5. Store decimal 195.427 in a double-length 12-bit word; use one word for the integral part and truncate as necessary.

6. A 12-bit word, using twos-complement form, contains 1100 1110 1110. What is its decimal value?

7. An 8-bit word, which uses twos-complement form for storing negative numbers, contains 0011 0101. What is its decimal value?

8. Express decimal 172 in a 12-bit word. Now show how to divide it by 32, giving your decimal answer in

   (i)  truncated form

   (ii) rounded form

9. Express decimal 37 in a 12-bit word. Multiply by 32 and convert your answer to decimal.

10. Use BCD to add decimal 79 and 536.

# 5 Floating-point numbers

## OBJECTIVES

When you've worked through this Chapter, you should be able to:

— convert decimal values to scientific and normalised standard forms

— understand and use E notation

— express binary values in normalised floating-point form

— add, subtract, multiply and divide in binary floating-point arithmetic.

## INTRODUCTION

We now know that, though fixed-length arithmetic can give the degree of precision we want, it has limitations. The main one is that a single-length 12-bit word can hold integers only in the range −2048 to +2047; double-length working increases the range, but at the cost of storage space.

There are in the same way limitations upon the ranges of fractions and mixed numbers a single-length word can hold; again, while increasing the number of words increases the range, it does so at the expense of storage space.

The basis of our work in Chapter 4 was the 12-bit word; just the same arguments apply regardless of the size of the word. Thus, though a true 24-bit word (*not* the same thing as two 12-bit words because these ignore the second sign bit) can hold from −8,388,608 to +8,388,607, it still cannot handle some of the values likely to occur in scientific or commercial arithmetic. Examples include the thousands of millions of dollars of the budget of a country or large firm, and the distance from the earth to the sun (150,000,000km) or the weight of an electron, (0.00000000000000000000000009 grams).

The solution to the problem compromises between the need for precision and the need to reduce waste of storage space. Floating-point numbers (as the solution is called) allows a far greater range of values – integer, fractional or mixed numbers, – in a single-length word. Calculations in floating-point arithmetic are slower than those in fixed-length working (though save programmers effort, especially when working in assembly code). One way to overcome the loss of speed is to install special hardware to control and speed up floating-point calculations, even though this adds to the cost. Clearly, if an application involves a great deal of floating-point arithmetic, the extra cost is worthwhile.

As I've noted, the greatest need for floating-point working is when we deal with values much larger or smaller than normal.

## 5.1   NUMBERS IN STANDARD FORM

It was in scientific matters where such extreme values first arose – so the first attempt at simplifying numbers came to be called scientific notation.

This approach gives each value as the product of a mantissa with the right power of 10 (in decimal), called the exponent. Thus we write 57429 as $5.7429 \times 10^4$ where 5.7429 is the mantissa and the exponent is 4.

The value of the mantissa is always greater than or equal to 1 and less than 10. The exponent is always an integer, either positive or negative.

Using this notation gives the distance from the Earth to the Sun as $1.5 \times 10^8$km. Here the mantissa is 1.5 and the exponent is 8.

There is no reason why the mantissa should not also be negative. So a firm might have a loss of \$287,000,000 ie $2.87 \times 10^8$. In the same way, the charge on an electron is $-1.6 \times 10^{-19}$ units, the same as $-0.000,000,000,000,000,000,16$.

Unfortunately, scientific form as above isn't the most convenient simplification for computer storage. We use an adjusted version, called the normalised form; here the mantissa is, in effect, divided by 10 and the exponent goes up by 1 to compensate.

In this form, therefore, the mantissa is a fraction less than 1 but greater than or equal to 0.1; the exponent is still integral. I show the two examples from earlier (the Earth's distance from the Sun and the firm's debt) in Figure 5.1, giving in each case mantissa and exponent in normalised form. Note that it's usual to put a zero in front of the decimal point; this doesn't affect the storage. The figure also shows how

| Normalised Standard Form | Mantissa | Exponent | Computer Input/Output Form |
|---|---|---|---|
| $0.15 \times 10^9$ | 0.15 | 9 | 0.15E9 |
| $-0.287 \times 10^9$ | −0.287 | 9 | −0.287E9 |

**Figure 5.1   Mantissa-exponent form**

such numbers may appear in computer input and output – mantissa-exponent form with the letter E before the exponent.

Likewise, the electron charge −0.000,000,000,000,000,000,16 would have a mantissa of −0.16, and an exponent of −20; it would appear as −0.16E−20 on computer input-output.

**NOW TRY THESE ...**

Express each of the following values in normalised standard form. Then give both mantissa and exponent, and the way the number would appear in computer input-output.

| | | | |
|---|---|---|---|
| (i) | 7,400,000 | (v) | −8,200,000 |
| (ii) | 2,560,000,000 | (vi) | −55,400,000,000 |
| (iii) | 0.000,062,8 | (vii) | −0.000,27 |
| (iv) | 0.000,000,000,153 | (viii) | −0.000,000,079 |

## 5.2   NORMALISED STANDARD FORM IN BINARY

The same methods apply when extending the ideas of normalisation to binary quantities for computer storage, in that the mantissa will be a positive or a negative fraction with an absolute value greater than or equal to binary 0.1 but less than 1, whilst the exponent will be a positive or a negative integral value. It is important to note that since the mantissa may be positive or negative, one bit must be reserved for its sign, although the absolute value of the mantissa is held *without* recourse to twos complement form if negative.

There are however, two ways of storing the exponent. In the first it is held using the twos complement form, in which case its sign can be determined by examination of the sign-bit in the space allocated to the exponent. In the second way, usually called the 'excess 64 code', the value $2^{t-1}$ is added to the exponent (where $t$ is the number of bits used to store the exponent). In the situation where 7 bits are used to store the exponent, $2^6$ or 64 is added to its value (hence the name), which ensures that what is held is always seen as a non-negative 'pure' binary 7-bit quantity.

The example in Figure 5.2 shows the two alternative methods of storing the binary quantity −10110.1011 in a 24-bit word. Note that in each case the sign of the mantissa appears at the beginning but the 16 bits allocated to its absolute value come at the end; this leaves 7 bits for holding the exponent between the mantissa and its sign.

In the first case the exponent (101 or decimal 5) is held as though in twos complement form (as 0000101) but in the second 64 is added to the decimal 5 to give 69 and this is held as 1000101 in the excess 64 code representation.

Having considered a 24-bit word using 1 bit for the sign of the mantissa, 16 bits for its absolute value and 7 bits for the exponent consideration should now be given to what ranges of values it is possible to store in such a word using the normalised exponential form.

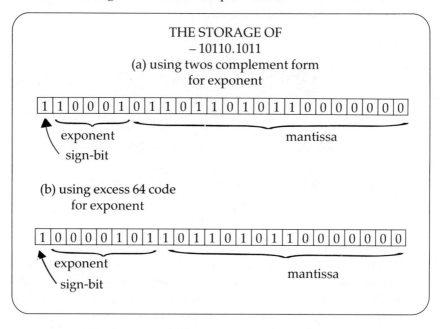

**Figure 5.2    Binary notation in normalised exponential form**

The 7-bit field allows values for the exponent from $-64$ to $+63$. The absolute value of the mantissa is in the range 0.0000 0000 0000 0001 to 0.1111 1111 1111 1111 binary; in decimal (to ten decimal places) this is from 0.000,015,258,7 to 0.999,984,741,2.

Concentrate first on positive values of the mantissa. We can store any decimal number from a smallest value of $0.000,015,258,7 \times 2^{-64}$ (which is *very* small) up to the largest value of $0.999,984,741,2 \times 2^{63}$, ie 9,223,231,299,000,000,000.

The numbers with a negative mantissa have a similar range but with negative values. However this means there's a very small gap between the two values $-0.000,015,258,7 \times 2^{-64}$ and $+0.000,015,258,7 \times 2^{-64}$. We can put zero in this gap by using a zero mantissa.

This method quite dramatically increases the range of values a 24-bit word can hold from the $-8,388,608$ to $+8,388,607$ range of fixed-point arithmetic. The disadvantage is lower precision.

**NOW TRY THESE ...**

1. Use normalised binary standard form – with a 12 bit word, one bit for the sign of the mantissa, six bits for the value of the mantissa, and

five bits for the exponent to store the decimal values

(i)    +59

(ii)   +0.35

(iii)  −39

(iv)   −0.26

2. Calculate the decimal range of values a 12-bit word can hold using normalised binary standard form − given one bit for the sign of the mantissa, seven bits for value, and four for the exponent.

3. Give the decimal range of values a 16-bit word can hold, using the normalised binary standard form, with one bit for the sign of the mantissa, seven bits for the value of the mantissa, and four for the exponent.

## 5.3   INTEGERS AND FLOATING-POINT ARITHMETIC

If a system holds numbers as fixed-point integers, adding, subtracting and multiplying them will give correct integer answers, as long as there's no overflow.

However, dividing two integers is quite likely to give a fraction in the answer. By trying to store the result of the division as an integer, truncation (towards zero) will occur to give an integer result. Using integer arithmetic, 15 divided by 7 gives 2, 9 divided by 11 gives 0, and −5 divided by 3 gives −1.

Some computer programming languages (such as Fortran) have integer results as standard; these lose the fractional parts of quotients, and the standard arithmetic rules of division no longer hold. Integer arithmetic is very fast; most programmers therefore use it where they can.

In most cases, however, computer calculations take place in floating-point form; the arithmetic associated with this is floating-point arithmetic, or "real" arithmetic. The word "real" is not a good word as it implies that anything else is "unreal" or "artificial"; in fact, in maths, "real numbers" are ones that can have a fractional part − the opposite of integers. The rules of floating-point arithmetic are outlined below.

### 5.3.1   Floating-point addition

When adding two numbers each in normalised binary standard form, there are two possibilities − the exponents are the same or they're different. This may seem obvious, but each involves a different method of calculation.

If the exponents are the same, addition simply involves adding the mantissas. The result has the same exponent as before − unless the mantissa has a value of 1 or more. In that case normalise the result as in Figure 5.3 (where decimal exponents are used solely for convenience).

$$(0.1011 \times 2^5) + (0.1001 \times 2^5)$$
$$= (0.1011 + 0.1001) \times 2^5$$
$$= 1.0100 \times 2^5$$
$$= 0.1010 \times 2^6$$

**Figure 5.3    Floating-point addition with the same exponent**

When adding the two mantissas the result (1.0100) is greater than is allowed (which must be fractional), therefore normalisation has to take place and the result truncated into four bits.

Where the exponents differ, a different method is applied. It is necessary, in this instance, to adjust the value with the smaller exponent by increasing the exponent to the size of the larger and decreasing the mantissa accordingly (see Figure 5.4). Again the mantissa has more bits than allowed – but at this stage no adjustment is made. Now the exponents are the same, and we can work as before.

$$(0.1001 \times 2^3) + (0.1110 \times 2^5)$$
$$= (0.001001 \times 2^5) + (0.1110 \times 2^5)$$
$$= 1.000001 \times 2^5$$
$$= 0.1000 \times 2^6 \text{ (after truncation)}$$

**Figure 5.4    Floating-point addition with different exponents**

You can see that adding floating point numbers may make the mantissa longer than allowed (four bits above); then we have to truncate. The result of adding may be loss of precision therefore.

### 5.3.2    Floating-point subtraction

This process is so similar to floating-point addition that there is no need for further explanation.

$$(0.1110 \times 2^7) - (0.1100 \times 2^7)$$
$$= 0.0010 \times 2^7$$
$$= 0.1000 \times 2^5$$

$$(0.1001 \times 2^8) - (0.1000 \times 2^5)$$
$$= (0.1001 \times 2^8) - (0.0001 \times 2^8)$$
$$= 0.1000 \times 2^8$$

**Figure 5.5    Floating-point subtraction**

The two examples in Figure 5.5 show the two cases; note in the first, the presence of non-significant zeroes in the intermediary mantissa (0.0010) and the need for normalisation.

### 5.3.3  Floating-point multiplication

This is even more straightforward. Multiply the mantissas and add the exponents to achieve the result. As before, you may need normalisation and truncation to obtain the final answer.

The two examples in Figure 5.6 outline the technique – can you fill the gaps?

$$(0.1101 \times 2^6) \times (0.1010 \times 2^4)$$
$$= 0.1000001 \times 2^{10}$$
$$= 0.1000 \times 2^{10}$$
$$\overline{\phantom{= 0.1000 \times 2^{10}}}$$

$$(0.1001 \times 2^7) \times (0.1111 \times 2^{-11})$$
$$= 0.10000111 \times 2^{-4}$$
$$= 0.1000 \times 2^{-4}$$
$$\overline{\phantom{= 0.1000 \times 2^{-4}}}$$

**Figure 5.6    Floating-point multiplication**

### 5.3.4  Floating-point division

Once again we have a quite simple process. This time divide the mantissas (as far as you need to get the correct number of significant digits), and subtract the exponents. Normalise and truncate as required, to produce the final answer. See Figure 5.7.

$$(0.1011 \times 2^7) \div (0.1101 \times 2^4)$$
$$= 0.1101 \times 2^3$$
$$\overline{(0.1111 \times 2^8) \div (0.1000 \times 2^{-4})}$$
$$= 1.111 \times 2^{12}$$
$$= 0.1111 \times 2^{13}$$
$$\overline{\phantom{= 0.1111 \times 2^{13}}}$$

**Figure 5.7    Floating-point division**

**NOW TRY THESE . . .**

Using decimal integer arithmetic, work out each of these

1.  (i)     $5 \times 17$                                (vi)    $-4 \div 2$

    (ii)    $93 + 162$                              (vii)   $-17 \div 5$

(iii)   493 − 76                    (viii) 28 ÷ 6

(iv)   12 ÷ 3                       (ix)   19 ÷ 21

(v)    10 ÷ 6                       (x)    −22 ÷ 6

2. Using floating-point addition, work out each of the following. Assume the mantissa has five bits, and retain decimal exponents for convenience.

(i)   $(0.10110 \times 2^4) + (0.10001 \times 2^4)$

(ii)  $(0.10011 \times 2^3) + (0.10010 \times 2^6)$

(iii) $(0.10001 \times 2^2) + (0.11101 \times 2^{-1})$

3. In just the same way, work out these

(i)   $(0.10110 \times 2^4) - (0.10001 \times 2^4)$

(ii)  $(0.10110 \times 2^7) - (0.10101 \times 2^4)$

(iii) $(0.11001 \times 2^3) - (0.10111 \times 2^{-1})$

4. Use floating-point multiplication to work out each of these, this time with four bits for the mantissa

(i)   $(0.1011 \times 2^3) \times (0.1001 \times 2^4)$

(ii)  $(0.1101 \times 2^4) \times (0.1111 \times 2^5)$

5. Now divide, using three bits for each mantissa

(i)   $(0.111 \times 2^5) \div (0.101 \times 2^3)$

(ii)  $(0.110 \times 2^4) \div (0.101 \times 2^{-3})$

6. Here are two 12-bit words –

0001 1010 1010

and 0001 1110 0101

They hold numbers in normalised binary standard form with the fields in the following order:

one bit for the sign of the mantissa

five bits for the exponent (twos-complement form)

six bits for the value of the mantissa.

Use floating-point addition, and give the result in the same form.

## REVISION EXERCISE A

The first five chapters of this book have concentrated on calculations used in a business data processing context and on the way computers do calculations. This revision section, therefore, provides fully worked examples covering these areas, plus others for you to try.

All the following examples have been taken from past examination papers set by the National Computing Centre, Manchester.

**First Example**

A company borrows $10,000. At the beginning of each year the bank adds interest to the remaining balance at the rate shown below.

The company repays $4000 at the end of the first year, then reduces its repayments by 10% per year.

(a) Complete the table

| Year | Remaining Balance | Interest Rate | Balance Outstanding After Adding Interest | Amount Repaid | Remaining Balance At End Of Year |
|------|-------------------|---------------|-------------------------------------------|---------------|----------------------------------|
|  | $ | % | $ | $ | $ |
| 1 | 10,000 | 20 | 12,000 | 4,000 | 8,000 |
| 2 | 8,000 | 15 |  |  |  |
| 3 |  | 12.5 |  |  |  |
| 4 |  | 7.5 |  |  |  |

(b) Calculate the total interest paid as a percentage of the total amount repaid, correct to one decimal place, after the four stages.

(c) Calculate the angles in a Pie chart relating original loan, total amount repaid and total interest paid to the nearest degree.

(d) Sketch the Pie chart.

**Solution**

As with all problems, the first task is to make sure you really understand the question being asked. The example given shows the whole of the Year 1 figures so, take full advantage of them.

In some ways this is a standard type of problem dealing with a loan and its repayments – however, note that the interest rate changes dramatically each year (far more indeed than is usual).

Make sure you really understand the calculations by following through the Year 1 figures. Start with $10,000 then calculate the simple interest for 1 year at 20% thus:

$$\frac{10,000 \times 20 \times 1}{100}$$

This gives just $2,000; therefore, the "balance outstanding after adding interest" is $10,000 + $2,000, or $12,000 (you can check this figure in the table once you have completed the calculation). If the company repays

$4,000, the "remaining balance at end of year" must be $12,000 − $4,000 or $8,000. The final stage is to note that the "remaining balance at the end of Year 1" must be the same as the "remaining balance at the start of Year 2"; this explains why the $8,000 also appears at the start of the second line.

In order to complete the table, continue with calculations using the method described above. The Year 2 interest calculated at 15% is

$$\frac{8,000 \times 15 \times 1}{100}$$

giving $1,200: the "balance outstanding after adding interest" becomes $8,000 + $1,200 or $9,200. The "amount repaid" will *not* be $4,000, since the company reduces its repayments by 10% per year – it is $4,000 less 10% which is $400 ie $3,600; therefore, the "remaining balance at end of "Year 2" is $9,200 − $3,600 = $5,600. This in turn is the balance at the start of Year 3.

The interest paid in Year 3 is

$$\frac{5,600 \times 12.5 \times 1}{100} = \$700$$

so the outstanding balance is $5,600 + $700 or $6,300. The amount repaid this time is 10% less than the $3,600 of the previous year; this comes to $3,600 − $360 or $3,240, and the remaining balance is $6,300 − $3,240 or $3,060. Again $3,060 is carried onto the next line.

Finally, we obtain the Year 4 figures. The interest this time is

$$\frac{3,060 \times 7.5 \times 1}{100} = \$229.50$$

so the outstanding balance is $3,060 + $229.50 or $3,289.50. The amount repaid, is 10% less than the previous $3,240, so is $2,916; the final remaining balance is $3,289.50 − $2,916 or $373.50. Having performed the calculations, the table should now appear as follows

| Year | Remaining Balance | Interest Rate | Balance Outstanding After Adding Interest | Amount Repaid | Remaining Balance At End Of Year |
|---|---|---|---|---|---|
| | $ | % | $ | $ | $ |
| 1 | 10,000.00 | 20 | 12,000.00 | 4,000.00 | 8,000.00 |
| 2 | 8,000.00 | 15 | 9,200.00 | 3,600.00 | 5,600.00 |
| 3 | 5,600.00 | 12.5 | 6,300.00 | 3,240.00 | 3,060.00 |
| 4 | 3,060.00 | 7.5 | 3,289.50 | 2,916.00 | 373.50 |

With problems you meet, there is often the possibility of making false assumptions. In the example we have used it could be assumed that the amount repaid is always 10% less than the previous year's figure – however, we can also read the question to imply that, having reduced the figure by $400 after the first year, the firm pays back the same in each year which follows. It is unfortunate that questions are open to misinterpretation but the safest approach (since you cannot ask questions during an examination) is to show clearly *exactly* how you have performed the calculation. The examiner will then be able to give you full credit for your calculations, as far as they are correct.

*Part (b)*

Now we come to part (b). The "total interest paid" involves adding the interest for each of the four years – $2,000 + $1,200 + $700 + $229.50 giving a total of $4129.50. Note that these figures do not appear in the table, but if you set your work out carefully, these figures will be easy to find. However, if you do not set out your work with care, you may have to re-calculate in an examination; this would take up valuable time.

Adding the entries in the fifth column gives the total amount repaid, a sum of $13,756. We can now find the percentage as in $\dfrac{4129.50 \times 100}{13756} = 30.0196$

The number of decimal places you arrive at may depend on the calculator (or the log tables) you are using and on the order in which you calculate the sum; however, the answer here is "correct to one decimal place", so 30.0% is the required value. Note that you must quote the zero after the decimal point – an answer of 30% is wrong as it is not given correct to one decimal place.

*Part (c)*

For the pie chart of part (c), we need to list the three quantities we are to show, ie:

|                     | $         |
|---------------------|-----------|
| Original loan       | 10,000.00 |
| Total amount repaid | 13,756.00 |
| Total interest paid | 4,129.50  |

The total is $27,885.50. Since a pie chart must show the total as 360°, each dollar relates to an angle of $360/27885.50$ degrees; thus the angles of the three sectors are

| Original loan | $\dfrac{\$10,000.00 \times 360}{27885.50} = 129°$ |
|---|---|
| Total amount repaid | $\dfrac{\$13,756.00 \times 360}{27885.50} = 178°$ |
| Total interest paid | $\dfrac{\$4,129.50 \times 360}{27885.50} = 53°$ |

You *must* check that the angles add up to 360° – if they do not, check your arithmetic. Here I give all angles to the nearest degree; do not be too surprised if your total is not exactly 360° – rounding errors can creep in sometimes.

*Part (d)*

Part (d) asks you to sketch the actual pie chart. Note the word "sketch" – you do not have to draw it with complete accuracy, but do take care to present the pie chart clearly.

Note that, in sketching the pie chart, you do not need to shade the sectors, but be sure to label each one correctly. (Note too, that this is not a good use of pie charts in real life – can you think why?)

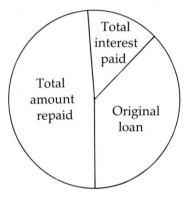

This first worked example may seem long, mainly because we have gone through each stage of the calculation in full, and given comments to aid your understanding. Now we look at another example.

**Second Example**

Two 4-bit registers add binary integers in twos-complement form. A 4-bit sum register and a 4-bit carry register hold the result.

(a) Show the contents of each of the four registers for the following calculations.

    (i)    $7 + 3$
    (ii)   $6 + (-2)$
    (iii)  $(-8) + 3$
    (iv)  $(-5) + (-4)$

(b) How can overflow be detected using the carry register?

(c) When overflow occurs, the system converts the result into a normalised floating point number of 12 bits: eg, 0 1010 1011010, where the first bit represents the sign of the mantissa (0 is positive), the next four bits are the integer exponent in twos-complement form, and the remaining seven bits are the normalised mantissa (ie the assumed point comes directly before the first bit). Show how the system would hold $-9$ in this form.

(d) Express the base 10 numbers 375 and 467 in BCD. Add them, showing clearly how you add using BCD. Show that the resulting BCD number represents the correct value.

## Solution

Part (a) of this problem is quite straightforward, it only requires knowledge of how to represent and add binary values. Since we deal with 4-bit registers throughout, we should show all values in four bits – for example, code $+3$ as 0011 rather than as 11.

(i)     Binary 0111 is 7 and binary 0011 is 3, so we have

$$
\begin{array}{r}
0111 \\
0011 + \\
\hline
\text{Sum } 1010 \\
\text{Carry } 0111
\end{array}
$$

(ii)    Binary 0110 is 6 and $-2$ is binary 1110 (be careful with negative values), so we have

$$
\begin{array}{r}
0110 \\
1110 + \\
\hline
\text{Sum } 0100 \\
\text{Carry } 1110
\end{array}
$$

(iii)   Binary 1000 is $-8$ and 3 is binary 0011, giving

$$
\begin{array}{r}
1000 \\
0011 + \\
\hline
\text{Sum } 1011 \\
\text{Carry } 0000
\end{array}
$$

(iv)    Since $-5$ is binary 1011 and $-4$ is binary 1100, we have

$$
\begin{array}{r}
1011 \\
1100 + \\
\hline
\text{Sum } 0111 \\
\text{Carry } 1000
\end{array}
$$

In each case, we have fully identified both the sum and the carry; in particular, see how the register holds all the carries from one column to the next. In ordinary arithmetic we might not do this as formally, but in computing we can use the results to our advantage.

To answer part (b), we need to identify what we mean by overflow; a

4-bit register can hold any value in the range from binary 1000 (the most negative) up to 0111 (the most positive-: this means from −8 to +7 in decimal. Hence the 4-bit register can cope only with values in the range −8 to +7.

Examine the four sets of part (a) of the question. You can see that the answers are, respectively, (i) 10, (ii) 4, (iii) −5 and (iv) −9. It is only in (ii) and (iii) that the values are in the range −8 to +7; in neither of these cases is there any overflow. However, the results of (i) and (iv) each give values outside the range, so overflow has taken place here. Looking at the carry register in each case we can see that if overflow has taken place, the first two bits of the carry are different from each other, but they are the same where there is no overflow. This then is the answer; overflow can be detected if the first two bits of the carry register are different.

Part (c) gives us a set of instructions – therefore all we have to do is follow them through. To represent −9 in normalised floating point format, put it into mantissa/exponent format first; remember that the mantissa must be in the range 0.5 to 1 (decimal) or .1 to 1 in binary – this means that −9 becomes − $\frac{9}{16}$ × 16, or − $\frac{9}{16}$ × $2^4$, in decimal terms. As there is a negative sign in the calculation, the first bit in the normalised floating point number must be 1; the next four bits must give the exponent (which is 4) in binary, ie 0100. We are left with expressing the mantissa $\frac{9}{16}$ as a 7-bit binary fraction, 1001 000. The overall result is that the normalised floating point representation of −9 has to be, using the given structure, 1 0100 1001000.

Part (d) of the question requires the use of BCD; the first two conversions are quite straightforward:

375 becomes 0011 0111 0101
467 becomes 0100 0110 0111

BCD addition appears in Chapter 4; using the values here, we get

0011 0111 0101
0100 0110 0111 +
0111 1101*1100*
    1°0111°0110
1000 0100 0010

which reads as 8 4 2, the correct value. * indicates something is not a valid BCD code, and $^c$ shows a carry from a previous column. In the example, by adding 0101 to 0111 we obtained 1100; clearly this is not a valid BCD code (since it does not represent a digit in the range 0 to 9), this is why 0110 is added. The same thing happens when we try to add 0111 and 0110 – these give a total of 1101, once again not a valid BCD code – but this time there is the 0110 to be added as well as the carry from the previous column which is why 0111 appears rather than 0110.

The result has already been seen to give the decimal value 842, which you can check is correct by adding 375 and 467.

**NOW TRY THESE . . .**

1. Three people contribute $5,000 in the ratio 1:2:5 to set up a company producing software. Apart from salaries and expenses they agree not to receive any repayment for four years.

   The following table shows value of sales, expenses and interest rate paid on the remaining balance for each of the four years.

| Year | Sales $ | Expenses $ | Interest rate on Balance after Sales and Expenses |
|------|---------|------------|---------------------------------------------------|
| 1 | 10,000 | 12,000 | 10.0% |
| 2 | 15,000 | 10,000 | 12.0% |
| 3 | 16,000 | 12,000 | 12.5% |
| 4 | 20,000 | 15,000 | 11.0% |

   (a) Calculate how much each person originally contributes.
   (b) Calculate the balance after sales and expenses, the amount of interest on this balance and the balance carried forward for each of the four years (to the nearest dollar).

   They then agree to leave $10,000 in the company and divide the rest, which is taxed at 33⅓%, in the same ratio as their contributions.

   (c) Calculate the amount of tax paid
   (d) Calculate how much each receives after tax
   (e) Produce pie charts to show
       (i)    the original contribution of the three people
       (ii)   the tax and the three repayments

2. (a) In a particular computer 8-bit registers hold numbers, using twos-complement for negative values.

       (i)    Write down the range of whole numbers a single register can hold
       (ii)   Show how the system holds −100
       (iii)  Show how it would find the value of 84 − 112
       (iv)   Show how overflow is detected if an attempt is made to add 100 to 50.

   (b) The register is now used with the assumed binary point as shown below:

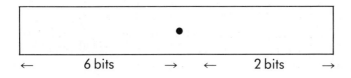

   ←        6 bits        →    ←      2 bits      →

    (i)     Write down the range of fractional numbers which a single register can now hold

    (ii)    For numbers in this range, what is the maximum absolute error in the representation?

    (iii)   Show the contents of the register as accurately as possible when representing the following values

         (1) 12.5

         (2) $-4\frac{1}{4}$

         (3) 1.7

    (iv)    What is the relative error in the representation of 1.7? (Give your answer to the nearest whole number).

3. A particular microcomputer handles 8-bit words in its ALU. These words can represent integers using the twos-complement system for negatives.

(a) Write down the 8-bit representations for $+25$ and $-25$.

(b) What range of integers can be stored in eight bits using this system?

Floating point numbers are stored using 16 bits in the format
         0 101011 110110111

The first bit is the mantissa sign bit, the next six bits are the exponent in excess-32 form and the final nine are the normalised mantissa.

(c) Express the decimal number $+20.25$ in this format

(d) Express the floating point number 0 011111 110000000 in decimal

In all calculations the computer truncates the mantissa to ten bits.

(e) Express the octal number $+325.2$ in this floating point format and find the relative error correct to the nearest whole number.

4. A 16-bit word length microcomputer represents numbers in normal-ised floating-point form. Of the 16 bits, the leftmost ten store the mantissa (with the binary point assumed to be after the leftmost bit). The mantissa is in twos-complement form. The remaining six bits store the exponent in excess-32 form.

Two typical numbers in this form are:

A     0100010011 100111

B     0110101000 100010

(a) Explain the meanings of the terms underlined

(b) Give the denary (decimal) forms of A and B

(c) Show how A and B would be added in floating-point form

(d) Convert your answer from adding A and B into denary and explain why the computer result differs from the correct sum of A and B.

# 6    Basic statistics

## OBJECTIVES

When you've worked through this Chapter, you should be able to:

— state some uses of statistical techniques

— state how qualitative and quantitative data differ, including continuous and discrete in the latter case

— convert a set of raw data to a frequency table

— give advantages and disadvantages of graphs compared to tables

— draw pictograms, pie charts and bar charts from frequency tables, and explain their values in practice

— draw and use histograms, frequency polygons, and cumulative frequency graphs

— draw and interpret time and scatter graphs.

## INTRODUCTION

A major task of any computer-based management information system is to accept a (potentially) very large volume of individual records and produce as output a well-organised and coherent summary. The tools and techniques of statistics help summarise the raw data, analyse it, and draw conclusions from it.

A firm may store data on the sales of their products over a period of time, so they can know which products are growing in popularity and which are falling. They will also want to find out where each product sells best.

Depending on the results, the firm may change production levels, marketing strategies, and deliveries to retail outlets. Such situations are common; statistical analytical techniques can cope with them.

In the computer department itself, the same techniques analyse machine downtime, regulate machine loading, and predict demand for consumable items like printer ribbons, paper, and disks. There's also a need to examine the efficiency of software packages, staff productivity levels, and the effectiveness of new products for the machine room before a decision is made to buy them.

At a more advanced level, statistics help people organise file and database structures, and to "fine-tune" systems so they work as well as possible.

Since most management information systems give screen-based output, people find graphical representations of data create a better understood analysis than tables of figures, though in most systems *both* have an important place. As most people absorb graphical output more quickly than tables of data, this is a major factor in the design of output – whether to screens or to printers.

The only limit to the successful development of this are the resolution of the screens in graphics mode and the level of statistical knowledge of the system's designers.

## 6.1   TYPES OF DATA

It may be useful to define the forms that data can take – as certain types of graphical representation are more suitable than others in different cases.

*Qualitative* data involves qualities we cannot measure such as colours, types of material, personal preferences in respect of music, books, and so on. If you survey the colours of clothing worn by a specific group of people, the results are qualitative (for example "red coat", "blue coat" and "yellow coat"). In the same way, materials (such as nylon, aluminium, paper) are qualitative.

We can measure the number of people *wearing* red coats – but we can't assign a numerical value to the concept of 'red'. If we can't place data in any particular order, for example, should red come before yellow or after it?, then the data is qualitative.

*Quantitative* data, however, can go into a well-defined sequence – shoe size 38 comes before size 40, which in turn comes before size 42, and so on. We can't assign to qualitative data the ideas of "greater" or "lesser" – such terms as these, which let us compare data items, can refer only to data which is quantitative. Quantitative data therefore includes length, volume, weight, temperature, etc – to each of these we can assign numerical values and place values in order.

Quantitative data can be divided into continuous and discrete types (see Figure 6.1). Continuous data allows every value in a range while discrete data allows for a limited number only. Continuous data includes time, length, weight; thus, in theory at least, we can measure any value of time between 6 and 7 seconds even if the value is 6.385218 seconds. Discrete items such as shoe sizes for example do not have intermediate values, therefore, 41, 42, 43, 44 etc are the sizes and 41.7 just cannot occur. Likewise paint may be bought in 0.25 litre, 0.5 litre or litre tins, but a tin of 0.3728 litres would not be practical. Volumes are usually continuous but in the case of tins of paint, the data is discrete.

Types of Data

Qualitative:

- colour

- types of cloth

- foods

- favourite singers

Quantitative:

Continuous:

- length of a road

- weight of a parcel

- age of a building

- temperature of a room

Discrete:

- shoe size

- clothing size

- number of people in a room

- sizes of tins of food

**Figure 6.1    Types of data**

## 6.2   TABLES

"Raw" data usually consists of large volumes of figures, often poorly laid out, so that they overwhelm the reader. The first stage in making data usable is to refine it into tabular (table) form – organised in order and summarised. Figure 6.2 presents a list of the quantities of paper used for each of 120 jobs run on a computer in a particular day. It is difficult, when figures are presented in this way, to extract information.

To present this in a more useful form, divide the numbers of sheets used into a number of classes, usually of equal size, such as 5–, 10–, etc. Now count (tally) how many jobs are in each class – use a single stroke for each job and a cross-stroke for every fifth one (to make counting easier later). When added, the total of the strokes in each class is its

**Number of sheets of printer paper used
on each of 120 jobs**

| | | | | | | | | | | | |
|---|---|---|---|---|---|---|---|---|---|---|---|
| 17 | 8 | 14 | 17 | 5 | 9 | 11 | 18 | 22 | 14 | 6 | 17 |
| 24 | 11 | 18 | 7 | 21 | 14 | 12 | 27 | 13 | 12 | 9 | 18 |
| 14 | 29 | 13 | 8 | 9 | 16 | 27 | 21 | 14 | 11 | 19 | 7 |
| 18 | 14 | 21 | 27 | 11 | 10 | 19 | 14 | 12 | 17 | 9 | 12 |
| 23 | 16 | 7 | 14 | 21 | 17 | 19 | 24 | 26 | 2 | 5 | 18 |
| 17 | 24 | 13 | 17 | 8 | 14 | 13 | 28 | 16 | 7 | 8 | 14 |
| 19 | 16 | 18 | 24 | 7 | 14 | 16 | 19 | 11 | 17 | 23 | 12 |
| 27 | 9 | 8 | 19 | 13 | 25 | 18 | 21 | 10 | 15 | 11 | 14 |
| 9 | 8 | 20 | 16 | 8 | 11 | 22 | 10 | 17 | 9 | 18 | 12 |
| 14 | 28 | 12 | 10 | 9 | 24 | 20 | 5 | 16 | 7 | 10 | 7 |

**Figure 6.2   List of data for tabulation**

frequency. This frequency is the number of times the particular class occurs in the distribution as a whole. The resulting table (with or without the tally marks) is known as a frequency table – it shows the frequency of each class in the original data. See Figure 6.3.

Note that 10– means 10 to 14 inclusive, as the data is discrete. The frequency of this particular class is 37 – there were 37 entries in the original table in the range 10 to 14 inclusive.

| Number of sheets of paper used | Tally | Frequency |
|---|---|---|
| 0– | l | 1 |
| 5– | l卌 卌 卌 卌 卌 l | 26 |
| 10– | 卌 卌 卌 卌 卌 卌 卌 ll | 37 |
| 15– | 卌 卌 卌 卌 卌 卌 l | 31 |
| 20– | 卌 卌 卌 l | 16 |
| 25– | 卌 llll | 9 |

Total of all frequencies = 120

**Figure 6.3   Frequency table**

**NOW TRY THESE . . .**

1. For each of the following, decide whether the data is qualitative or quantitative; if it is quantitative state whether it's discrete or continuous:

(a)  The temperature of the machine room

(b)  The number of boxes of printer paper delivered today

(c)  The makes of microcomputers used in a firm

(d)  The time taken to execute an instruction in a processor

(e)  The number of staff in a data processing department

(f)  The number of lines of code in each of a number of programs

(g)  The size of main memory in KB

(h)  The tasks of a systems programmer

(i)  The number of runs of a program needed to get a "clean" compilation

(j)  the salaries paid to staff in a data processing department

2. Here is a list of the salaries paid (in dollars) to the 70 staff in a data processing department.

| | | | | | | | | | |
|---|---|---|---|---|---|---|---|---|---|
| 314 | 65 | 381 | 174 | 219 | 78 | 156 | 198 | 274 | 315 |
| 279 | 82 | 186 | 287 | 153 | 158 | 341 | 287 | 164 | 236 |
| 183 | 176 | 291 | 310 | 264 | 109 | 316 | 192 | 112 | 206 |
| 194 | 319 | 354 | 264 | 154 | 322 | 213 | 352 | 219 | 341 |
| 263 | 174 | 207 | 158 | 291 | 371 | 150 | 171 | 286 | 136 |
| 374 | 163 | 148 | 78 | 273 | 286 | 163 | 253 | 172 | 118 |
| 286 | 293 | 376 | 107 | 241 | 159 | 88 | 164 | 154 | 209 |

Using categories of 60−, 80−, 100−, etc up to 380−, conduct a tally, and so produce a frequency table for the data.

3. A benchmark test on each of 50 microcomputers gave the following times, in seconds, to perform certain tasks.

Time taken in seconds to
perform a certain task

| | | | | | | | | | |
|---|---|---|---|---|---|---|---|---|---|
| 416 | 289 | 517 | 275 | 496 | 316 | 417 | 316 | 309 | 453 |
| 374 | 361 | 428 | 538 | 299 | 414 | 586 | 480 | 516 | 347 |
| 288 | 351 | 500 | 550 | 463 | 512 | 542 | 314 | 531 | 376 |
| 459 | 308 | 486 | 345 | 406 | 419 | 599 | 398 | 319 | 428 |
| 374 | 410 | 292 | 290 | 353 | 327 | 417 | 484 | 418 | 572 |

Using categories of 275−, 300−, 325−, etc up to 575−, conduct a tally and produce a frequency table for the data.

## 6.3  PICTURING DATA

Most people find a diagram can quickly give far more information than can a table of figures; "one picture is worth a thousand words" is often true here. A table may contain a considerable amount of detailed information, but it tends to be dull and to lack impact. A diagram, if used effectively, gives an immediate overview of the contents of the table; and information can be absorbed more easily, even if the diagram tends to lack some of the finer detail. It is common, in practice, therefore, to produce both diagram and table, to provide the combination of impact, overview and detail required by the user.

There are a number of different types of diagram people use to produce the right impact.

### 6.3.1  Pictograms

The results of a survey showed that 4000 visual display units each cost between $600 and $700. This could be shown using four pictures of a VDU, each standing for 1000 machines. Figure 6.4 shows the full survey table and a pictogram.

| Cost of VDU ($) | Frequency |
|:---:|:---:|
| 600 − | 4000 |
| 700 − | 5500 |
| 800 − | 2000 |
| 900 − 1000 | 500 |

Figure 6.4   A pictogram

The point of the pictogram (also called ideograph or isotype chart), is that the reader can easily identify the symbols with the item whose frequency is shown. These symbols can be subdivided but it's not wise to do so beyond the half-unit. (Otherwise problems arise regarding the accuracy of the drawing).

The pictogram is quite versatile – it depends largely on the imagination of the artist, and copes equally well with data which is qualitative or quantitative. All the same, it is open to abuse.

In Figure 6.5, the symbol on the left stands, as before, for 1000 VDUs, and the one on the right is twice as high (and in proportion elsewhere). As it is twice as high it could stand for 2000 VDUs; alternatively, as it takes up four times the area on the page (since both height and width are double) it could stand for 4000. There's also the argument that, since its volume would be eight times that of the original (height and width and depth are all double) it could stand for 8000. To avoid this kind of problem, decide on one symbol of a given size and use it throughout the pictogram; do not use others of different sizes, unless they can be clearly identified in the key.

1000 VDUs                                          2000?
                                                   4000?
                                                   8000?

**Figure 6.5    An ambiguous pictogram**

### 6.3.2    Pie charts

The pie chart uses a circle for the whole distribution; individual sectors represent the classes. The size of the circle isn't critical.

The angle at the centre of each sector is proportional to the frequency of the value that sector represents; as the area of the sector is proportional to this angle also; it can be used to stand for the frequency.

Therefore the frequency can be identified directly with the angle at the centre of the sector or with the sector area or with the arc length of the sector.

Figure 6.6 shows how to create a pie chart; note that, as the total frequency (for the whole distribution) is 80, this must be proportional to the angle of the whole circle, 360°. Thus each person is represented by a sector angle of 360°÷80, ie 4½°.

For a sector to represent 18 people (the operators) it must have an angle of 18 × 4 ½° or 81°; calculate the others in the same way. The angle for data preparation staff must also be 81°, and for data control it is 22½°, for programmers it's 94½°, for analysts 67½°, and for managers it's 13½°. Note that you should add all the angles to check they total 360°.

**Distribution of staff in Computer Centre**

| Class | Number of staff |
|---|---|
| Data preparation personnel | 18 |
| Data control personnel | 5 |
| Operators | 18 |
| Programmers | 21 |
| Analysts | 15 |
| Managers | 3 |

Total = 80

Angle for analyst sector $\frac{15}{80} \times 360° = 67\frac{1}{2}°$

**Figure 6.6   Data table converted into a pie chart**

In general people draw pie charts so the sectors appear in order of size. This is for visual effect only. However, occasions do arise when we need two or more pie charts in the same diagram, usually for the purpose of comparison.

For example, the previous pie chart showed the distribution of 80 staff in a data processing department in 1985; the second diagram shows the same department in 1990, when there were a total of 135. Since the two pie charts will appear side by side, it's important to ensure they do achieve the correct visual comparison. The eye is strongly influenced by area so the areas of the two circles are in the same ratio as the staff totals, 80:135. Thus, if the radius of the smaller, 1985, circle is 40mm, the radius of the larger, 1990, circle is

$$40 \times \sqrt{\frac{135}{80}} = 52 \text{ mm (correct to 1 mm)}$$

The sizes of the sectors for the 1990 circle are expressed in precisely the same way as before. The table below provides the data for 1990 and the angles.

| Class | Number of staff in 1990 | Sector Angle |
|---|---|---|
| Data preparation personnel | 25 | 67° |
| Data control personnel | 8 | 21° |
| Operators | 32 | 85° |
| Programmers | 36 | 96° |
| Analysts | 31 | 83° |
| Managers | 3 | 8° |
| TOTAL | 135 | 360° |

Table 6.1   Distribution of staff data for 1990

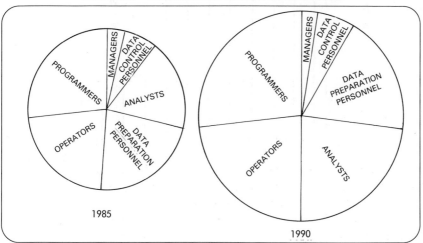

Figure 6.7   Comparison pie charts

Figure 6.7 shows two pie charts, drawn as indicated. A full comparison can easily be made of each year as well as between years.

### 6.3.3   Bar charts

Bar charts are an alternative method of representing data that could be shown on a pictogram or pie chart, thus they are equally suited to qualitative or quantitative data representations.

The main difference is the use of "bars" instead of sets of pictures or sectors of a circle. The bars are of equal width so their areas are proportional to their lengths; thus the frequency for each is shown either by height or by area. The vertical scale at the left of the chart in Figure 6.8 indicates frequency and is linear, so equal intervals on the scale stand for equal changes of frequency. The bars themselves stand on a horizontal axis with gaps between them, and with labels to show what each represents. It is common to arrange bars either in ascending or descending order of size but this is not essential. Also bar charts may be drawn with the bars running across the page with the axes inter-changed.

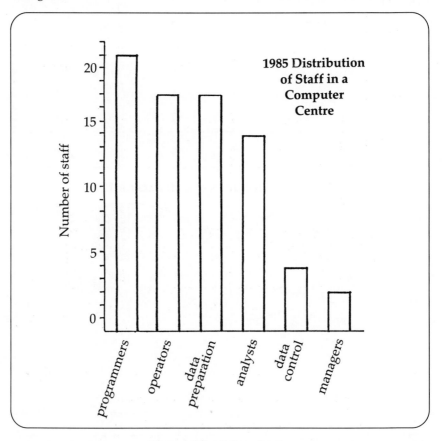

**Figure 6.8   A bar chart**

Sometimes you may want to use a bar chart to compare classes whose frequencies are roughly the same size. To draw them full-scale would produce bars of much the same length. To resolve this problem, it is acceptable to insert a break in the bars (see Figure 6.9). This means that a larger scale can be used to show differences more clearly. Note that you can do this with pictograms too, but not with pie charts.

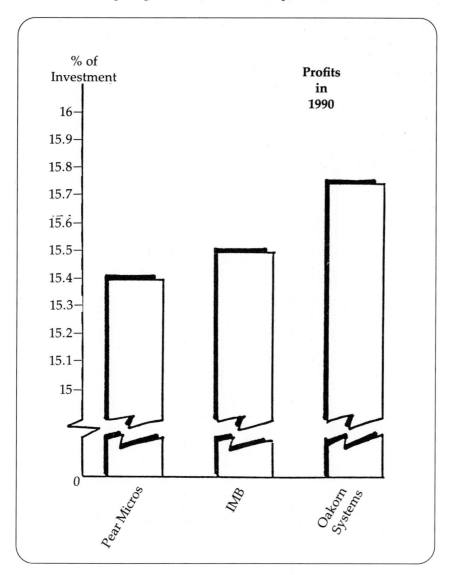

**Figure 6.9    Bar chart with breaks for clarity**

Returning to the 1985 staff figures, we may also wish to know the numbers of males and females in each class. This can be achieved by sub-dividing the bars, to give what some call a component bar chart. There may be more than two sub-divisions in each class – shading and a key are, therefore, essential.

This type of chart lets you compare the composition of the sub-divisions within a class; you can also compare the sub-divisions with each other on a class-by-class basis – and still compare the classes themselves. Figure 6.10, therefore, illustrates not only the male-female division within each class, but also the distribution of each sex within the department – providing supplementary information to the original "global" purpose of the chart.

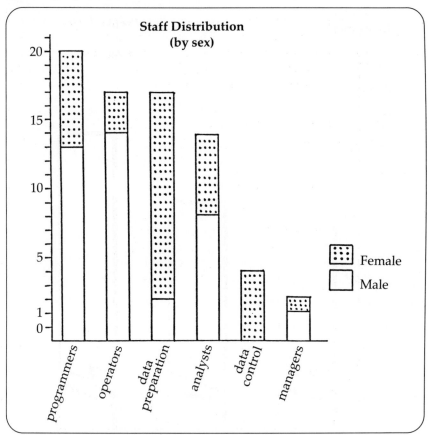

**Figure 6.10    A component bar chart**

There are many other types of bar chart but it is not necessary to cover these at this stage.

### 6.3.4   Histograms and frequency polygons

The graphs defined so far can be used for either qualitative or quantitative data. Those we turn to now apply to quantitative data only.

The histogram is rather like a bar chart to look at, though, there are no gaps between the bars (which are still of equal width), and the horizontal axis has a linear scale. The range of values of each class appears on the horizontal scale – so the order of classes depends on the numerical order of the values. The vertical axis shows the frequency of each class.

Figure 6.11 shows a histogram of the number of hardware items distributed by age; for instance, some 600 items in a department between six and eight years old, while there are none in the 0–2 year old class.

The data here, identifying the age of equipment (called the independent variable) is continuous. Thus the classes of 2–4, 4–6, etc share boundaries (in this case four years) – four years is the upper limit of one class and the lower limit of a second class. In such cases we put half of the items exactly four years old into each class.

The histogram shown has another feature. The mid-points of the tops of the bars have been plotted and joined by a series of straight lines to create what we call a frequency polygon. Though there are no bars between the years 0–2 and 14–16, the spaces are identified with a zero frequency and points are plotted on them to close off the polygon.

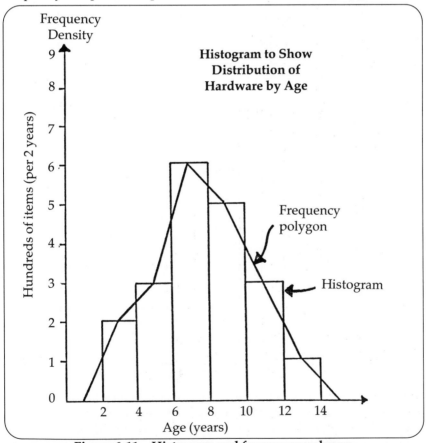

Figure 6.11    Histogram and frequency polygon

Figure 6.12 is a histogram associated with discrete data; here the variable (the number of people) dealt with is integral, so that classes of 0–4, 5–9, 10–14, etc are a good choice. However, rather than have a gap between the boundaries (eg at 4 and 5) we make a common boundary (4½) between the 0–4 and 5–9 categories and similarly elsewhere.

| Number of people in each department | Number of Departments |
|---|---|
| 0–4 | 5 |
| 5–9 | 8 |
| 10–14 | 14 |
| 15–19 | 17 |
| 20–24 | 12 |
| 25–29 | 8 |
| 30–34 | 6 |
| 35–49 | 6 |

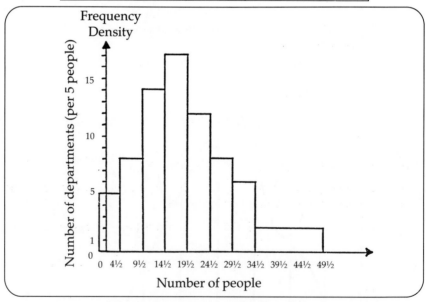

**Figure 6.12  Histogram showing the importance of area**

The other feature here is the presence of a class whose width is not the same as that of the others in the class: 35–49 is three times as wide as the others. In a histogram it's the area of the bar, not its height, which represents its frequency – since the frequency of the 35–49 category is 6, the height of the bar must be one third of 6, ie 2, to compensate for the treble width. This is why the vertical axis is labelled "frequency density" rather than frequency – it really refers to the frequency per "standard unit of bar-width".

**NOW TRY THESE . . .**

1. The data below refers to the number of people employed in computing jobs in a particular town.

| | |
|---|---|
| Programmers | 250 |
| Data preparation personnel | 150 |
| Systems Analysts | 175 |
| Operators | 300 |
| Managers | 25 |

Create a pictogram to show the data.

2. This list shows the number of computers manufactured by each company in a small area of the country.

| | |
|---|---|
| IBM | 12 |
| ICL | 7 |
| Unisys | 4 |
| Tandem | 5 |
| Bull | 9 |
| Hewlett Packard | 7 |
| DEC | 14 |
| Data General | 2 |

Illustrate the data using (i) a pie chart (ii) a bar chart

3. Create a component bar chart to show the following distribution of jobs undertaken by six companies last month.

| Company | Batch jobs | Real-time jobs | Maintenance |
|---|---|---|---|
| Art Sales | 8 | 24 | 6 |
| Bannerjee | 4 | 9 | 1 |
| Chicken Farms | 3 | 17 | 3 |
| Data House | 9 | 12 | 6 |
| Ed Con | 16 | 14 | 4 |
| Fat Choy | 12 | 10 | 7 |

4. Produce pie charts for time lost (in hours) in May 1988 and May 1990.

| Month | Industrial Action | Hardware Faults | Software Faults | Human Error | Total |
|---|---|---|---|---|---|
| May 1988 | 6 | 7 | 15 | 3 | 31 |
| May 1990 | 2 | 5 | 34 | 8 | 49 |

5. Draw a histogram and on it a frequency polygon to show the following data for monthly salaries. (First decide whether the data is continuous or discrete).

| Salary Range ($) | Number of staff |
|---|---|
| 0–100 | 7 |
| 100 – 200 | 12 |
| 200 – 300 | 19 |
| 300 – 400 | 27 |
| 400 – 500 | 14 |
| 500 – 600 | 8 |
| 600 – 700 | 2 |

6. The following data gives the number of runs taken to get a program working for each of 30 programming students. Again, draw a histogram and on it a frequency polygon to represent the figures.

| Number of runs | Number of students |
|---|---|
| 1 – 3 | 4 |
| 4 – 6 | 6 |
| 7 – 9 | 9 |
| 10 – 12 | 4 |
| 13 – 15 | 3 |
| 16 – 21 | 4 |

## 6.4   CUMULATIVE FREQUENCY

Sometimes a frequency distribution, as has been explained so far, is not enough. The total frequency up to a particular value on the horizontal axis (the value of the relevant variable) may be needed.

For example, Table 6.2 summarises the number of lines of code in the programs in the library file. It shows that 24 programs have between 150 and 174 lines of code. However, we may want to know how many have

less than 175; this is the sum of the frequencies in the classes 100−, 125−
and 150 − a cumulative frequency of 3 + 12 + 24 = 39.

| Lines of code | Number of programs |
|---|---|
| 100 − | 3 |
| 125 − | 12 |
| 150 − | 24 |
| 175 − | 42 |
| 200 − | 51 |
| 225 − | 39 |
| 250 − | 30 |
| 275 − | 21 |
| 300 − | 12 |
| 325 − 349 | 6 |

**Table 6.2   Breakdown of number of lines of code in different programs**

| Lines of code (less than) | Cumulative frequency |
|---|---|
| 100 | 0 |
| 125 | 3 |
| 150 | 15 |
| 175 | 39 |
| 200 | 81 |
| 225 | 132 |
| 250 | 171 |
| 275 | 201 |
| 300 | 222 |
| 325 | 234 |
| 350 | 240 |

**Table 6.3   Cumulative frequency table**

First build what we call a cumulative frequency distribution table (Table 6.3) – count up the total frequency below each of the boundary values, including the lower limit of the first class as well as the upper limit of the last. The total frequencies for values less than 100, 125, 150, etc will need to be found. Since there is nothing below 100 the cumulative frequency less than 100 is 0; for less than 125 it is 3; for less than 150 it is 3 + 12 = 15, and so on. The final cumulative frequency – less than 350 – is the total of all the original frequencies, ie 240. You can use this to check for errors.

The table shows that 15 programs have fewer than 150 lines of code each and that 201 have less than 275 lines each. To produce the corresponding cumulative frequency curve, plot the values from the cumulative frequency table. The cumulative frequency (or *cf*) of 15 goes against the *x* value of 150, 201 against 275, and so on – until all the values have been plotted. Once the points are on, draw the curve as smoothly as possible. See Figure 6.13.

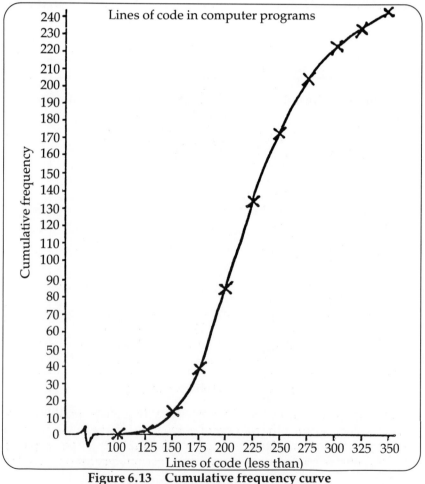

**Figure 6.13    Cumulative frequency curve**

Note that the horizontal axis is broken at the left to give a better scale.

To find how many programs contain fewer than any given number of lines of code just read off the values : other uses for such a curve will be introduced later.

## 6.5   TIME SERIES GRAPHS

People often need to record how a measure changes with the passage of time. For instance, at school you may have noted the temperature each day, or the amount of rainfall, to see how they change over the year. Likewise a firm may wish to plot the sales figures of a product week by week to see where any peaks and troughs exist, and find evidence of any pattern that can relate to time of year, etc.

To show this as a graph, we use a time series graph (sometimes called a historigram), with time along the horizontal axis and the values of the variable on the vertical axis – in Figure 6.14.

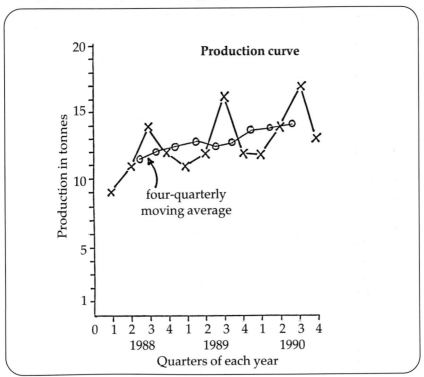

**Figure 6.14   A time series graph**

Always plot points against the time to which they relate, or, if they are average values, against the mid-point of the time interval, or, if they are totals for a period, against the end-point of the period. Since points other than those plotted have no meaning, use straight lines to join the points.

Time series graphs can show up "seasonal" variations – where the values of the variable tend to peak or trough at fairly regular intervals. Examples are ice-cream sales reaching a peak in the hot season, or the sales of meat being lowest on Mondays.

We can suppress these seasonal variations with a suitable moving average; the one shown in Figure 6.14 is a four-quarterly moving average. Note that we plot these at the centre of the period to which they relate; they are calculated by averaging the four consecutive figures which cover a year – ie quarter one to quarter four in 1988, then quarter two of 1988 to quarter one of 1989, etc. Join these points by lines to give a smooth curve which shows the trend – the way the variable really changes with time (ie, without the confusions caused by the peaks and troughs of any seasonal variation).

## 6.6  SCATTER DIAGRAMS

A time graph shows how one variable relates to time; people also wish to see how one variable relates to other variables. The kind of

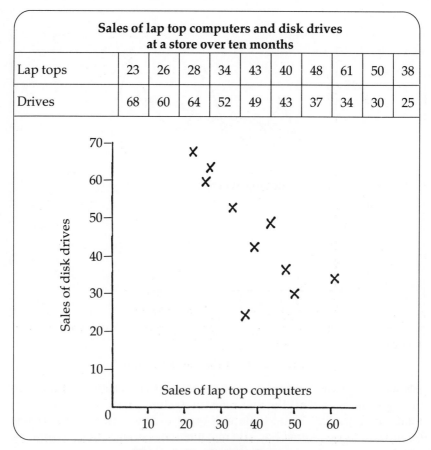

| Sales of lap top computers and disk drives at a store over ten months | | | | | | | | | | |
|---|---|---|---|---|---|---|---|---|---|---|
| Lap tops | 23 | 26 | 28 | 34 | 43 | 40 | 48 | 61 | 50 | 38 |
| Drives | 68 | 60 | 64 | 52 | 49 | 43 | 37 | 34 | 30 | 25 |

Figure 6.15   Scatter diagram

distribution which gives this consists of a set of pairs of values called a bivariate distribution. Figure 6.15 gives such a distribution and its scatter diagram. We put the two variables along the two axes and plot points from the table.

The scatter diagram is no more than a set of points scattered between the axes (hence the name). It's unlikely that the points will lie conveniently along some curve or straight line, but they may approximate to one. Generally, if high values of one variable seem to go with high values of the other (and low with low), we describe the variables as being directly correlated; this implies that an increase in one will cause an increase in the other.

If, however, high values of one variable tend to go with low values of the other, and vice versa (as in Figure 6.15) the variables are inversely correlated and an increase in one tends to produce a decrease in the other. Sometimes there is no obvious pattern at all; in this case there's no correlation between the two variables.

**NOW TRY THESE ...**

1. An analysis of the ages of the 120 staff of a computer department gives the following results.

| Age | Number |
|-----|--------|
| 20 – | 12 |
| 25 – | 17 |
| 30 – | 21 |
| 35 – | 18 |
| 40 – | 14 |
| 45 – | 13 |
| 50 – | 12 |
| 55 – | 9 |
| 60 – 65 | 4 |

Produce a cumulative frequency distribution table from the above data and so construct a cumulative frequency diagram. Use this to find how many employees were aged:

(i)  less than 33

(ii) less than 47

(iii) between 33 and 46 inclusive

2. Use the following information about machine downtime to draw up a time series graph. Identify any patterns that emerge.

Downtime in minutes per day

|          | Mon | Tues | Wed | Thurs | Fri | Sat |
|----------|-----|------|-----|-------|-----|-----|
| Week 1   | 97  | 23   | 68  | 68    | 93  | 71  |
| Week 2   | 48  | 6    | 86  | 104   | 93  | 51  |
| Week 3   | 71  | 45   | 71  | 64    | 87  | 119 |
| Week 4   | 115 | 51   | 123 | 118   | 128 | 106 |

3. The following bivariate distribution links the number of times a system has been run since it was first tested (x) with the number of errors it is known to contain (y) for twelve well-documented systems.

| System | A  | B  | C  | D  | E  | F  | G  | H  | I  | J  | K  | L  |
|--------|----|----|----|----|----|----|----|----|----|----|----|----|
| X      | 17 | 83 | 62 | 31 | 75 | 91 | 51 | 49 | 12 | 34 | 81 | 9  |
| Y      | 18 | 6  | 12 | 15 | 8  | 4  | 7  | 11 | 21 | 16 | 5  | 12 |

Draw a scatter diagram. Is there any evidence of correlation between x and y?

4. The following bivariate distribution shows the relationship between the mean temperature in °C(x) in the machine room and the number of minutes of downtime recorded (y) for each ten consecutive days:

| Day | A  | B  | C  | D  | E  | F  | G  | H  | I  | J  |
|-----|----|----|----|----|----|----|----|----|----|----|
| x   | 20 | 21 | 18 | 22 | 17 | 20 | 21 | 23 | 17 | 24 |
| y   | 5  | 8  | 10 | 11 | 13 | 4  | 9  | 13 | 14 | 16 |

Plot a scatter diagram. Is there any evidence of relationship between temperature and amount of downtime?

# 7 Is it probable?

## OBJECTIVES

When you've worked through this Chapter, you should be able to:

— state what people mean by the probability of an event

— give and work out examples

— state the sum of a complete set of probabilities

— work out compound probabilities, involving either AND or OR with up to three individual parts

— draw and use probability trees for AND compound cases.

## INTRODUCTION

Several aspects of the work of a data processing department will, sooner or later, involve the use of probability. For example, you may run a computer simulation (where the computer creates models of situations too dangerous, time-consuming or difficult to produce in real life). Then, the program (or the user) must assess how likely may be each of a number of possible outcomes at each stage of the simulation.

Likelihood is probability. Also, in many aspects of operational research you may need to be able to calculate probabilities – so the "best" information is provided to management to help in making decisions regarding the viability of a proposal, or in working out how long a certain project is likely to take.

Here's a third example. When people determine the size and nature of back-up hardware to guard against machine downtime in critical real-time situations (such as the control of an industrial process), they assess the risks involved and try to work out the likelihood of obvious types of failure.

Probability theory is, in fact, a very wide field, but is only covered briefly in this chapter.

## 7.1  RELATIVE FREQUENCY HISTOGRAMS

Histograms were used in Chapter 6 to compare the frequencies achieved by different classes in a particular distribution. However, the histograms did not show how to compare one class in a distribution with a different class in a second distribution because the two distributions might be of totally different sizes.

To see this more clearly think about the following:

— Computer A has 25 hours of downtime out of 2000 hours of running

— Computer B has 6 hours of downtime out of 100 hours of running

We cannot assume that B is more reliable than A simply because it has less recorded downtime – those figures don't reflect the total running time. In fact, it could be said that A is the more reliable – it has 1.25% of downtime compared to the 6% of machine B.

When trying to compare many different classes in two or more distributions, a relative frequency histogram (based on the same idea as the percentage comparison just used) avoids the problems of the more straightforward histogram.

To create a relative frequency histogram, find the relative frequency for each class; this means you divide each actual frequency by the total of all the frequencies for the whole distribution.

If one class has a frequency of 12 and the total of all frequencies in the distribution is 200, that particular relative frequency is $^{12}/_{200} = 0.06$. Once you've worked this out for each class, draw the histogram using the relative rather than the absolute frequencies.

The total of all the relative frequencies for a given distribution will always be exactly 1 – no matter what the distribution is, how many classes it contains, or what the total of the actual frequencies is.

So now we can compare individual parts of two relative frequency histograms – for example, those of Figure 7.1, which show the ages of hardware in two workshops. You can see at once that there is a far higher proportion of hardware aged between 4 and 5 years in workshop W8 (a relative frequency of 0.35 – 35% as a percentage) than in workshop W6 (where the relative frequency is 0.1). Had the actual number of machines of that age been relied upon then the respective sizes of the two workshops and the quantity of hardware in each might have affected the conclusions.

## 7.2   RELATIVE FREQUENCY AND PROBABILITY

Relative frequency measures how one particular class occupies the distribution as a whole and in what proportion.

Staying with Figure 7.1, we ask "How likely is it that an item, chosen at random from workshop W8, will be between 4 and 5 years old?" The answer would be the proportion of workshop W8 equipment between 4

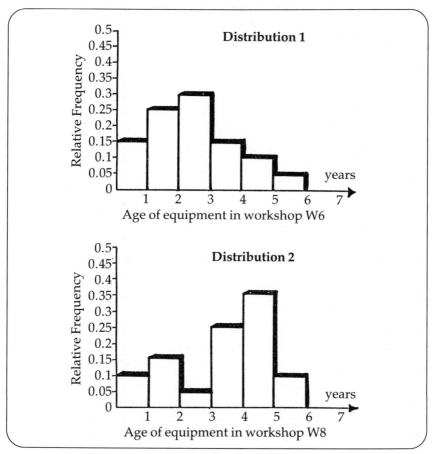

**Figure 7.1    Relative frequency histograms**

and 5 years old; we call such a likelihood a probability; in this case its value is 0.35.

So a relative frequency histogram gives the probability for each class. You can see that the smallest value any probability can take is zero (as in the case of 6–7 year old equipment); the maximum is 1 – if all the items are in the same range.

The phrase "chosen at random" means that all items are equally likely to be chosen – there is no reason for any preference (or bias) for any item. If the item were chosen by entering the workshop and taking the piece nearest the door, this might create bias – as this might be the position usually occupied by the last item to come into the room and, as such, the youngest. Again, neither size nor colour should influence the choice.

An ideal way of choosing might be to give each item a number and to draw the number at random from a container. This is a reasonably fair way of avoiding bias, if the machine whose number you draw becomes the one chosen "at random" from the workshop.

## 7.3   DEFINING PROBABILITY

We can formally define probability using the statement given in Figure 7.2.

> If an "experiment" has N equally likely outcomes, and an "event" involves E of these outcomes, the probability of that "event" is
>
> $$\frac{E}{N}$$
>
> ie  $P = \dfrac{E}{N}$  where P is the probability of success

**Figure 7.2    Defining probability**

The idea of "experiment" may seem an odd choice of phrase; it refers simply to any situation in which there can be one of a number of outcomes. Consider a few simple examples to make the definition clear.

Firstly, imagine a set of 52 items of hardware from which we can choose at random any one, which could be (with equal probability) a printer, modem, disk drive or tape deck. The "experiment" involves choosing an item from the set, and the outcomes are the different types of hardware.

However, one printer is set to handle 9600 baud transmission, as is one modem, one disk drive and one tape deck. Since there are 52 items ($E = 52$) of which 13 are printers ($N = 13$), the probability of drawing a printer at random is $^{13}/_{52}$ or $^{1}/_{4}$. Similarly, since there are four 9600 baud items ($N = 4$) the probability of drawing one at random is $^{4}/_{52}$ or $^{1}/_{13}$. The probability of choosing a 9600 baud printer ($N = 1$) is $^{1}/_{52}$.

When rolling a traditional six-sided die, there are six equally likely outcomes. The probability of throwing a 5 is $^{1}/_{6}$ (since $E=6$ and $N=1$), and the probability of throwing an even number ($N=3$ since there are three such outcomes) is $^{3}/_{6}$ or $^{1}/_{2}$. Not surprisingly, the probability of throwing a 7 would be 0 (since $N=0$), a value representing total impossibility. Alternatively the probability of throwing a number between 1 and 6 inclusive ($N=6$) is $^{6}/_{6}$, or 1, a value which shows absolute certainty.

The word "success" implies getting a desired outcome, such as an even-numbered face on the die; probability defined in this manner suggests the likelihood of achieving that success. We call this probability $p$. Also, $q$ is the probability of "failure", ie of failing to achieve "success".

Since it's absolutely certain that if an event is not a success it must be a failure, the two probabilities must add up to 1 (we see success and failure as complementary events). Hence:

$$p + q = 1$$

Using our example, if the test involved throwing the six-sided die and "success" is throwing a 3, then (with $N=6$ and $E=1$) $p=\frac{1}{6}$. Failure means not throwing a 3, ie throwing instead any other number so that (with $N=5$ and $E=6$) $q=\frac{5}{6}$. You can see that $p + q = 1$.

Many people use $P(E)$ to stand for the Probability of achieving an Event, with the particular event often stated in the brackets. Unless there's any chance of confusion, we shall take $P(E) = p$. Where some confusion is possible, values such as $p_1$, $p_2$, $p_3$, etc are used to refer to different probabilities in the same experiment.

As we can carry out an experiment more than once, we call each experiment a "trial". If the die is thrown 12 times, there are 12 trials of the same experiment. We can never say in advance what the outcome of any trial will be but we can, by theory, practical work of a mixture of both, identify all the possible outcomes and give each a probability that indicates which outcomes are either more or less likely.

If the probability of getting two heads when two coins are thrown is $\frac{1}{4}$, we can be sure that (while the event may not actually happen once on every four throws), it will tend to happen on a quarter of all throws as the number of trials gets larger.

### NOW TRY THESE . . .

1. A programmer noted the results of writing 20 programs. The results were that

2 compiled correctly on the first run

7 compiled correctly on the second run

5 compiled correctly on the third run

4 compiled correctly on the fourth run

2 compiled correctly on the fifth run

Find the probabilities that his next program will compile correctly

(i)    on the first run

(ii)   on the second run

(iii)  on the third run

(iv)  before the fifth run

(v)   after the third run (but not earlier)

(vi)  at all

(vii) but not on the first run

2.  The operations manager keeps a log of the downtime records of the 30 VDUs in her department. These indicate that

17 VDUs have never failed

8 VDUs have each failed on one occasion

4 VDUs have each failed on two occasions

1 VDU has failed on three occasions

On the basis of this data, give the probabilities that a micro chosen at random from the 30 would

(i)    never fail

(ii)   fail once

(iii)  fail twice

(iv)   certainly fail

(v)    fail two or three times

(vi)   fail four times

### 7.4   COMBINING PROBABILITIES

Events can sometimes be the result of linking two or more events in some way. The resulting events are then called compound events. For example, you may want to know the probability that a system will fail at the same time as the person who designed it is on holiday – these are two quite independent events, but we can find the probability of each happening.

This type of probability involves two (or more) events which must happen at the same time. We can describe this as ". . . both event A and also event B . . .". We assume that A and B are independent events, so the result of A happening in no way alters the probability that B will happen or the other way round. (If they aren't independent, we must use a slightly different approach.)

The probability of the compound event is the product of the respective probabilities:

$$P(A \text{ and } B) = P(A) \times P(B)$$

To discuss this, let us return to the example of throwing a six-sided die. If there are two trials, the result of the first can have no effect on that of the second; therefore, these are two independent events.

If you want to find the probability of throwing a 5 on the first throw and a 2 on the second, multiply the respective probabilities together – $\frac{1}{6}$ $\times \frac{1}{6} = \frac{1}{36}$ – the required probability is $\frac{1}{36}$.

Consider next the data processing example.

The probability that the system will fail is $\frac{1}{20}$ and that of the system designer being on holiday is $\frac{1}{10}$ – so the probability that both will happen at the same time is $\frac{1}{20} \times \frac{1}{10} = \frac{1}{200}$. In the same way, the probability that the system will fail when he is not on holiday is $\frac{1}{20} \times \frac{9}{10}$ $= \frac{9}{200}$, as the probability of his not being on holiday must be $1 - \frac{1}{10} = \frac{9}{10}$ (ie "failure" of the "he is on holiday" event).

If, also, the probability that the engineer is out on a call is $\frac{2}{3}$, then the probability of a system failure when both the designer is on holiday and the engineer is out on a call is $\frac{1}{20} \times \frac{1}{10} \times \frac{2}{3} = \frac{1}{300}$. This is a very small value, so quite an unlikely (but not impossible) event.

Check the probability that the system will fail and the designer is not on holiday and the engineer is not out on a call. This is $\frac{1}{20} \times \frac{9}{10} \times \frac{1}{3}$ or $\frac{3}{200}$.

## NOW TRY THESE ...

A microcomputer is to be delivered by a local supplier. The probability that they will send the wrong model is $\frac{1}{5}$. There's a probability of $\frac{3}{4}$ that the machine delivered will work properly, and a probability of $\frac{1}{3}$ that there is a fault on the system disk. Find the probabilities that

(i)   the correct model arrives

(ii)  the correct model arrives but does not work properly

(iii) the correct model arrives with no fault on the system disk

(iv)  the wrong model arrives, but it works properly

(v)   the wrong model arrives, does not work properly and there's a fault on the system disk

(vi)  the correct model arrives, works correctly, with no fault on the system disk

(vii) the supplier sends the wrong model on two consecutive occasions

(viii) the supplier sends the wrong model on two consecutive occasions, but then sends the correct model on the third delivery

## 7.5   EITHER ... OR ...

Another type of compound probability involves one or other of two events taking place, but not necessarily both. We describe this in words as "... either event A or event B ..." – this includes the case of both events taking place.

We can extend cases involving more than two events, again to give the probability that one or more of them takes place (it does not matter how many, as long as it's at least one).

However, this time, the events must be what we call mutually exclusive; for example, tossing a coin "heads" or "tails" are mutually exclusive – the success of one automatically guarantees the failure of the other.

To see this, look back at the problem of throwing a six-sided die. The probability of throwing a 5 is $\frac{1}{6}$ and the probability of throwing a 3 is also $\frac{1}{6}$. Hence the probability of throwing *either* a 5 *or* a 3 is $\frac{1}{6} + \frac{1}{6} = \frac{1}{3}$ since the two events are mutually exclusive.

Let's consider the possible causes of the system failure. Maybe the executive will be unable to cope with an interrupt, with a probability of $\frac{1}{15}$ (event A), or a failure may occur at the disk controller (event B), with probability $\frac{1}{20}$. There's also the possibility that the system cannot partition main memory (event C), with a probability of $\frac{1}{30}$. (These figures are far higher than are likely on a real system, but their values make for easier calculation, and it's convenient to assume they're mutually exclusive).

The probability of system failure because of either event A or event B is $\frac{1}{15} + \frac{1}{20} = \frac{4}{60} + \frac{3}{60} = \frac{7}{60}$. The probability of either event A or event B or event C is $\frac{1}{15} + \frac{1}{20} + \frac{1}{30} = \frac{4}{60} + \frac{3}{60} + \frac{2}{60} = \frac{9}{60} = \frac{3}{20}$; this includes the possibility that two or even all three events occur.

In other words, for compound probability, multiply the individual probabilities for AND; add the individual probabilities for OR.

**NOW TRY THESE . . .**

1. A data validation program may reject fields for one or more of three possible reasons; these are, with their respective probabilities of occurrence

(i)   wrong data type, $\frac{1}{6}$

(ii)  wrong value range, $\frac{1}{5}$

(iii) wrong format, $\frac{1}{10}$

Find the probabilities that the program rejects a field because of

(iv)  wrong data type or wrong value range

(v)   wrong data type or wrong format

(vi)  wrong value range or wrong format

(vii) wrong value range or wrong data type or wrong format

Now give these following probabilities

    (viii)the field isn't rejected at all

    (ix)  the field is rejected for all three reasons

2.  Candidates in a data processing examination may fail, pass, obtain a merit, or obtain a distinction, with probabilities of 0.2, 0.5, 0.2 and 0.1 respectively.

Find the probabilities of

    (i)   not failing at all

    (ii)  obtaining either a merit or a distinction

    (iii) failing to obtain either a merit or a distinction

Subash and Jean both take the examination. What are the probabilities that

    (iv) both fail

    (v)  Subash fails and Jean obtains a pass

    (vi) Subash fails and Jean passes or Subash passes and Jean fails

    (vii) Subash does not fail but Jean does or both get merits

## 7.6   PROBABILITY TREE

The probability tree provides a picture of a compound probability situation. Consider the two events – a system crashes, with a probability of $\frac{1}{10}$, and the chief operator is away, with a probability of $\frac{3}{14}$ (Figure 7.3). The tree shows all the possible outcomes, including those which depend on the system crashing and/or the operator being away. There are four possible outcomes from these two events; the tree shows these at the right-hand side, with their respective probabilities. This case involves only two events, but we can easily extend a probability tree to cater for more events (though it may become unwieldy as the number of events increases). It is quite common when dealing with two events, to use $p_1$ and $p_2$ to refer to their 'success' probabilities and $q_1$ and $q_2$ for the probabilities of failure.

It is absolutely certain that one of the four outcomes must occur – so a useful check is to see that the four probabilities do add up to 1 (as they do here).

This tree shows the probability that the system will crash while the chief operator is not away is $\frac{11}{140}$. Therefore, the probability that either the system crashes when the operator is not away or it fails to crash when the operator is away is $\frac{11}{140} + \frac{27}{140}$ (by the addition rule), ie $\frac{38}{140}$ or $\frac{19}{70}$. (The order in which you present these does not matter).

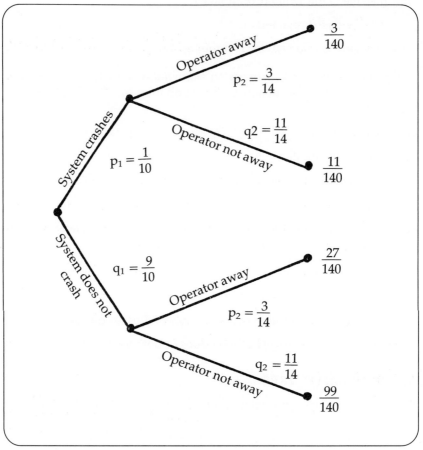

**Figure 7.3   Probability tree**

**NOW TRY THESE . . .**

1. Produce a probability tree to show the four outcomes and their respective probabilities involving two events. The first event is that a microcomputer from a local supplier arrives, but they have sent the wrong model – a probability of ⅕. The second event is that the machine delivered is working properly – a probability of ¾.

2. Extend the tree diagram in question 1 to include a third event – that the system disk is faulty, a probability of ⅓.

3. Produce a probability tree to show the eight outcomes of an experiment that involved the three events that

(i)   the system fails with a probability of ¹⁄₂₀

(ii)   the system designer is on holiday with a probability of ¹⁄₁₀

(iii)  the engineer is out on call with a probability of ⅔.

# 8 Calculating averages

**OBJECTIVES**

When you've worked through this Chapter, you should be able to:

— state how mean, median and mode differ, and give simple examples

— work out the mean of a set of discrete values

— find the median of an odd or even set of values

— state the mode of a set of values

— obtain mean and median from a frequency distribution

— assess the mode of a frequency distribution.

**INTRODUCTION**

The word "average" is, to say the least, a very loose term. It refers, in general, to the taking of a single value or quantity to be representative of, usually, a large number of such values or quantities. The problem is that there's no single way to get such a value; it has to be chosen. The choice depends partly on the nature of the values in the set (eg whether they are qualitative or quantitative), and partly on the purpose for which the average is required.

Often the word "average" is the same as what we call the mean (sometimes called the arithmetic mean). However, other types of average exist, such as the median and the mode.

**8.1 THE MEANING OF MEAN**

Here is a set of eight numbers

$$7 \quad 21 \quad 13 \quad 17 \quad 23 \quad 18 \quad 9 \quad 20$$

Add them, then divide the total (128) by the number of items (8). This gives the mean as $^{128}/_8 = 16$.

Clearly you can only use this particular average with quantitative data. Note that the mean may or may not equal any of the original values.

Note, too, that the presence of even one value which is very different from the others may distort the value of the mean. For example, take the set of values

$$3 \quad 3 \quad 4 \quad 4 \quad 4 \quad 4 \quad 5 \quad 5 \quad 6 \quad 6 \quad 6 \quad 176$$

The mean is the total (226) divided by the number of items (12), giving 18.83 (to two decimal places). This is in no way typical of the first 11 items in the set – for the twelfth item, 176, is so much out of keeping with all the others that it distorts the picture.

Figure 8.1 shows another example. To calculate the average speed of key-punch operators in a data processing department, a formula is required. Let $x$ be a typical speed (there are 14 $x$-values in this sample), and $\Sigma x$ (pronounced sigma x) stand for the sum of the $x$-values. The letter $N$ represents the number of $x$-values in the set (14 in this case). Lastly, $\bar{x}$, read as x-bar, is the mean of the $x$-values.

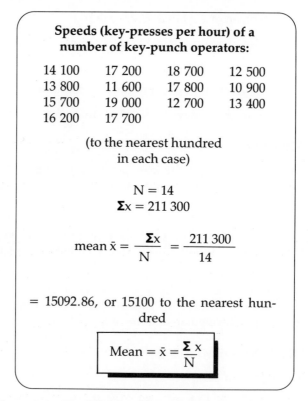

**Figure 8.1    Establishing the mean of a set of data items**

The original values are "to the nearest 100", the $\bar{x}$-value is rounded up to the same level; it makes no sense to quote a mean with more precision than the original data. Note also that the mean has the same unit as the original data; therefore, when you work out a mean, ensure the data has the same units. For instance, don't mix minutes with seconds or hours – convert to the same unit.

Use the mean of 15,100 key-presses per hour to estimate the time it might take six of the operators, chosen at random, to punch a volume of data of 500,000 characters. The average output of six operators is $6 \times 15,100 = 90,600$ characters per hour. The task will therefore take $500,000/90,600 = 5.52$ hours, or about 5½ hours.

Take a second group of 29 operators, with a mean speed of 12,300 characters per hour. How can we find the mean speed of the combined group (43 people)? We don't know the speeds of the members of the second group, but can work out the total of their speeds which is $29 \times 12,300 = 356,700$. We know the total of the speeds of the first group is 211,300. Thus the total of the speeds of the combined group is $356,700 + 211,300$, ie 568,000. Divide that by 43 to give the mean – 13,200 key-presses per hour.

Note that the value is not the result of adding together the two means and dividing by two – since it must take into account the number of people in each group. Thus, the result of 13,200 is closer to 12,300 than to 15,100 as there are more people in the slower group.

**NOW TRY THESE . . .**

1. Following are the numbers of boxes of printer paper used each day in a seven-day period.

$$12 \quad 14 \quad 17 \quad 16 \quad 24 \quad 13 \quad 7$$

(i)   Find the average number of boxes used per day

(ii)  How many days are 400 boxes likely to last?

2. The response times of 11 terminals, to the nearest 0.1 second, are

$$2.3 \quad 1.6 \quad 2.9 \quad 3.6 \quad 4.1 \quad 2.6 \quad 2.7 \quad 3.1 \quad 3.8 \quad 2.7 \quad 2.8$$

(i)   What is the mean response time?

Changing the system software gives these response times

$$1.8 \quad 1.3 \quad 3.1 \quad 3.2 \quad 3.8 \quad 2.8 \quad 2.7 \quad 3.0 \quad 3.5 \quad 2.1 \quad 1.8$$

(ii)  Find the new mean response time.

(iii) Use your results to find the percentage reduction in response time.

3. A group of 12 programmers with a mean experience of five years of Cobol joins a larger group of 17 with a mean experience of 7.2 years. What is the mean experience of the new combined group?

**8.2   MEDIAN**

Returning to the group of key-punch operators. If you need to select one person as a "typical" member of the group, to test a new keyboard, clearly you should not choose the fastest or the slowest but someone whose speed is "near the middle". The data shows that not one of the 14 staff has a speed exactly equal to the mean. Try the following approach.

Arrange the values in order of size, lowest to highest. Choose as the average the one that occurs in the middle of the list, calling it this time the median.

For $N$ items, the median is the $\frac{1}{2}(N+1)$th value. If $N$ is an odd number, this will give one unique value. If $N$ is even, for example ($N=14$), the median is the $7\frac{1}{2}$th value – exactly half way between the 7th and the 8th values. Of course, in the case of our 14 key-punchers, there isn't a $7\frac{1}{2}$th person in the list – choose either the seventh or the eighth. In this case, maybe the eighth is better – the speed is closer to the mean. The 14 values, in order of size, are

10900   11600   12500   12700   13400   13800   14100   15700   16200

17200   17700   17800   18700   19000

The 7th and 8th values are, respectively, 14100 and 15700 so the median speed is $\frac{1}{2}$ (14100 + 15700) = 14900 even if, as in this case, no person happens to work at that exact speed.

Figure 8.2 takes a case, relating to processor sizes of microcomputers, in which the value of $N$ is odd.

Processor sizes of some microcomputers:

128KB 32KB 64KB 256KB 96KB

Put into ascending sequence and,

since there are five values ($N=5$),

select the $\frac{1}{2}(5+1)$th value –

ie select the 3rd:

32KB 64KB 96KB 128KB 256KB
                 ▲
             Median

**Figure 8.2   The median of a set of items**

The median has some major advantages; it's easier to calculate than the mean, and doesn't depend so much on individual values. Thus the median of the following items

3   4   7   8   12   15   8164

is exactly the same as the median of these items below

3   4   7   8   12   15   17

Figure 8.3 looks at benchmark test times, the value of $N$ being even.

Times (in seconds) to complete a benchmark test:

24   37   19   27   25   34   30   22

Put into ascending sequence and, since

there are eight values ($N=8$), we need the

½ (8+1)th, ie 4½th value−

the mean of the 4th and 5th values:

19   22   24   25   27   30   34   37

4th 5th

Median = $\dfrac{25+27}{2}$ = 26 seconds

**Figure 8.3    The median of an even number of items**

This has a disadvantage, however, as the value of the median doesn't at all reflect the values of anything but the middle term(s) in a data set, whereas the mean depends on each value.

Lastly, note that if we cannot quantify the data but can list it in order of priority or preference, there is a median but no mean.

**NOW TRY THESE . . .**

1. Here are the ages in years of the 13 staff in the systems section of a computer department

37   26   29   42   28   51   23   32   49   29   35   41   38

Put the ages in order of size and find the median.

2. The run-times (in minutes) of 12 jobs are

43   28   37   21   16   59   18   24   37   41   12   29

What is the median run-time?

**8.3   THE MODE**

The mode of a set of values is the most common value in the list, ie the "most popular" one. As this completely ignores the values of the data items, it's specially well suited to qualitative data.

The table in Figure 8.4 shows the results of a survey of programming languages.

If two most popular values appear with equal frequencies, both values are modes – the distribution is then said to be bimodal.

The number of firms using different
programming languages

| Language | Frequency |
|----------|-----------|
| ALGOL | 4 |
| BASIC | 13 |
| COBOL | 27 |
| DIBOL | 3 |
| FORTRAN | 10 |
| PASCAL | 8 |
| RPGII | 14 |
| SNOBOL | 1 |

The mode is COBOL since it has the highest frequency

Clearly, if a survey of a different group of firms were to be used, the results might be different, and the mode might change

Figure 8.4    The mode of a set of items

Apart from its ease of working out, the mode is of value for planning purposes. If (all other factors being equal), you had to choose a language for training a group of new students, the most popular language (here Cobol) is a wise choice. If you wanted to train the students in two languages, the most popular, Cobol, and the second most popular, RPGII, would provide the best coverage – the trainees would then be able to work in 41 of the 80 companies in the survey. Note, however, that the choice of language may depend on factors other than popularity.

**NOW TRY THESE . . .**

1. Give the mode of the following set of values:

6  8  5  12   6  8  16  5  9  3  12

4  9  6   5  13  7   9  8  2  5   1

2. The operators were asked to choose the colour of the walls of their new rest room; the 47 people chose thus:

| beige | 12 |
|---|---|
| blue | 3 |
| lemon | 8 |
| mustard | 4 |
| pink | 9 |
| white | 11 |

What was the mode?

## 8.4   THE MEAN OF A FREQUENCY DISTRIBUTION

As defined earlier, the mean is almost the same by definition in the case of a frequency distribution.

For example, say the $x$-value 17 occurs with a frequency of 3 (ie $f=3$); then each of the three 17s must contribute to the total. To find the mean in this case, set the data out in a table. The columns are $x$, $f$ and $fx$ (the product of $f$ and $x$). With $x=17$ and $f=3$, $fx$ is 51, for instance. Next, replace the $N$ we had before by $\Sigma f$ – to give the total number of items in the set. Figure 8.5 shows such a table. Previously we had the mean $\bar{x}$ as

$\bar{x} = \dfrac{\Sigma x}{N}$   Now the formula is $\bar{x} = \dfrac{\Sigma fx}{\Sigma f}$

**Age at last birthday quoted by 100 trainees**

| Age $x$ | Frequency $f$ | $fx$ |
|---|---|---|
| 17 | 3 | 51 |
| 18 | 8 | 144 |
| 19 | 14 | 266 |
| 20 | 21 | 420 |
| 21 | 24 | 504 |
| 22 | 13 | 286 |
| 23 | 7 | 161 |
| 24 | 6 | 144 |
| 25 | 3 | 75 |
| 26 | 1 | 26 |
|  | $\Sigma f = 100$ | $\Sigma fx = 2077$ |

Mean $\bar{x} = \dfrac{\Sigma fx}{\Sigma f}$

Mean age $= \dfrac{2077}{100} = 20.77$ years

or, to nearest year, 21

**Figure 8.5   The mean of a frequency distribution**

Here's how to reduce tedious arithmetic (especially where the $x$-values are large so the $fx$ calculations are unwieldy). Decide on a "working zero" ("assumed mean"). We call this $x_0$ and choose it to be somewhere near where you expect the mean to lie.

The accuracy of the choice does not matter – it is far more important to choose so that when you subtract $x_0$ from each of the $x$-values, to give the values for the difference $x - x_0$ or $d$ as simply as possible. It is best if the values of $d$ are all whole numbers, some positive and some negative – then it's easiest to work out $fd$, which we need instead of $fx$. Lastly, since we have reduced every $x$-value by $x_0$, the formula for $x$ adds $x_0$ back on again at the end. See Figure 8.6.

Note that, since the $fd$ column is likely to include both positive and negative values, having these separate reduces the risk of error. In

## Number of attempts to make a program compile

### Select $x_0=9$

| Number of attempts $x$ | Frequency $f$ | $d=x-x_0$ | $fd$ |
|---|---|---|---|
| 6 | 17 | −3 | −51 |
| 7 | 29 | −2 | −58 |
| 8 | 36 | −1 | −36 |
| 9 | 47 | 0 | 0 |
| 10 | 31 | 1 | 31 |
| 11 | 26 | 2 | 52 |
| 12 | 13 | 3 | 39 |
| 13 | 12 | 4 | 48 |
| 14 | 12 | 5 | 60 |
| 15 | 11 | 6 | 66 |
| 16 | 9 | 7 | 63 |
| 17 | 7 | 8 | 56 |
| | $\Sigma f = 250$ | | $\Sigma fd = 270$ |

$$\text{Mean } x = x_0 + \frac{\Sigma fd}{\Sigma f}$$

$$x = 9 + \frac{270}{250} = 9 + 1.08 = 10.08$$

Mean = 10 (to nearest integer)

**Figure 8.6   Using a working zero**

Figure 8.6, $\Sigma fd$ is the sum of the positive $fd$ values less the negative $fd$ values ($415 - 145 = 270$).

Often it is easiest to use as $x_0$ the value of $x$ with the highest frequency (ie the modal value), as done here; while this doesn't always lead to the simplest arithmetic it's a fairly reliable choice.

We need one further step when dealing with grouped frequency distributions in which the class widths are equal. Take the mid-interval value of each class as the $x$-value, the rest of the work being as before. Now the d column is likely to consist of a set of values with a common factor (usually the same as the class width). Calling this common factor (or 'unit') $u$ it is possible to divide the $d$-values by $u$ (to scale down all the numbers in later columns); this gives a $d^1$-column (with $d^1 = d/u$). This time the final column contains $fd^1$ values; these are all equally scaled-down versions of what would normally have been fd values, thus simplifying the arithmetic. At the calculation stage for $\bar{x}$ reverse the scaling down (ie multiply by $u$ in Figure 8.7) and then add back $x_0$.

In Figure 8.7, $u$ is given as 5 – the most obvious common factor for the $d$-column – after choosing $x_0 = 37\frac{1}{2}$ (the modal value).

### Ages of people in a firm
Select $x_0 = 37\frac{1}{2}$ and $u = 5$

| Age range (years) | Mid-intend interval value ($x$) | Frequency $f$ | $d = x - x_0$ | $d^1 = \dfrac{d}{u}$ | $fd^1$ |
|---|---|---|---|---|---|
| 15– | 17½ | 12 | −20 | −4 | −48 |
| 20– | 22½ | 14 | −15 | −3 | −42 |
| 25– | 27½ | 23 | −10 | −2 | −46 |
| 30– | 32½ | 31 | −5 | −1 | −31 |
| 35– | 37½ | 33 | 0 | 0 | 0 |
| 40– | 42½ | 28 | 5 | 1 | 28 |
| 45– | 47½ | 22 | 10 | 2 | 44 |
| 50– | 52½ | 15 | 15 | 3 | 45 |
| 55– | 57½ | 12 | 20 | 4 | 48 |
| 60– | 62½ | 8 | 25 | 5 | 40 |
| 65–70 | 67½ | 2 | 30 | 6 | 12 |
| | | $\Sigma f = 200$ | | | $\Sigma fd^1 = 50$ |

$$\text{Mean } x = x_0 + u\,\frac{\Sigma fd^1}{\Sigma f}$$

$$\therefore x = 37\frac{1}{2} + 5.\frac{50}{200}$$
$$= 37.5 + 1.25 = 38.75$$
$$\text{Mean} = 38.75 \text{ years}$$

**Figure 8.7  The mean of a group frequency distribution**

In dealing with grouped frequency distributions, take special care to distinguish between discrete and continuous data when you determine the mid-interval values.

**NOW TRY THESE . . .**

1. Here are the numbers of phone calls to a help desk during 50 days of working

| No of calls/day, $x$ | No of days, $f$ |
|---|---|
| 17 | 4 |
| 18 | 8 |
| 19 | 19 |
| 20 | 12 |
| 21 | 5 |
| 22 | 2 |

Find the mean number of telephone calls per day over this period.

2. The number of pages of printed output ($x$) for each of 100 jobs run at the operations centre are

| No of pages output, $x$ | No of jobs, $f$ |
|---|---|
| 73 | 7 |
| 74 | 12 |
| 75 | 15 |
| 76 | 23 |
| 77 | 17 |
| 78 | 12 |
| 79 | 9 |
| 80 | 3 |
| 81 | 2 |

Choose a suitable working mean and so calculate the mean number of pages of output per job.

3. The table shows the number of transcription errors detected each hour, x, for each of 80 recorded hours in a data preparation department.

| No of errors, x | No of times found, f |
|---|---|
| 1 – 50 | 6 |
| 51 – 100 | 12 |
| 101 – 150 | 19 |
| 151 – 200 | 21 |
| 201 – 250 | 16 |
| 251 – 300 | 6 |

Choose a suitable working mean and unit size to estimate the mean number or errors detected per hour.

4. Estimate the mean annual salary of these 200 employees of a large computer bureau.

| Salary ($) | Number of employees |
|---|---|
| 3000 – | 6 |
| 4000 – | 7 |
| 5000 – | 25 |
| 6000 – | 49 |
| 7000 – | 56 |
| 8000 – | 31 |
| 9000 – | 14 |
| 10000 – 11000 | 12 |

## 8.5   THE MEDIAN OF A FREQUENCY DISTRIBUTION

In all cases in which the data isn't grouped, you can find the median by inspection (as before), by quoting the $\frac{1}{2}(N+1)$th value when the data is in order of size. For instance:

| x | f |
|---|---|
| 17 | 3 |
| 18 | 5 |
| 19 | 18 |
| 20 | 36 |
| 21 | 15 |
| 22 | 4 |

If we arrange the 81 values as 17 17 17 18 18 18 18 18 19, and so on, the ½(81+1)th (ie the 41st) will be 20 – so the median is 20. It so happens that this time the median is the same as the mode; this is not always (or even often) true.

If, however, the data is grouped so you cannot tell the actual individual values, you have to estimate the median – produce a cumulative frequency distribution, and draw a cumulative frequency diagram, as in Figure 8.8.

In this case there are 300 items, so the median would be the ½(301)th value, or 150 ½th value. In fact, as $N$ is large, we take the ½($N$)th value instead. (The discrepancy is too small to bother about).

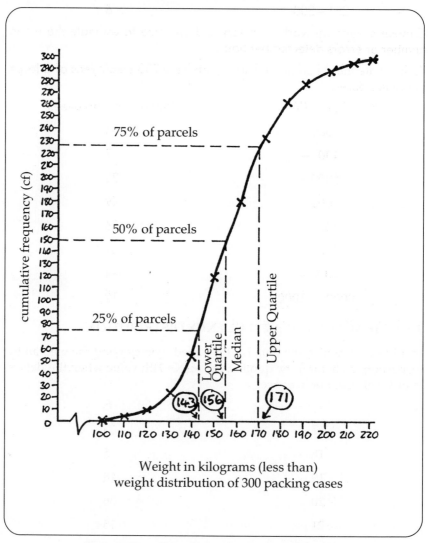

**Figure 8.8   Cumulative frequency diagram**

To obtain the median, simply search for 150 on the *cf*-axis, go across to the curve, then look down to the *x*-axis to give the median directly – in this case 156kg.

Two other values of importance in the next chapter are the lower and the upper quartiles. The lower quartile is the ¼*N*th value (in this case, the 75th) and the upper quartile is the ¾*N*th value (here the 225th) – the two quartiles and the median divide up the whole distribution into four equal groups. The lower quartile therefore has a quarter of all the data values below it (and three quarters above); the upper quartile has three quarters of all the data values below it (and only one quarter above). In this case, we can read off the lower and upper quartiles as 143kg and 171kg respectively.

## NOW TRY THESE ...

1. Find the median of the following distribution of estimates made by 115 operators as to the ideal size for an operations shift team.

| Size, x | No of estimates, f |
|---------|--------------------|
| 3 | 16 |
| 4 | 24 |
| 5 | 27 |
| 6 | 29 |
| 7 | 16 |
| 8 | 3 |

2. Create a cumulative frequency table and then a cumulative frequency diagram. Now estimate the median of the following survey of the salaries of 200 people in a computer bureau.

| Salary ($) | No of people |
|------------|--------------|
| 4000 – | 7 |
| 5000 – | 19 |
| 6000 – | 38 |
| 7000 – | 45 |
| 8000 – | 34 |
| 9000 – | 27 |
| 10000 – | 21 |
| 11000 – 12000 | 9 |

## 8.6    THE MODE OF A FREQUENCY DISTRIBUTION

When dealing with data which isn't grouped, the mode (like the median) can be found by inspection – it's simply the $x$-value with the highest value of $f$.

If, however, the data is grouped, we can be sure only that the modal class (rather than the mode) is the group or class with the highest frequency; as we don't know the individual values in each class, we cannot possibly work out which one value occurs more frequently than any other.

To see this, look at the following part of a grouped distribution (involving whole values of $x$ only).

| $x$ | $f$ |
|---|---|
| 51–55 | 12 |
| 56–60 | 16 |
| 61–65 | 10 |

Clearly, 56–60 must be the modal class – but, since we don't know the original x-values, it is not possible to tell where the mode lies. It's quite possible that no one value in the 56-60 class occurs more than four times – yet maybe 63 occurs ten times. If this is the case, then 63 is a contender for the mode, even though it doesn't lie in the modal group.

Nevertheless, if an estimate has to be made of the mode with no knowledge other than the details of the grouped distribution, you

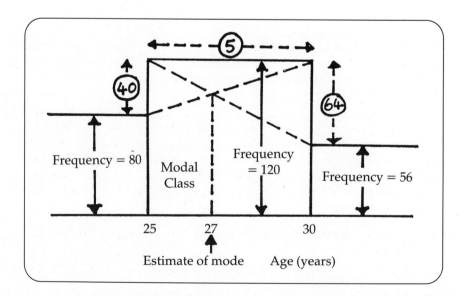

**Figure 8.9    Estimating mode using a histogram**

would have to assume that it lies in the modal class – and that it occupies a position that depends on the values in the distribution table. This can be done either graphically or by calculation. The graphical method is shown in Figure 8.9, as a histogram. Note the way in which lines pass from the tops of the two cells adjoining the modal class; they intersect above what becomes the estimate of the mode.

**NOW TRY THESE . . .**

1. Find the mode of this distribution

| $x$ | $f$ |
|---|---|
| 92 | 7 |
| 93 | 19 |
| 94 | 26 |
| 95 | 34 |
| 96 | 15 |

2. Estimate the mode of this distribution of ages of staff in a computer department.

| Age (years) | No of staff |
|---|---|
| 20 – | 7 |
| 25 – | 18 |
| 30 – | 21 |
| 35 – | 28 |
| 40 – | 19 |
| 45 – 50 | 7 |

## 8.7   SUMMARY

Clearly, each of the three forms of average has some advantages and some disadvantages. The mode is the only one we can use with qualitative data, for example. The mean uses every data value but can easily be distorted by extreme values; the median and mode effectively ignore all other values so aren't distorted by them. This also means that whereas the mean is sensitive to changes in the data, however small, the other two are not.

A "formula" connects the three values, but should be treated as a guideline only. It is

$$\text{mode} = \text{mean} - 3(\text{mean} - \text{median})$$

In fact, the mean is the only "average" with a "proper" formula.

# 9　Measures of spread or dispersion

## OBJECTIVES

When you've worked through this Chapter, you should be able to:

— explain the need for a measure of the spread of a set of data values

— find the range and inter-quartile range of a data set

— find a data set's standard deviation

— find variance and give its unit.

## INTRODUCTION

We met an average way to identify one item to be representative of (or be typical of) a group. However, it doesn't tell us all we need to know about a distribution, since it is quite possible for two sets of values to have exactly the same mean but be very different in nature.

Consider the four distributions in Figure 9.1; the mean is given for each.

Distribution A:　5,　6,　7,　8,　9,　10,　11

Mean is 8

Distribution B:　5,　5,　5,　8,　11,　11,　11

Mean is 8

Distribution C:　1,　2,　3,　8,　13,　14,　15

Mean is 8

Distribution D:　14,　15,　17,　19,　20

Mean is 17

**Figure 9.1　The means of different distributions**

Distributions A, B and C each have seven values and the same mean yet differ in other ways: A has an even distribution of values between the two extremes (5 and 11), while in B the values spread with the same extremes, with extremely heavy bunching at the ends. In C the end-points

111

are further apart yet the values still cluster close by them without affecting the mean at all. With D the difference between the extremes is the same as in A and B yet the mean is quite different.

We need a second meaning to help describe a distribution. This should identify how the values are spread out; it must reflect the fact that the values in C are far more widely scattered than in the other three cases, and it should also distinguish between the uniformity of distribution seen in A and the clustering around the extremes of B. Just as was found with averages, there is no single way of measuring this spread (or dispersion) but several, each with different characteristics.

## 9.1  THE RANGE

The range is by far the simplest measure of spread. Find it for any distribution by subtracting the smallest data value in the set from the largest. Figure 9.2 gives the ranges for the above sets A, B, C and D.

Distribution A Range is 6

Distribution B Range is 6

Distribution C Range is 14

Distribution D Range is 6

**Figure 9.2    Range**

We can at once see that B and C are more readily distinguished from each other; both have the same mean (8) but the greater spread of C shows in its range of 14 compared to the 6 of B. Observe also that A and D have the same range yet different means.

However, the range totally fails to distinguish between A and B – they have equal means and equal ranges but, as already indicated, the data in B clusters more around the two extremes. Thus the range cannot cope with what happens between the extremes. All the same, it gives a simple measure of spread even if it cannot provide the degree of discrimination needed in all cases.

Extreme "untypical" values can distort both the mean and the range. In the case of distribution A, if 11 is replaced by 17, to give distribution:

$$5 \quad 6 \quad 7 \quad 8 \quad 9 \quad 10 \quad 17$$

the mean changes from 8 to $8\frac{6}{7}$ and the range doubles from 6 to 12. Had we altered values between 5 and 11 of distribution A, the range would not have changed at all.

## 9.2   INTER-QUARTILE RANGE

Section 8.5 introduced the upper and lower quartiles of a grouped frequency distribution. The difference between these values is the inter-quartile range. Thus in Figure 8.8 with lower and upper quartiles of 143 kg and 171 kg, the inter-quartile range is 171 − 143 kg; like the range, this has the same unit as the data items.

Inter-quartile range is a slightly better measure of spread than the range, as any "untypical" values will almost certainly appear in the lowest or the highest 25% of the data values − so they will not distort the result. However, it still suffers from many of the same problems as experienced with the range, and as it is not convenient to draw up cumulative frequency diagrams just to find the inter-quartile range, this is not widely used.

If a distribution is not grouped, finding the two quartiles is fairly easy. They are the $\frac{1}{4}(N+1)$th and the $\frac{3}{4}(N+1)$th values (or the $\frac{1}{4}N$ and $\frac{3}{4}N$ values when the number of data items, $N$, is large). So if 15 items are

   10   3   12   16   5   2   8   17   11   13   6   8   12   16   4

re-arrange in order like this;

   2   3   4   <u>5</u>   6   8   8   10   11   12   12   <u>13</u>   16   16   17

the lower and upper quartiles being underlined. Here, $N = 15$, the lower quartile = $\frac{1}{4}$(16)th = (4th) value, and the upper quartile = $\frac{3}{4}$(16)th = (12)th value. For this distribution, the inter-quartile range is $13 - 5 = 8$. Should any values below 5 or above 13 change eg, 17 becoming 2139, there is no change in the inter-quartile range, though the range changes from 15 to 2137 in the process.

### NOW TRY THESE . . .

1. Find the range and the inter-quartile range of

   29   7   15   23   11   14   36   8   14   17   21

2. If the value of 36 in question 1 is changed to 39, state the effect on;

   (i)   the range

   (ii)   the inter-quartile range

3. The semi-inter-quartile range is half the inter-quartile range. Give the semi-inter-quartile range of:

   741   865   637   801   782   871   915

4. For the following set of data values find:

   (i)   the range

   (ii)   the inter-quartile range

(iii)  the semi-inter-quartile range

    23  17  29  36  15  6  18  24  32  41

    14  27  33  18  24

5.  If the 17 in question 4 changes to 15, what effect would this have on:

(i)    the range

(ii)   the inter-quartile range

(iii)  the semi-inter-quartile range

## 9.3  STANDARD DEVIATION

Standard deviation is a measure of spread which overcomes the problems of both range and inter-quartile range. You may think it's hard to work out – but as it is almost a by-product of finding the mean for a grouped frequency distribution, in most cases there is little extra calculation involved.

A good measure of spread will:

(i)    take every data value into account;

(ii)   weight data values according to frequency.

The standard deviation fits these criteria, and it is worked out using these stages

(a)   find the mean, $\bar{x}$, of the data items.

(b)   find the deviation d $= x - \bar{x}$ for each of the data items $x$ from $\bar{x}$.

(c)   Take the square of each deviation, $d^2$.

(d)   Find the mean of $d^2$ values.

(e)   Obtain the square root of this value.

Note in particular that stage (b) gives the deviations; some of these values are positive and some negative – the squaring undertaken in (c) eliminates the signs. Compensation for squaring is made at the last stage by taking the square root.

Occasionally people refer to the variance of a set of values; this is simply the square of the standard deviation. In Figure 9.3, variance at stage (d) appears as 18.61; in other words we find variance while working out standard deviation.

Standard deviation, like both range and inter-quartile range, has the same unit as the original data. The unit of variance, on the other hand, is the square of the original unit; thus if the data items were all lengths in metres, the variance would be in square metres.

The standard deviation, together with the mean, lets us usefully

Data values:
3  6  7  9  9  11  12  13  14  19

(a) Their mean is 10.3

(b) Deviations from the mean:

−7.3  −4.3  −3.3  −1.3  −1.3  0.7  1.7  2.7  3.7
and 8.7 respectively

(c) The squared deviations:

53.29  18.49  10.89  1.69  1.69  0.49  2.89  7.29

13.69 and 75.69 respectively

(d) The mean of these squared deviations is

186.1 divided by 10 ie, 18.61

(e) Standard deviation is square root of 18.61 = 4.314

**Figure 9.3   Calculation of standard deviation**

compare two or more data sets. Together with probability, these two measures are the basis of much statistical work (although not covered in this book). Here is a second example for finding standard deviation and variance. The set of response times, measured in seconds, for 11 terminals linked to a mainframe are

5.3  3.2  2.6  2.9  3.4  4.7  6.8  2.9  3.7  5.1  4.8

The sum of the values is 45.4, so the mean is 4.13 (to 2 decimal places). The deviations of the values from the mean are therefore

1.17  −0.93  −1.53  −1.23  −0.73  0.57  2.67  −1.23  −0.43  0.97  0.67

The squares of the deviations are

1.3689  0.8649  2.3409  1.5129  0.5329  0.3249
7.1289  1.5129  0.1849  0.9409  0.4489

The sum of the squared deviations is 17.1619.

Next the mean of the squared deviations is $17.1619/11 = 1.560$ (so variance is 1.56 sec$^2$). The standard deviation is the square root of 1.560 which is 1.249 sec (1.25 seconds to 2d.p.). Thus, for this distribution, the mean is 4.13 seconds and the standard deviation is 1.25 seconds.

As noted earlier, if you have a frequency distribution you can find the standard deviation as a by-product of working out the mean. Take this data set.

| $x$ | 4 | 8 | 12 | 16 | 20 | 24 | 28 | 32 | 36 | 40 |
|-----|---|---|----|----|----|----|----|----|----|----|
| $f$ | 1 | 7 | 15 | 31 | 22 | 19 | 13 | 6  | 4  | 2  |

The table in Figure 9.4 uses a working mean $x_0$ of 16 and a unit size of 4. It has the usual form for finding the mean, plus an extra column for $fd'^2$. This is the product of the two previous columns, $d'$ and $fd'$.

The formula we now use for standard deviation is slightly more involved, as you may expect, but by using the values in the table it is easy to work out. An important advantage of the table is the use of the

Select $x_0 = 16$ and $u = 4$

| No of people in group $(x)$ | Frequency $(f)$ | $d = x - x_o$ | $d^1 = \dfrac{d}{u}$ | $fd^1$ | $fd^{12}$ |
|---|---|---|---|---|---|
| 4 | 1 | $-12$ | $-3$ | $-3$ | 9 |
| 8 | 7 | $-8$ | $-2$ | $-14$ | 28 |
| 12 | 15 | $-4$ | $-1$ | $-15$ | 15 |
| 16 | 31 | 0 | 0 | 0 | 0 |
| 20 | 22 | 4 | 1 | 22 | 22 |
| 24 | 19 | 8 | 2 | 38 | 76 |
| 28 | 13 | 12 | 3 | 39 | 117 |
| 32 | 6 | 16 | 4 | 24 | 96 |
| 36 | 4 | 20 | 5 | 20 | 100 |
| 40 | 2 | 24 | 6 | 12 | 72 |
| | $\Sigma f = 120$ | | | $\Sigma fd' = 123$ | $\Sigma fd'^2 = 535$ |

$$\text{Standard deviation} = u \sqrt{\frac{\Sigma fd'^2}{\Sigma f} - \left(\frac{\Sigma fd'}{\Sigma f}\right)^2}$$

$$\text{Standard deviation} = 4 \sqrt{\frac{535}{120} - \left(\frac{123}{120}\right)^2}$$

$= 4 \ \sqrt{4.4583 - 1.0506}$

$= 4 \ \sqrt{3.4077} \ = 4 \times 1.8460 = 7.384$

or 7.38 to 2 decimal places

**Figure 9.4   Finding standard deviation with table**

working mean; this was not used in the previous analysis (of response times) and it does make the calculation very much easier.

Note also that the data in the example is not grouped, thus leading to an exact value for the standard deviation.

With grouped data, though, the mid-interval value for each group serves as the $x$-value and the value of the standard deviation can only be approximate as values are distributed within each group.

The formula for standard deviation involves the factor $u$; if there is no division of $d$-values by $u$ to obtain $d^1$ values; then $u = 1$. Further, note that in this formula $x_0$ does not appear at all – the working mean plays absolutely no part in finding standard deviation even though we use it to obtain the mean. The variance is still the square of the standard deviation, in this case $(7.384)^2 = 54.52$ or $54.5$ to 1d.p.

## NOW TRY THESE...

1. Here are the times, in minutes, taken to run a spreadsheet on eight different microcomputers.

$$6.1 \quad 7.3 \quad 5.4 \quad 6.9 \quad 8.7 \quad 5.3 \quad 6.4 \quad 8.3$$

What are the mean and the standard deviation of these values? State clearly the unit of each. Also give the variance of the times, with its unit.

2. Work out the mean, the standard deviation and the variance of the values (in $) of orders received by a consultant.

| $x$ | 50 | 100 | 150 | 200 | 250 | 300 | 350 | 400 | 450 | 500 |
|---|---|---|---|---|---|---|---|---|---|---|
| $f$ | 2 | 7 | 15 | 21 | 16 | 14 | 12 | 8 | 4 | 1 |

3. A survey of the ages of 200 freelance programmers gave this set of values.

| Age Years | No of Programmers |
|---|---|
| 16– | 12 |
| 20– | 37 |
| 24– | 32 |
| 28– | 24 |
| 32– | 19 |
| 36– | 16 |
| 40– | 18 |
| 44– | 12 |

| 48– | 17 |
| 52–56 | 13 |

Estimate the mean and the standard deviation of the ages.

## 9.4  CONCLUSION

Just as the mean is the most useful measure of average, standard deviation is widely used to measure spread and both are important in more advanced statistical work.

While range is not as common as standard deviation its great advantage is that it can be found very quickly; this has some useful side effects. All too often, carelessness in working out standing deviation leads to values that are wildly inaccurate. One very simple check (that works in a large number of cases, but not all) is to see if standard deviation lies between approximately one eighth and one quarter of the range; if so then the standard deviation is at least roughly right, even if not necessarily arithmetically correct. You may use this test solely to check that the standard deviation you have calculated is at least of a size appropriate to the data values – so it avoids putting forward values which are totally and obviously wrong.

### REVISION EXERCISES B

This section deals with Chapters 6 to 9, ie with aspects of statistics. There is a mix of worked examples and questions for which we supply answers only.

### First Example

Four hundred computer components were tested until they failed. The frequency distribution table recording the month when each failed was:

| Months to failure | 0–9 | 10–19 | 20–29 | 30–39 | 40–49 | 50–59 | 60–69 | 70–79 | 80–99 |
|---|---|---|---|---|---|---|---|---|---|
| Frequency | 44 | 56 | 64 | 78 | 60 | 40 | 36 | 18 | 4 |

a) Use the data to calculate the mean life expectancy of a component and the standard deviation.

b) Draw a cumulative frequency graph; from this estimate the percentage of the components which failed within ONE standard deviation of the mean.

### Solution

*Part (a)*

When calculating mean or standard deviation from a frequency distribution table, first examine the values which are the subject of the table (the so-called "x- values") – are they discrete or continuous? In this particular case, the values are "Months of failure". In the table these range from 0 to 99; clearly we are numbering the months, so that the value 47 refers to the 47th month from the start of testing. For this reason we could not possibly have such a month as $3\frac{1}{2}$ – it wouldn't make any sense at all – these values must be discrete.

It is also wise to check that the frequency values really do add up to the total stated – all too often people do not make this sort of check and assume that everything is correct. In this case, the frequencies indeed add up to 400; the careful reader will already have checked this – even authors make mistakes!

We can now begin to set out the table ready for all the calculations:

| Month | Frequency (f) | Mid-interval value (x) |
|---|---|---|
| 0-9 | 44 | $4\frac{1}{2}$ |
| 10-19 | 56 | $14\frac{1}{2}$ |
| 20-29 | 64 | $24\frac{1}{2}$ |
| 30-39 | 78 | $34\frac{1}{2}$ |
| 40-49 | 60 | $44\frac{1}{2}$ |
| 50-59 | 40 | $54\frac{1}{2}$ |
| 60-69 | 36 | $64\frac{1}{2}$ |
| 70-79 | 18 | $74\frac{1}{2}$ |
| 80-99 | 4 | $89\frac{1}{2}$ |

Note that the last group, from 80 to 99, is wider than the others, hence the rather different mid-interval value.

Now we can get on with the next stage – coding the x- values to make the arithmetic simpler. Select the working zero to begin with. In this case $34\frac{1}{2}$ has been chosen since it corresponds with the grouping with the highest f-value; as stated in the text, this is not the only possible choice, but is usually the simplest to use. Once we have subtracted the working zero from each of the mid-interval values (to give us the values of d), we should choose a number that goes into all the "d" values exactly to give d. The most reasonable choice here is 5; the table now becomes:

| Month | f | x | d | d' |
|---|---|---|---|---|
| 0-9 | 44 | $4\frac{1}{2}$ | −30 | −6 |
| 10-19 | 56 | $14\frac{1}{2}$ | −20 | −4 |
| 20-29 | 64 | $24\frac{1}{2}$ | −10 | −2 |
| 30-39 | 78 | $34\frac{1}{2}$ | 0 | 0 |
| 40-49 | 60 | $44\frac{1}{2}$ | 10 | 2 |
| 50-59 | 40 | $54\frac{1}{2}$ | 20 | 4 |
| 60-69 | 36 | $64\frac{1}{2}$ | 30 | 6 |
| 70-79 | 18 | $74\frac{1}{2}$ | 40 | 8 |
| 80-99 | 4 | $89\frac{1}{2}$ | 55 | 11 |

The next stages, calculating $fd'$ and $fd'^2$ are straightforward. We need to total the $f$, the $fd'$ and the $fd'^2$ columns. Note that the best way to calculate $fd'^2$ is by multiplying the value of $d'$ by the value of $fd'$. This gives:

| Month | $f$ | $x$ | $d$ | $d'$ | $fd'$ | $fd'^2$ |
|---|---|---|---|---|---|---|
| 0-9 | 44 | $4\frac{1}{2}$ | $-30$ | $-6$ | $-264$ | 1584 |
| 10-19 | 56 | $14\frac{1}{2}$ | $-20$ | $-4$ | $-224$ | 896 |
| 20-29 | 64 | $24\frac{1}{2}$ | $-10$ | $-2$ | $-128$ | 256 |
| 30-39 | 78 | $34\frac{1}{2}$ | 0 | 0 | 0 | 0 |
| 40-49 | 60 | $44\frac{1}{2}$ | 10 | 2 | 120 | 240 |
| 50-59 | 40 | $54\frac{1}{2}$ | 20 | 4 | 160 | 640 |
| 60-69 | 36 | $64\frac{1}{2}$ | 30 | 6 | 216 | 1296 |
| 70-79 | 18 | $74\frac{1}{2}$ | 40 | 8 | 144 | 1152 |
| 80-99 | 4 | $89\frac{1}{2}$ | 55 | 11 | 44 | 484 |
|  | 400 |  |  |  | 68 | 6548 |

We can now obtain the mean as

$34\frac{1}{2} + (5 \times 68/400) = 34\frac{1}{2} + 0.85 = 34.5 + 0.85 = 35.35$

The standard deviation is

$5 \times \sqrt{6548/400 - (68/400)^2} = 5 \times \sqrt{16.37 - 0.0289} = 5 \times \sqrt{16.3411}$
$= 5 \times 4.0424 = 20.212$

Finally, before giving the solutions, be sure that each is given in appropriate units and to sensible levels of precision. The original month values are given as whole numbers – it would be reasonable to quote the mean and the standard deviation to no more than one place of decimals each; also they both have the same units as $x$.

Mean = 35.4 months and standard deviation = 20.2 months

## Solution

*Part (b)*

Part (b) requires the drawing of a cumulative frequency graph; in order to do this first we need a cumulative frequency (cf) table, based directly on the information contained in the original frequency distribution table. Such a table is based on "less than" values, and in this case is as follows:-

| Month ($x$) (less than) | cf |
|---|---|
| 0 | 0 |
| 10 | 44 |
| 20 | 100 |
| 30 | 164 |

| | |
|---|---|
| 40 | 242 |
| 50 | 302 |
| 60 | 342 |
| 70 | 378 |
| 80 | 396 |
| 100 | 400 |

The graph must now be carefully drawn, to a sensible scale (chosen so the graph almost fills the graph paper). The cf axis always runs parallel to the left side of the paper, with the "less than $x$" axis parallel to the bottom. Please draw the graph as accurately as you can; the following figure illustrates how the graph should look.

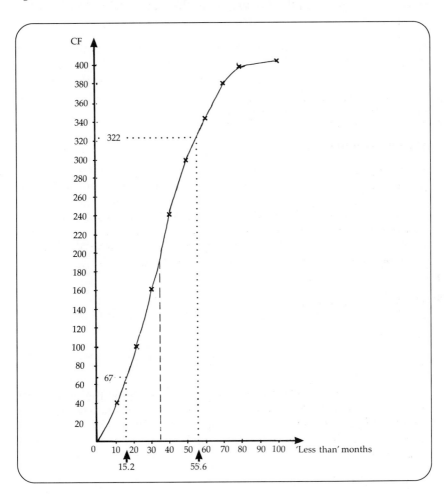

Cumulative frequency graph

Once you have plotted the points, join them carefully with a smooth curve.

The resulting shape is quite typical of cumulative frequency graphs. We are asked to estimate the percentage of components that failed "within ONE standard deviation of the mean". We know both mean and standard deviation, so one standard deviation below the mean is where $x = 35.4 - 20.2 = 15.2$ months, and one standard deviation above has $x = 35.4 + 20.2 = 55.6$ months; both points have been marked on the $x$ axis of the graph. Lines have then been drawn parallel to the cf axis from 15.2 and from 55.6, to cut the curve at two points; also across to the cf axis from these two points to cut the axis at cf $= 67$ and 322 respectively.

Hence 322 components failed in less than 55.6 months and 67 in less than 15.2 months; therefore, $322 - 67 = 255$ components (out of 400) failed within ONE standard deviation of the mean; $100 \times {}^{255}/_{400} = 64\%$ to the nearest integer.

There is one final point to make. The graph used in the example has the cf scale set as *linear* – each step up the axis stands for an equal quantity, in this case 20 components. However, people often look at the values of cf in the table (0, 44, 100, 164, 242, etc) and mark these at consecutive steps on the cf axis – this is totally wrong.

## Second Example

(a) A computer system uses a disk cache to speed up access to a random file. The hit rate is the percentage of times that a request for file access relates to a record already read into the cache. The following table shows the percentage hit rates for various cache sizes.

| Cache size (kilobytes) | 10 | 20 | 30 | 40 | 50 | 60 | 70 | 80 | 90 | 100 |
|---|---|---|---|---|---|---|---|---|---|---|
| Hit rate (%) | 1 | 3 | 10 | 20 | 35 | 60 | 75 | 90 | 95 | 100 |

(i)   Plot a graph of the data.

(ii)  Use your curve to estimate the cache size required to ensure a hit rate of 50%

(iii) What is the probability that the next record requested will be in the cache if the cache size is 32K?

(b) Another measure of the effectiveness of a cache is the number of consecutive hits for a given cache size. The table below gives the frequencies of *successive hits* using a 50K cache.

| Number of successive hits | 2 | 3 | 4 | 5 | 6 | 7 | 8 | 9 and over |
|---|---|---|---|---|---|---|---|---|
| Frequency | 14 | 10 | 7 | 4 | 2 | 2 | 1 | 0 |

(i)  Draw a histogram of the data

(ii) Calculate the mean and standard deviation, correct to two decimal places.

## Solution

In looking at a question like this, many people ask themselves what they understand by cache storage; if they are unfamiliar with it, they ignore the question completely. This is most unfortunate – the question expects no understanding of cache memory at all; it simply involves drawing graphs and making quite straightforward deductions from them, together with standard calculations.

*Part (a)*

Part (a) starts with drawing the graph; this involves deciding what goes on the $x$ and $y$ axes. Although it may not matter too much, there is a right and a wrong choice; decide which of "cache size" and "hit rate" follows from the other. In this case, we would be given a particular cache size and the hit rate follows, not the other way round. In the jargon, the "cache size" is the independent variable ($x$) and "hit rate" is the "dependent" variable ($y$) – hence we use the $x$ axis for the cache size and the $y$ axis for the hit rate.

Now draw the graph with great care (see next page).

The values for the hit rate make this graph slightly awkward to draw, since they do not lie in a simple sweeping curve – however, draw as smooth a curve as possible.

Next, to answer (ii), a hit rate of 50% on the hit-rate axis corresponds to a cache size of 56K; as shown, this involves drawing a straight line across from 50% on the hit-rate axis until it meets the curve, and then drawing "down" from this point onto the cache-size axis.

Part (iii) refers us to a probability; from the 32K cache size value, draw a line "up" to the curve, then "across" to the hit-rate axis. We obtain a value of 11%; this means (according to the wording of the question) that in 11% of cases "a request for file access relates to a record which has already been read into the 32K cache". Hence the probability required must be 0.11 (we give probabilities as fractions of 1).

*Part (b)*

Part (b) asks for a histogram using some different data. The "Number of successive hits" is a discrete item of data and goes on the $x$ axis, with the $y$ axis being used for the frequencies. The histogram should be drawn on graph paper and appears as shown on page 125.

The shaded areas make the graph stand out better, though this is not a requirement of the question.

The next stage is to find the mean and the standard deviation; in this example there is no need to code the values of the variable $x$ (representing the number of successive hits) as the arithmetic is easily manageable.

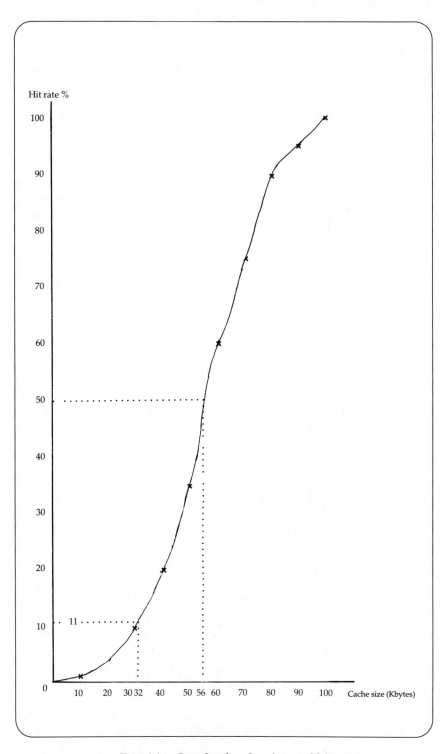

**Part (a)    Graph of cache size and hit rate**

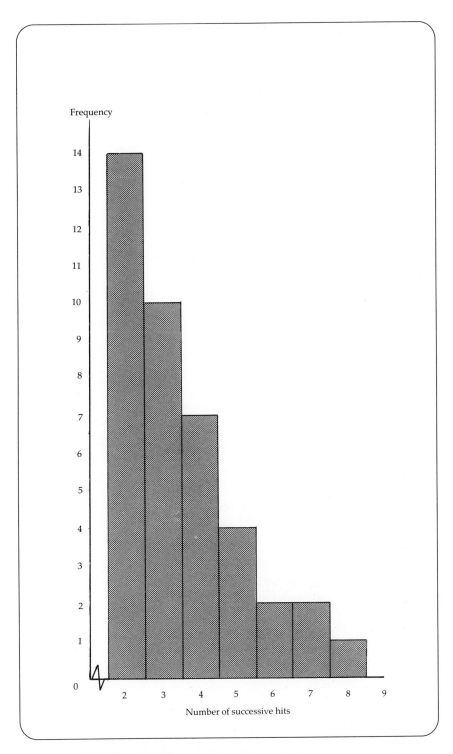

**Part (b)    Histogram of frequency and successive hits**

The table below demonstrates this point.

| $x$ | $f$ | $fx$ | $fx^2$ |
|---|---|---|---|
| 2 | 14 | 28 | 56 |
| 3 | 10 | 30 | 90 |
| 4 | 7 | 28 | 112 |
| 5 | 4 | 20 | 100 |
| 6 | 2 | 12 | 72 |
| 7 | 2 | 14 | 98 |
| 8 | 1 | 8 | 64 |
| | 40 | 140 | 592 |

Using these values, $\Sigma x = 40$, $\Sigma fx = 140$ and $\Sigma fx^2 = 592$ we can see that

$$\text{Mean} = \frac{\Sigma fx}{\Sigma f} = \frac{140}{40} = 3.5 \text{ and also that}$$

$$\text{Standard deviation} = \sqrt{\frac{\Sigma fx^2}{\Sigma f} - \left(\frac{\Sigma fx}{\Sigma f}\right)^2} = \sqrt{\frac{592}{40} - \left(\frac{140}{40}\right)^2}$$

$$= \sqrt{14.8 - 12.25} = \sqrt{2.55} = 1.60 \text{ (to two decimal places)}.$$

Hence mean is 3.50 and standard deviation is 1.60, in each case to two decimal places. (Note that the value of 3.5 for the mean is actually only to one decimal place, not as specified in the question).

**NOW TRY THESE . . .**

1. The following data relates to the sales in two separate periods made by the sales staff of Premier Software Products.

| Sales ($) | Period 1 | Period 2 |
|---|---|---|
| up to 500 | 84 | 60 |
| 501 to 1000 | 86 | 80 |
| 1001 to 1500 | 122 | 165 |
| 1501 to 2000 | 86 | 110 |
| 2001 to 3000 | 16 | 55 |
| 3001 to 4000 | 6 | 30 |

(i)  Calculate the relative (percentage) cumulative frequencies for each period.

(ii)  Draw (on one graph) cumulative frequency curves for the two periods.

(iii)   Use your graph to find the median sales and inter-quartile range for each period.

(iv)   Write a short report interpreting the results obtained.

2.  A sample was taken of the output from a machine producing 2cm diameter rods. The diameters of the sampled rods are as follows.

| | | | | |
|---|---|---|---|---|
| 2.40 | 2.17 | 2.14 | 2.14 | 2.01 |
| 2.12 | 2.05 | 1.94 | 2.45 | 1.81 |
| 1.85 | 2.10 | 1.88 | 2.25 | 1.80 |
| 2.05 | 1.84 | 2.06 | 1.94 | 2.16 |
| 1.62 | 2.26 | 2.03 | 1.92 | 1.63 |
| 2.05 | 1.91 | 2.07 | 1.92 | 1.85 |
| 2.02 | 1.96 | 2.09 | 1.56 | 2.01 |
| 1.93 | 1.98 | 2.15 | 1.76 | 1.95 |

(i)   Classify the data using class sizes of 0.1 cm (ie $1.5 \leq x < 1.6$ etc) and produce a frequency table of the number of rods in each class.

(ii)   Draw a histogram of the frequency distribution.

(iii)   Calculate cumulative relative frequencies (as percentages).

(iv)   Draw the corresponding cumulative frequency ogive (curve).

(v)   From your curve determine the median and interquartile range.

(vi)   All rods with diameters outside the range 1.85 to 2.15 are considered unsuitable for sale. Use your curve to estimate the percentage of rods rejected.

3.   A survey was taken of the time taken to repair computers when an engineer was called out under a maintenance contract. A cumulative frequency was formed as follows.

| Time taken (hours) | <5 | <10 | <15 | <20 | <25 | <30 | <35 | <40 | <45 |
|---|---|---|---|---|---|---|---|---|---|
| Cumulative frequency | 28 | 45 | 81 | 143 | 280 | 349 | 374 | 395 | 400 |

(i)   Draw a cumulative frequency curve.

(ii)   Estimate how many repairs took less than 18 hours.

(iii)   4% of repairs took $x$ hours or longer. Estimate x.

(iv)   Taking equal class intervals 0-, 5-, 10-, .... construct a frequency distribution and draw a histogram.

4.   The following data sample shows the marks distribution for a

school examination in 1987. The marks were all positive whole numbers between 0 and 100.

| Marks | Number of students |
|---|---|
| 0 – 9 | 5 |
| 10 – 19 | 10 |
| 20 – 29 | 9 |
| 30 – 39 | 30 |
| 40 – 49 | 35 |
| 50 – 59 | 39 |
| 60 – 69 | 41 |
| 70 – 100 | 31 |

(i)   Draw a histogram to represent this data.

(ii)  Calculate the mean and standard deviation for this data sample.

(iii) From your histogram find the mode and mark it on the histogram.

(iv)  Compare the use of the mode and mean as measures of average.

# 10 Algebraic terminology and simple manipulations

## OBJECTIVES

When you've worked through this Chapter, you should be able to:

— explain simple algebraic expressions and equations in words

— state what variables and subscripted variables are

— relate the symbols $=$, $*$, $/$, $+$, $-$, and $\uparrow$ (or $**$) to arithmetical meanings

— simplify expressions with powers

— explain how equations and inequations differ, with examples

— state the rules of precedence and use them correctly

— change the subject of an equation

— add two equations.

## INTRODUCTION

In the programming language Cobol you meet instructions like

MULTIPLY HOURS-WORKED BY RATE-OF-PAY GIVING GROSS-PAY

and you have very little trouble understanding their meaning. However, as soon as we write this as $G = H*R$, many people become very worried. Both statements mean the same thing – the second simplifies, not the relationship itself, but the way of writing it. It uses symbols, eg letters, for the quantities involved ($G$ for GROSS-PAY etc) $*$ for 'multiplied by', and $=$ for 'is equal to' (or 'gives').

This is part of the language of algebra – a neat, clear, quick and convenient way to express relationships between quantities. If you worry about it, that is partly because of lack of familiarity and partly because you do not appreciate that it is no more than a shorthand way to express a relationship, rather than using flowing text with which you are more familiar.

Of course, what algebra can achieve is much more than this, but the first step has to be a degree of comfort with the language.

129

## 10.1  MIND YOUR LANGUAGE!

The $G = H*R$ statement is an equation, as the "equals" sign shows. It tells us that the two quantities are equal to one another, ie, that $G$ and the product of $H$ and $R$ have exactly the same value – or that working out that product can give the value of $G$.

Since $H$ and $R$ will not always have the same values, we call them variables – so $G$ must also be a variable.

Now look at the equation $T = 0.15*P$; here $T$ stands for the amount of tax due on price $P$, assuming a rate of 15%. $T$ and $P$ are again variables but the third quantity, 0.15, is a constant as it always has the same value. The same relationship in Cobol is

MULTIPLY PRICE BY 0.15 GIVING TAX-DUE

Algebra uses other symbols than * and =. Here is a longer list

=   is equal to, gives

*   times, multiplied by

/   divided by

+   added to

−   minus, subtract

If you are used to programming in Basic, Fortran or Pascal (for instance), you will recognise these symbols at once.

In Section 2.3 (and later), we met the word "power" or "exponent". $X^4$ is "$X$ to the power of 4", meaning $X*X*X*X$. Using the power (4 in that case) is simply a shorthand for expressing the idea of 4 $X$s multiplied together. It is not the same as $X$ times 4, which would be $X*4$ or $4*X$.

Perhaps it is a pity that $X$ appears as often as it does; by tradition, people use it far more than any other symbol to stand for a variable, to many people, "$X$" and "algebra" mean almost the same.

When we use exponents, we meet such things as $X^1$ (a way of writing $X$ itself) and $X^0$ which always has the value 1. Please see the following example.

$$5^3 = 5*5*5 = 125$$
$$7^4 = 7*7*7*7 = 2401$$
$$3^1 = 3$$
$$6^0 = 1$$
$$(7.9)^1 = 7.9$$
$$(8.326)^0 = 1$$

In most programming languages we cannot express exponents this way – all instructions must be "at line level". Then you may find $X^4$ given as X**4 or as $X \uparrow 4$ depending upon the language. So treat $**$ or $\uparrow$ as meaning "to the power of".

Say a program uses variable $A$ to represent a person's age; as long as we do not use $A$ in the same program for a second quantity there is no risk of confusion. However, if the program has to read in record after record and note the age of each person, you could scarcely use $A$ for each one at the same time.

In such a case we may use 'subscripted variables' putting $A_1$, $A_2$, $A_3$, etc, for the various ages. Here the numbers 1, 2, 3, are the subscripts. Again as programming languages tend not to allow "below the line" values, you find $A(1)$, $A(2)$, $A(3)$, etc, instead of $A_1$, $A_2$, $A_3$, etc,.

We always use this approach when we have an array to hold such values; the advantage is that, whilst it keeps the individual values separate from each other it retains the idea that each value stands for the same quantity, but for each of a number of cases.

When programming, you will also find that the subscript itself may be variable, as in $A(N)$, to allow for more useful program control for instance in Basic

FOR N = 1 TO 20

READ A(N)

NEXT N

reads the value of $A(1)$, then $A(2)$, etc, up to $A(20)$ and stores the values into the elements of the array $A$.

## 10.2   THE RULES OF ALGEBRA

In algebra outside the context of a program, $5f$ represents the product of the constant 5 and the variable $f$. Since a computer would try to handle $5f$ as an address instead of as a product, we must include the multiplication sign in program expressions – in this case writing $5 * F$ (note the common use of upper case letters).

The next step is $5f + 7f$. This means "five lots of $f$ added to seven lots of $f$" – making $12f$. In the same way eg,

$$11b + 6b = 17b$$

$$11b - 6b = 5b$$

$$10a - 3a + 9a = 16a$$

$$13xy + 5xy - 27xy = -9xy$$

Here, we simplify expressions that involve a number of "like items" added together using simple arithmetic. "Like terms" means terms of the same kind – you cannot simplify $7c + 4d$ that way.

Multiplying gives no such problems – can you see that $7c * 4d = 28cd$? Can you see why?

On the other hand, multiplying terms with powers can be more tricky. The first example is easy, $7c^2 * 4d^3 = 28c^2d^3$. Yes? But what about $7c^2 * 4c^3$? If the variables are the same, add the powers: $7c^2 * 4c^3 = 28c^{2+3} = 28c^5$.

Work through the following example.

$$\text{What is } 5ab^2c^3 * 6a^2b^4c$$

$$= 30\, a^1b^2c^3a^2b^4c^1 \text{ (remember that } x \text{ and } x^1 \text{ mean the same thing)}$$

$$= 30a^{1+2}b^{2+4}c^{3+1}$$

$$= 30\, a^3b^6c^4$$

Now check that you agree that $4a^2b * 7b^2c^3$ is $28a^2b^3c^3$.

In much the same way we can divide algebraic expressions. First $28e \div 4f = 7e \div f$. Next, with powers, subtract where before we added to multiply, eg,

$$28e^3 \div 4e^2 = 7e^{3-2} = 7e$$

$$32a^5b^6 \div 4a^2b^4 = 8a^{5-2}b^{6-4} = 8a^3b^2$$

$$x^3 \div x^5 = x^{3-5} = x^{-2}\, (=1 \div x^2)$$

But we cannot do anything like that with $x^6 \div y^3$ for instance.

You may meet expressions like $(5x^2y^3)^3$. This is the same as writing $(5x^2y^3) * (5x^2y^3) * (5x^2y^3)$, so gives $125x^6y^9$. Other examples are $(x^5)^4 = x^{20}$, $(y^7)^2 = y^{14}$ and $(a^4)^3 = a^{12}$ – in general $(x^a)^b = x^{ab}$.

Brackets are common in algebra, for example $3a(2a + 5b)$. Simplify this by multiplying first the $2a$ by the $3a$ and then the $5b$ by the $3a$ – and adding the results – to give $6a^2 + 15ab$. In the same way, $5x(4x - 3y)$ gives $20x^2 - 15xy$. More examples below.

$$3p(2p - 6q) = 6p^2 - 18pq$$

$$5x^2\,(2x - 3y) = 10x^3 - 15x^2y$$

$$7ab(bc - 2a^2 - c) = 7ab^2c - 14a^3b - 7abc$$

What about $(x + 3)\,(2x - 5)$? Treat as $x(2x - 5) + 3(2x - 5)$ – the $x$ and the $+3$ are the two terms from the first bracket. That now gives $2x^2 - 5x + 6x - 15$ or (since $- 5x + 6x$ simplifies to $x$) $2x^2 + x - 15$. At this point remember that if you multiply two numbers, the product is positive if both numbers are positive or if both numbers are negative; it is negative if the two numbers differ in sign. Thus

$$-3 * -6 = +18$$

$$+2 * +5 = +10$$

$$+2 * -7 = -14$$

$(3x-2)*(2x-7)$ becomes $3x(2x-7)-2(2x-7)$ which is

equal in turn to $6x^2 - 21x - 4x + 14 = 6x^2 - 25x + 14$. Look below for more examples.

eg    $(x - 6)(2x + 3) = x(2x + 3) - 6(2x +3)$
$= 2x^2 + 3x - 12x - 18 = 2x^2 - 9x - 18$

eg    $(a + 5b)(a - 2b) = a(a - 2b) + 5b(a - 2b)$
$= a^2 - 2ab + 5ab - 10b^2 = a^2 + 3ab - 10b^2$

eg    $(x^2 - 3)(2y - 7) = x^2 (2y - 7) - 3 (2y- 7)$
$= 2x^2y - 7x^2 - 6y + 21$

You may also meet a bracket raised to a power, eg, $(2x - 3)^2$. This is just the same as $(2x - 3) (2x - 3)$ giving $4x^2 - 6x -6x +9 = 4x^2 - 12x +9$

**NOW TRY THESE . . .**

1. Work out each of the following

    (a)  $5^4$            (e)  $49^0$

    (b)  $3^5$            (f)  $17^1$

    (c)  $2^6$            (g)  $2.3^2$

    (d)  $8^3$            (h)  $2.3^0$

2. Simplify each of the following as far as you can

    (a)  $3x + 7x + 15x$

    (b)  $6a + 5a - 2a$

    (c)  $3x + 8x - 4y$

    (d)  $7ab - 2ab + 9ab$

    (e)  $8a^2 + 3a - 5a$

    (f)  $15a^3 - 7a^3 + 2a^3$

    (g)  $16abc - 4abc + 18bc$

3. $x = 2, y = 4$ and $z = 5$. Work out the following

    (a)  $7xy$

    (b)  $2xyz$

    (c)  $3x^2z$

    (d)  $8xy + 3yz$

    (e)  $4x^2yz$

4.  Simplify each of the following as far as you can

   (a)  $3x^2 * 5x^4 * 2x$

   (b)  $8a^2b * 3ab^2c$

   (c)  $16x^2y^4 / 4xy^3$

   (d)  $81x^2y^6z^4 \div 12x^2y^2z$

   (e)  $6a^2b^2c * 5abc * 2b$

   (f)  $72a^7b^6c^4 \div 18a^7bc^8$

5.  $x = 3$ and $y = 7$. Find the values of

   (a)  $2xy - x$          (d)  $x^2 + y^2$

   (b)  $5x$               (e)  $(xy)^0$

   (c)  $6x^{-1}$          (f)  $y^2 + x^3$

6.  Simplify each of these products.

   (a)  $4x(2x - 3y)$

   (b)  $5a(6a + 3b)$

   (c)  $6a(a + b) - 3(ab - a^2)$

   (d)  $(2a + b)(a - 3b)$

   (e)  $(4x - 1)(2x - 5)$

   (f)  $(2x + 5)(3x + 1)$

   (g)  $(3x - 4)^2$

   (h)  $(4x + y)(4x - y)$

   (i)  $(3a - 7b)(2a + 3b)$

   (j)  $(a + 2b)^2 - 5ab$

## 10.3   EQUALITY AND INEQUALITY

At the beginning of this chapter the idea was introduced of an equation as being a way of stating that two expressions have exactly the same value. This is true for $8*3=24$, for $^{35}/_7 = 5$ and for $18 + 17 - 2 = 33$; it is just as true for $2x + 3 = 19$, even if we do not know the value of $x$. This equation says that the value of $x$ is unknown, but that the value of $2x + 3$ is the same as the value of 19. In fact, there is one value of $x$ for which the equation is true. We'll come back to this shortly.

Some equations are more involved; in the case of $4x^2 - 3x = 85$ there are two values of $x$ for which it is true. Again we'll come back to this – finding the "solution" of the question.

Indeed some equations have a very large number of possible solutions.

For example, $x^4 - 2x^3 - x^2 + 2x = 0$, is true if $x$ is $-1$ or $0$ or $+1$ or $+2$ (four values in all); it is not true for any other value of $x$.

Some equations have no solutions however. This may appear strange – surely there has to be a solution? – but some equations genuinely have no solutions, just as some real-life problems have none.

Most people's experience of algebra has involved dealing primarily with equality – but in fact this is a very limited aspect of the relationship between two expressions. I might claim to be exactly 32 years old but there are far more people in the world older than 32 and far more younger than 32 than ever there are who are exactly 32. Inequality is far more common than equality, so we should think about it.

In dealing with equality, we used the symbol = to mean "is equal to". Now meet the symbols > for "is greater than" and < for "is less than". There are also ≥ for "is greater than or equal to" and ≤ for "is less than or equal to".

Statements such as $x > 5$ are inequations, like equations they are true for some values of $x$ and not for others. In this case an infinity of values of $x$ makes the inequation true for all values from 5.0 . . . 01 upwards. On the other hand the equation $x = 5$ is true for only one value of $x$. Inequations can be far more involved than this – for example, $8y^2 - 6y < 7$. In each case, to provide a solution needs one of various techniques to be used.

Inequations are common, for example in solving management problems, eg, using linear programming or other optimisation techniques. For this reason they often turn up within software used in management information systems.

## 10.4   TAKING PRECEDENCE

Look at $x + y^2$. If $x$ is 3 and $y$ is 7 do you agree the value is 52? If you do, it is because you know that you should work out $7^2$ before adding the 3.

On a totally strict left to right basis we would add the 3 and the 7 getting 10, before coming to the power 2, making $10^2$ ie, 100. We know this is wrong, only because we know that you should work out the $7^2$ before adding the 3. In other words, there is a precedence in the order in which we carry out calculations.

Computer calculations follow rules of precedence too. Starting with the highest priority, they deal with

(i)   brackets

(ii)   powers (exponents)

(iii)   multiply and divide

(iv)   add and subtract

To see how this works, work through $3x^2 - 7x + 3$ when $x = 2$ (note this would be 3*x**2 − 7*x + 3 in a computer). So we want the value of

$$3 * 2^2 - 7 * 2 + 3$$

As there are no brackets the first step is to work out the power – to calculate $2^2$, which is 4. This gives

$$3 * 4 - 7 * 2 + 3$$

Next go to the third level of the priority list, and work out all multiplications and divisions. This is done on a strict left to right basis, so work out $3 * 4$ to give 12, ie

$$12 - 7 * 2 + 3$$

Now find the second product $7 * 2$ to give 14, hence

$$12 - 14 + 3$$

Finally the last level of priority is to deal with all additions and subtractions, again on a strict left to right basis. This gives first

$$-2 + 3$$

and then $+ 1$

On the next example find the value of

$(2^2x - 7)$ ($\frac{4}{5} + 6$) with $x = 4$.

1. Take the first bracket $2 * 4^2 - 7$

2. Dealing with the power gives us $2 * 16 - 7$

3. Working out the product yields $32 - 7$

4. Carry out the subtraction and the result is 25

5. The second bracket is $\frac{4}{5} + 6$

6. With no powers, first divide to get $0.8 + 6$

7. Now we have 6.8

8. The original expression becomes $25 * 6.8$ and the result is 170.

**NOW TRY THESE . . .**

Use the rules of precedence on a step by step basis to find the value of

    (a)   $3x^3 - 6x^2 - 2x + 12$ when $x = 5$

    (b)   $(4x + 2)(3x - 5)$ with $x = 1.7$

    (c)   $(\frac{2x}{5} - 6)(x - 7)^2$ with $x = 8.2$

## 10.5   WORKING WITH EQUATIONS

An equation presents two quantities which we know are equal. Therefore, you can do anything you like to the two sides and they will remain equal – as long as what you do to one side, you do to the other. So you can add to each side, or take from it, the same value; multiply both by the same value, or divide; or raise to the same power – in all cases, the equation remains true, as long as you take care.

Manipulating equations (as we call this) leads to methods of solving equations. We will discuss this in greater detail in Chapter 11, but as an example, solve the following

$$5x - 12 = 14$$

Add 12 to each side            $$5x - 12 + 12 = 14 + 12$$

or $5x = 26$

Divide both sides by 5         $$5x \div 5 = 26 \div 5$$

$$x = 5.2$$

In order to decide what to do to each side consider the equation

$$C = \frac{5}{9}(F - 32).$$

We want to "make $F$ the subject of the equation" – that is to get $F$ on its own on one side of the equation. We need to list the operations originally carried out on F to create the right hand side of the equation. They are:

subtract 32

multiply by 5

divide by 9

Now, reverse each operation (ie multiply instead of divide, etc), and present them in the reverse order

multiply by 9

divide by 5

add 32

Doing these operations on C, the existing subject of the equation, first of all gives 9C, then $9C \div 5$ and finally $(9C \div 5) + 32$. This is the formula for F, ie

$$F = \frac{9C}{5} + 32$$

Please note that this is just the same as treating both sides the same way. For a second example of this "operation" technique, make $t$ the subject of $v = u + 10t$. The operations performed on $t$ are:

multiply by 10

add $u$

Invert these and put in the reverse order give

subtract $u$

divide by 10

Thus, starting with $v$ we get initially $v - u$ then $(v - u)/10$ so that

$$t = \frac{v - u}{10}$$

You should also be able to add equations and you will need the technique in Section 11.2. Really, it is the same idea as adding the same value to both sides of one equation.

For instance add $x^2 - 7x = 14$

to $7x + 9 = 15$

This gives $x^2 - 7x + 7x + 9 = 14 + 15$

or $x^2 + 9 = 29$

so that $x^2 = 20$

## NOW TRY THESE...

1. By listing the operations performed on $x$, make $x$ the subject of the equation $y = 7x - 4$

2. Make $u$ the subject of the equation $x = ut + 16t^2$

3. Add $5x + 6y = 35$

and     $4x - 6y = 21$

4. Add $x^2 - 7x + 3 = 0$

and     $7x - 5 = 0$

5. Solve the equation $4x - 7 = 1$ (ie, work out $x$)

# 11 Solving equations

## OBJECTIVES

When you've worked through this Chapter, you should be able to:

— solve simple linear equations in a single variable

— solve pairs of simultaneous linear equations by algebra and by drawing

— check whether a quadratic equation has real solutions

— solve quadratic equations by formula

— solve simple inequations.

## INTRODUCTION

We have seen that an equation involves an equals sign (=) between two expressions (eg 4, $x-3$, $16a^2z$). The equals sign tells us that the two expressions have the same value. As long as the same operations are carried out on both sides, the equation will remain the same.

In Chapter 10 we explored the use of this rule for changing the subject of an equation – for example, making $r$ the subject when $A = \pi r^2$. The solution is $r = \sqrt{A/\pi}$.

This same technique is also used to solve equations. Solving an equation means finding the value(s) of its unknown variable for which the equation is true. The whole of this chapter is devoted to this technique.

## 11.1 LINEAR EQUATIONS

First we look at equations with only one variable (and no powers of it) and some constant values. All such linear equations have the form $Ax = B$, where $A$ and $B$ are constants. Alas, many equations of this type do not appear so at first – they need simplification. Thus $7 = 1/x$ does not look as if it is linear, but, if you multiply both sides by $x$, you get $7x = 1$, which has the form we want.

139

With $x$ and $y$ as variables, the following are linear equations in $x$. Check by simplifying as needed.

$$5x + 3 = 17$$
$$4(x - 7) = 5(1 - 2x)$$
$$\frac{3}{x + 2} = 4$$

However, the following equations are not linear equations in $x$.

$$4x + 2y = 7$$
$$3x^2 + 4x = 5$$
$$5xy = 6$$
$$\frac{3}{x} - 2 = 6x$$

If $Ax = B$, to obtain the solution simply divide both sides by $A$, to give $x = B/A$; thus, to solve any simple equation, the real problem is to twist it into the $Ax = B$ form. The techniques you need for doing this appear in the examples which follow.

First is an equation in $x$ which involves the use of brackets:

$$5(x - 3) + 16 = 7x - 3(2x - 3)$$

This method involves getting rid of the brackets as shown in Chapter 10. The result is

$$5x - 15 + 16 = 7x - 6x + 9$$

Tidy up by taking $-15 + 16 = 1$ and by taking $7x - 6x = x$ to give

$$5x + 1 = x + 9$$

The next step is to collect all the "$x$" terms to the left hand side and to put all the constant terms, such as $+1$ and $+9$, onto the right hand side. Subtract $x$ from both sides to give
$$5x + 1 - x = x + 9 - x$$

which becomes

$$4x + 1 = 9$$

Then subtract 1 from each side to get

$$4x + 1 - 1 = 9 - 1$$

which becomes

$$4x = 8$$

This is now of the $Ax = B$ form with $A$ equal to 4 and $B$ equal to 8. The solution is $x = \frac{8}{4}$ or $x = 2$.

In general you will carry out such tasks as subtracting $x$ from each side and 1 from each side (or the equivalent in other equations) as a single step – in this case I set it out in separate stages to make it clearer.

The next example involves fractions; its solution needs the act of "cross-multiplication." If in an equation one fraction on the left equals one fraction on the right, such as

$$\frac{P}{Q} = \frac{R}{S},$$

then "cross-multiply" to turn it into $PS = QR$ – this will then be easier to work with. Our sample equation is

$$\frac{4}{2x-5} = \frac{3}{6-5x}$$

"Cross-multiplying" leads to:

$$4(6 - 5x) = 3(2x - 5)$$

Note that brackets have been inserted to make the multiplication clear.

Taking out the brackets gives

$$24 - 20x = 6x - 15$$

Take $6x$ from each side and 24 from each side to give

$$24 - 20x - 6x - 24 = 6x - 15 - 6x - 24$$

or

$$-26x = -39$$

This is now in the $Ax = B$ format, so $x = {}^{-39}\!/_{-26}$ or $^{39}\!/_{26}$, which is $^3\!/_2$, and the solution is $x = 1.5$. With experience, people devise many "short cuts" for solving equations; at first, it is probably best to avoid them and stick to straightforward techniques. Our next example involves both fractions and brackets – but as there is not simply one fraction on each side we can't cross-multiply this time. Instead, we multiply both sides of the equation by the lowest common multiple of the denominators of the fractions. Here is the equation:

$$\frac{1}{4}(2x - 7) - \frac{1}{3}(x + 5) = \frac{3}{8}(5 - 3x)$$

Multiply throughout by the lowest common multiple of 4, 3 and 8, which is 24, to get

$$6(2x - 7) - 8(x + 5) = 9(5 - 3x)$$

or

$$12x - 42 - 8x - 40 = 45 - 27x$$

collecting terms gives

$$4x - 82 = 45 - 27x$$

or

$$4x + 27x = 45 + 82$$

and

$$31x = 127$$

This leads to

$$x = {}^{127}\!/_{31} \text{ or } x = 4.097 \text{ (to 3 d.p.).}$$

## NOW TRY THESE ...

Solve each of the following equations for $x$:

1   $3x = 18$

2   $4x + 9 = 29$

3   $7x + 2 = 38 - 2x$

4   $2(3x - 1) = 5(1 - 2x)$

5   $3(1 + x) - 2(2x - 3) = 4(x + 3)$

6   $4(2x - 7) + 3(1 + 5x) = 8(2x - 1)$

7   $\dfrac{4}{3x} = \dfrac{8}{9}$

8   $\dfrac{x + 3}{4} = \dfrac{x - 1}{3}$

9   $\dfrac{1}{x - 7} = \dfrac{3}{2x + 5}$

10   $\dfrac{1}{3}x + 6 = \dfrac{9}{2}$

11   $\frac{1}{2}(x - 6) + \frac{1}{3}(2x + 4) = \frac{1}{4}(x - 3)$

12   $\frac{1}{5}(2x - 6) - \frac{1}{2}(x + 3) = 7$

## 11.2   SIMULTANEOUS EQUATIONS

The equation $3x = 12$ has a unique solution: $x = 4$. However, the equation $3x + 4y = 12$ has two variables ($x$ and $y$) – any solution must state values both for $x$ and for $y$.

In this case, $x = 4$, $y = 0$ is a solution – but so too are $x = 2$, $y = 1.5$; or $x = 0$, $y = 3$; or $x = 12$, $y = -6$, etc. In other words, one linear equation in two variables has an infinite number of equally valid solutions. A second equation in $x$ and $y$, such as $5x + 12y = 4$, also has an infinity of solutions such as $x = 11$, $y = -4.25$; $x = 14$, $y = -5.5$, etc. However, while each equation on its own has an infinity of solutions, we can usually find one solution which is common to both, in this case $x = 8$, $y = -3$. This solution, shortened to $(8, -3)$ is the solution to the pair of linear simultaneous equations.

$$3x + 4y = 12$$

$$5x + 12y = 4$$

How then can we obtain this unique solution of such a pair of equations?

There are two techniques to be explored; the first uses an algebraic approach, and the second (simpler but less accurate) uses drawing methods. We shall stay with equations of two variables (such as $x$ and $y$) which do not involve such terms as $x^2$, $xy$ and $y^2$.

Firstly, consider a pair of equations;

(1) $6x + 7y = 44$

(2) $4x - 7y = 6$

Note that the term in $y$ is the same in each case, though with different signs. This is particularly convenient; adding equations (1) and (2) gives $10x = 50$, and the $y$ terms vanish completely.

With no $y$ term present, we can find $x$ at once so that $x = {}^{50}\!/_{10}$ or $x = 5$. Putting this value into equation (1) gives $30 + 7y = 44$; from this we find $7y = 44 - 30 = 14$, or $y = 2$.

You must check that the solution is correct; if we put $x = 5$, $y = 2$ into equation (2); the left-hand side is $20 - 14$ or 6, which agrees with the right-hand side and confirms the solution. (It is essential not to check the solution with the same equation as was used to find the value of y).

In this particular example, $7y$ is in both equations, but with different signs, so we added. Where there are two equal terms with the same sign, we subtract the equations instead.

Suppose we have to solve

(1)   $4x + 9y = 3$

(2)   $4x + 2y = 10$

Both $x$ terms are equal and have the same sign, therefore we subtract giving

$$7y = -7$$

so that $y = -1$. Putting $y = -1$ into equation (2) gives $4x - 2 = 10$ or $4x = 12$, so $x = 3$.

Check with $x = 3$, $y = -1$ in equation (1): the left-hand side becomes $12 - 9$ or 3 which matches the right-hand side; the solution is $(3, -1)$. Always check the result — there are several stages in the process where things can go wrong. And don't forget that using the same equation for checking as for substitution will not work.

What about cases in which two equal terms are not present?

We can manipulate the equations to make equal terms appear, then work as before! Now try the following

(1)  $3x - 2y = 10$

(2)  $4x + 5y = 21$

Make the $y$ terms equal by multiplying (1) by 5 and (2) by 2. This gives

$$15x - 10y = 50$$

$$8x + 10y = 42$$

Addition yields $23x = 92$, so $x = 92/93 = 4$. Put $x = 4$ into equation (1): $12 - 2y = 10$, so $-2y = 10 - 12 = -2$, or $y = 1$. Check with $x = 4$, $y = 1$ in equation (2): the left-hand side becomes $16 + 5$ which is 21, the same as on the right. The solution is (4,1). Multiplying equations (1) and (2) by 5 and 2 respectively was performed by considering the lowest common multiple of the coefficients of $y$, ie 2 and 5, which is 10, and then deciding how to multiply each to produce 10.

The $x$ terms could have been made equal just as easily. The coefficients are 3 and 4, so their lowest common multiple is 12. Therefore, multiply equation (1) by 4 and equation (2) by 3 to give

$$12x - 8y = 40$$

$$12x + 15y = 63$$

We now need to subtract to give $-23y = -23$ from which we get $y = 1$. Check the $x$ value and obtain the solution as before.

Finally, consider the equations below

(1)  $3x + 10y = 44$

(2)  $7x - 15y = -89$

The lowest common multiple of 10 and 15 is 30, so multiply (1) by 3 and (2) by 2:

$$9x + 30y = 132$$

$$14x - 30y = -178$$

Addition produces $23x = -46$ and $x = -2$. Substitute $x = -2$ into equation (1): giving $-6 + 10y = 44$ or $10y = 50$, ie $y = 5$. Check the result by substituting $x = -2$, $y = 5$ in equation (2) – making the left-hand side $-14 - 75$ or $-89$, confirmed by the right-hand side. The solution is $(-2, 5)$.

## 11.3  SOLVING SIMULTANEOUS EQUATIONS BY DRAWING

Consider this pair of equations:

(1)  $2x + 5y = 25$

(2)  $5x - 3y = 16$

We can draw each equation as a straight line on standard graph paper. For instance, take equation (1), the values (0, 5), (5, 3), (10, 1), (15, −1), etc all satisfy this equation and we can plot all these points as they lie on a straight line. While you need plot only three points for a straight line, you can take any value of $x$ you like, find the corresponding value of $y$, and plot the pair to confirm the point does indeed lie on the line.

A different set of points satisfies equation (2), such as (2, −2), (5, 3), (8, 8), (11, 13), (14, 18), etc. Both lines are plotted on the graph in Figure 11.1. The point where the lines cross must lie on both lines – it is the only point to do so; thus its coordinates are the $(x, y)$ values that satisfy both equations, and therefore define the solution.

The graph in Figure 11.1 shows that $x = 5$, $y = 3$ is the solution of the pair of equations.

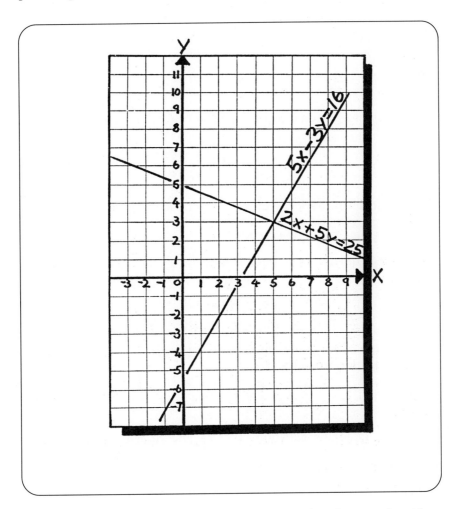

**Figure 11.1    Solving linear simultaneous equations by use of graphs**

Though you may find this approach to be more involved than the algebraic method, its virtue is that you can use it even with equations like these:

(1)  $x^3 - 6y^2 = 5xy$

(2)  $x^2 + 7y = xy^2$

An algebraic solution would be very clumsy here, if not impossible – but the graphical approach is fairly quick and accurate, depending on the care taken when plotting the graph.

### NOW TRY THESE ...

1. Using algebra, solve the following

   (a)  $3x - 5y = 22$
       $7x + 5y = 18$

   (b)  $8x + 3y = 46$
       $5x + 7y = 39$

   (c)  $3x - 5y = 22$
       $7x + 5y = 18$

2. Plot the following onto a graph and find the solution as accurately as you can

$$2x + 3y = 8$$

$$4x - y = 9$$

3. Use a graph to check one of your answers to question 1.

### 11.4   QUADRATIC EQUATIONS

A quadratic equation in $x$ contains terms in $x^2$, $x$ and a constant. Two examples are:

$$5x^2 - 3x + 7 = 0$$

$$x^2 + 12x - 16 = 0$$

However, the $x$ term or the constant may be missing – but if there is an $x^2$ term the equation is quadratic. Like these:

$$5x^2 + 4x = 0$$

$$6x^2 - 13 = 0$$

To solve a quadratic equation involves finding which two $x$ values satisfy it. A linear equation has only one solution, but a quadratic has two. For example, the equation

$$x^2 - 5x + 6 = 0$$

is satisfied either by $x = 2$ or by $x = 3$, but by no other value of $x$. Note that $(x + 3)(x - 7) = 5x(2x - 3)$ is also a quadratic equation. To show this, we must simplify; first by multiplying out the brackets, to get

$$x^2 + 3x - 7x - 21 = 10x^2 - 15x$$

and then collecting terms, to give

$$x^2 - 10x^2 - 4x + 15x - 21 = 0$$

or

$$-9x^2 + 11x - 21 = 0$$

There are three prime methods for solving quadratic equations: by a process called factorisation, by use of a formula, and by graph.

Now we shall look at the factorisation process. If asked to multiply together $(3x - 2)$ and $(x + 5)$ we would get $3x^2 + 13x - 10$, and if asked to solve the equation $3x^2 + 13x - 10 = 0$ (which is quite clearly a quadratic equation in $x$), this could be rewritten as $(3x - 2)(x + 5) = 0$ since we *already* know that the quadratic expressions $3x^2 + 13x - 10$ can be expressed as the product of the two linear expression $3x - 2$ and $x + 5$.

Now, if two quantities are multiplied together and produce 0 then one or other (or both) of the quantities must itself be 0. Thus either $3x - 2 = 0$ or $x + 5 = 0$; in the former case $x = \frac{2}{3}$ and in the latter case $x = -5$. Hence $x = -5$ or $x = \frac{2}{3}$ must be the two values of $x$ which satisfy the original quadratic equation.

To check these results try substituting the two values into the left-hand side of the original equation:

$$3(-5)^2 + 13(-5) - 10 = 3(25) - 65 - 10$$

$= 75 - 65 - 10 = 0$ so that $x = -5$ satisfies the equation.

$$\text{Equally} \quad 3(\tfrac{2}{3})^2 + 13(\tfrac{2}{3}) - 10 = 3(\tfrac{4}{9}) + \tfrac{26}{3} - 10$$
$$= \tfrac{4}{3} + \tfrac{26}{3} - 10 = 10 - 10 = 0$$

so that $x = \frac{2}{3}$ also satisfies the equation.

It follows therefore that if the linear factors of the quadratic expression can be obtained (in the example, $3x^2 + 13x - 10$), then we can solve the equation quite straightforwardly (which, in this case is $3x^2 + 13x - 10 = 0$) by setting each linear expression equal to 0 and solving the two linear equations. Unfortunately, not all quadratic equations do factorise but for those that do, the technique outlined below will always work.

If considering the general quadratic equation as $ax^2 + bx + c = 0$ in which $a$, $b$ and $c$ have constant values (so in the previous case $a = 3$, $b = 13$ and $c = -10$) then first the product $ac$ has to be found. The next step is to list all the possible pairs of factors which give $ac$, so that if $ac = 12$ we would list (1, 12) (2,6) (3,4) (−1, −12) (−2, −6) (−3, −4) which gives us all such pairs (integer values only). Then, *from this list* select the pair which add together to give $b$. Using the $ac = 12$ example and given that $b$ is 7, the pair would have to be (3, 4) since not one of the other pairs add up to give 7. At this point the equation is rewritten but replacing the $bx$ term, so if we did indeed have $7x$, it would be rewritten as $3x + 43x$, using the factor pair selected. The process is shown here for the equation $6x^2 + 7x + 2 = 0$ (in which $a = 6$, $b = 7$ and $c = 2$), so that $ac$ is indeed 12 and $b$ is indeed 7:

$$6x^2 + 3x + 4x + 2 = 0$$

Now factorise the left-hand side taking the first two terms together and then the second two terms together to produce:

$$3x\,(2x + 1) + 2(2x + 1) = 0$$

A common factor, $2x + 1$, has emerged so the equation can now be written as:

$$(2x + 1)(3x + 2) = 0$$

from which either $2x + 1 = 0$ or $3x + 2 = 0$, hence we shall obtain the two solutions as $x = -\frac{1}{2}$ or $x = {}^-\frac{2}{3}$.

The example given in Figure 11.2 shows a simpler equation but uses exactly the same method.

eg   $x^2 - 8x + 15$ Find numbers which
multiply together to give $+ 15$
:- (1, 15) (5, 3), (−1, −15) (−5, −3)
Select the pair which add to give
$-8 \therefore -5, -3$
Rewrite the expression
$x^2 - 5x - 3x + 15$
and factorise in pairs
$x\,(x - 5) - 3\,(x - 5)$
$= (x - 5)\,(x - 3)$
Hence to solve $x^2 - 8x + 15 = 0$
we have $(x - 5)\,(x - 3) = 0$
$\therefore x - 5 = 0$ or $x - 3 = 0$
$\therefore x = 5$ or $3$

**Figure 11.2   Factors of quadratic expressions**

In this example we have $a = 1$, $b = -8$ and $c = 15$ so that the product $ac$ is 15; the rest follows from the earlier example directly.

The next example given in Figure 11.3 is slightly longer because it uses $a = 3$, $b = -19$ and $c = -14$ so the factors of $ac$ (ie of $-42$) take rather longer to list and it also takes longer to find which pair add up to the value of $b$, but the process is identical to that used on the first two examples.

$3x^2 - 19x - 14$
Factors of 3 times
$-14$ ie $-42$
Are:- $(1, -42)$ $(-1, 42)$ $(2, -21)$
$(-2, 21)$ $(3, -14)$ $(-3, 14)$, $(6, -7)$
$(-6, 7)$
Those which add to give
$-19$ are $2, -21$
$\therefore 3x^2 + 2x - 21x - 14$
$= x(3x + 2) - 7(3x + 2)$
$= (3x + 2)(x - 7)$
$\therefore$ To solve $3x^2 - 19x - 14 = 0$
We have $(3x + 2)(x - 7) = 0$
$\therefore x = -\frac{2}{3}$ or $7$

**Figure 11.3  Example of solving a quadratic equation**

Note that a quadratic equation in a single variable will always have either:

> 2 different solutions (as in each example so far seen); or
> 2 equal solutions; or
> no real solutions at all.

The '2 equal solutions' case is exemplified by $x^2 - 6x + 9 = 0$ which can be factorised to give $(x - 3)(x - 3) = 0$ so that $x = 3$ or $x = 3$, ie the same value twice over. Occasionally the case of 'no real solutions' may be encountered. This has been dealt with more fully earlier in this section.

It should also be recognised that if factors of $ac$ that add together to yield $b$ cannot be obtained then that particular equation is not capable of being factorised in which case an alternative method of solution is used, usually being that by formula.

The graphical approach is covered in Chapters 12 and 13, so we will look at the formula method at this stage.

Here is the formula for solving the quadratic equation $ax^2 + bx + c = 0$

$$x = \frac{-b \pm \sqrt{b^2 - 4ac}}{2a}$$

Using the formula above we can see how this quadratic equation can be solved. It is easy to see how mistakes could be made; however, the process is quite automatic.

Using this formula try solving $x^2 + 3x - 11 = 0$. In this case we have $a = 1, b = 3$ and $c = -11$, so:

$$x = \frac{-b \pm \sqrt{b^2 - 4ac}}{2a}$$

$$= \frac{-(3) \pm \sqrt{(3)^2 - 4(1)(-11)}}{2(1)}$$

$$= \frac{-3 \pm \sqrt{9 + 44}}{2}$$

$$= \frac{-3 \pm \sqrt{53}}{2}$$

$$= \frac{-3 + 7.280}{2} \text{ or } \frac{-3 - 7.280}{2}$$

$$= \frac{4.280}{2} \text{ or } \frac{-10.280}{2}$$

$$= 2.14 \text{ or } -5.14 \text{ to three significant figures in each case.}$$

There are two answers – we noted before that a quadratic can have two solutions. In fact,

if $b^2 > 4ac$ we get two different solutions,

if $b^2 = 4ac$ there are two equal solutions,

if $b^2 < 4ac$ there are no real solutions at all

Thus, $x^2 - 8x + 16 = 0$ has $a = 1$, $b = -8$ and $c = 16$. So $b^2$ is 64 and the value of $4ac$ is $4(1)(16) = 64$. Since $b^2 = 4ac$ this equation has two equal solutions.

In the case of $3x^2 + 2x + 15 = 0$, $a = 3$, $b = 2$ and $c = 15$; $b^2$ is 4 and $4ac$ is $4(3)(15) = 180$; here $b^2 < 4ac$ which means that we cannot solve this equation. If, when applying the formula to a quadratic equation you find a negative value inside the square root no solutions to the equation exist, so you can go no further.

**NOW TRY THESE . . .**

1. Use the formula to solve these quadratic equations, in each case to 3 significant figures (s.f.)

(a) $x^2 - 2x - 3 = 0$

(b) $x^2 + 7x - 2 = 0$

(c) $2x^2 + 9x - 7 = 0$

(d) $3x^2 - 6x + 2 = 0$

(e) $5x^2 - 8x - 1 = 0$

2. Use the factorisation method to solve each of the following:

(a) $x^2 + 6x + 5 = 0$

(b) $x^2 + 2x - 24 = 0$

(c) $2x^2 + 7x + 3 = 0$

(d) $3x^2 - 8x + 5 = 0$

(e) $6x^2 + 7x + 2 = 0$

(f) $12x^2 + 17x - 5 = 0$

(g) $15x^2 + x - 2 = 0$

(h) $30x^2 + x - 20 = 0$

3.  For each of the following quadratic equations, check whether it has two different solutions, two equal solutions or no real solutions.

(a)  $3x^2 - 4x + 2 = 0$

(b)  $x^2 - 10x + 25 = 0$

(c)  $2x^2 - 7x + 1 = 0$

(d)  $4x^2 + 2x - 3 = 0$

(e)  $4x^2 - 20x + 25 = 0$

## 11.5  SIMPLE INEQUATIONS

The concept of inequations was raised in Chapter 10, and as they often appear in the context of linear programming (a commonly used management technique), it is appropriate to expand on this concept.

The rules for handling inequations and equations are very similar, but there are some differences. You can add/subtract equal quantities to or from both sides of an inequation, and you can multiply or divide both sides by the same positive quantity.

Thus $x + 4 > 2$ is the same as $x > 2 - 4$ or $x > -2$; if $3x > 6$, then $x > 2$.

However, you can multiply/divide both sides of an inequation by a negative value only if you change the sign of the inequation in the process. So, for $-2x > 7$, dividing both sides by $-2$ gives $x < -3.5$; if we multiply the inequation $x/3 < -5$ by $-3$, we get $-x > 15$.

You can also add unequal quantities to the two sides of an inequation, as long as you add the larger quantity to the side which is already the larger. So, if $x > y$, then $x + 4 > y + 3$.

The examples in Figure 11.4 illustrate both the solution of very simple inequations and also how to show the solutions on a number line; note that in the first case, $x > 3$, the shaded area indicating the solution set, does not include $x = 3$. However in the third case $x \geqslant 3.5$ the value $x = 3.5$ is circled to show that it is in the solution set.

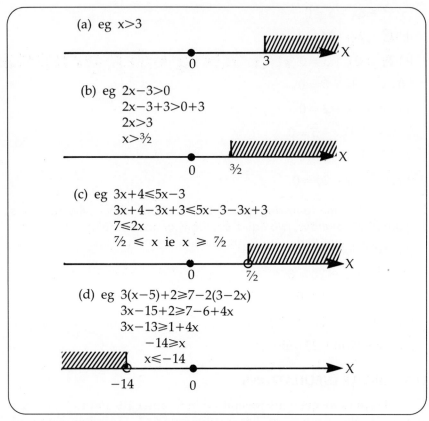

**Figure 11.4    Examples of solution of inequations**

# 12 Working with graphs

## OBJECTIVES

When you've worked through this Chapter, you should be able to:

— state what a function is, and give examples

— outline the nature and purpose of graphs of functions

— set up a table of values for any function over a stated range

— describe the standard system of graph axes

— use a table of values to plot the graph

— read useful values from a graph

— recognise and describe linear, quadratic and cubic polynomial, and exponential curves

— sketch curves of these types.

## INTRODUCTION

It's very important to be able to draw graphs. They are of great value for many kinds of report as they are able to show data and relationships quickly and with great effect. That being the case, many programs used in business offer graphs as one form of output – therefore, programmers need to be familiar with graphical representation of data.

First, though, we need to examine the concept of a function.

## 12.1  THE IDEA OF A FUNCTION

You are now used to writing down statements like $y = 2x^2 - 7x + 3$ and classing them as equations. It is now time to consider an alternative way of treating expressions like those on the right-hand side of the equation.

Any expression which contains $x$ as the only variable, we call a function of $x$; this means its value depends only on the value of $x$. Therefore, rather than use "$y = $" as above, we can state that the expression is a particular function of $x$, written as $f(x)$. In this case, $f(x) = 2x^2 - 7x + 3$.

An immediate advantage is that this lets us write $f(2)$ to mean the value of $f(x)$, when $x = 2$. Hence $f(2) = 2(2)^2 - 7(2) + 3 = 8 - 14 + 3 = -3$.

Likewise, $f(1) = 2(1)^2 - 7(1) + 3 = 2 - 7 + 3 = -2$, and $f(4) = 2(4)^2 - 7(4) + 3 = 32 - 28 + 3 = 7$.

The letter $f$ stands for "function". Once a particular function has been defined as $f(x) = $ "something", we can discuss the function $f$ itself by referring to the values it takes for different values of $x$. We talk about the "behaviour" of $f$ as $x$ varies.

If we need to refer to a number of different functions, we use letters other than $f$. So $f(x)$ stands for one function of $x$ and $g(x)$ and $h(x)$ are two others. Thus we could have $f(x) = 2x + 7$ and $g(x) = 3x^2 - 2x + 6$. Also we can create new functions by joining functions which have already been defined; $f(x) + g(x)$, as $2x + 7 + 3x^2 - 2x + 6 = 3x^2 + 13$ is a new function in terms of the others. We can define $h(x) = 3x^2 + 13$ or $h(x) = f(x) + g(x)$.

**NOW TRY THESE ...**

1. $f(x) = 3x^2 - 2x + 5$. Find the values of

   (i)   $f(0)$

   (ii)  $f(2)$

   (iii) $f(-1)$

2. $g(x) = \dfrac{x + 5}{2x - 1}$ Give the values of

   (i)  $g(2)$

   (ii) $g(-4)$

3. $f(x) = 6x^2 - 3x + 2$ and $g(x) = 7x + 5$. Work out

   (i)   $f(x) + g(x)$

   (ii)  $f(x) - g(x)$

   (iii) $2g(x)$

## 12.2   WHAT IS A GRAPH?

We can describe a graph as a visual method of showing the behaviour of a function.

A graph can easily show how the value of $x$ changes as the value of $f(x)$ changes – for example, does $f(x)$ change slowly or rapidly? Is $f(x)$ increasing or decreasing as $x$ increases?

Most people find the graph, with its visual impact, far easier to "digest" than a table of values of $f(x)$ and $x$ – or indeed, than the statement that "$f(x) = $ ...".

A graph can also show for what values of $x$ the function reaches its highest or its lowest values if indeed it has any; it can show where you can find specific values of $f(x)$ and can demonstrate when the function is increasing or decreasing as $x$ increases.

Likewise a graph can illustrate when two functions have the same value; this is covered in Chapter 11 in the graphical solution of simultaneous equations.

On occasion, a graph may be the only way to describe a function, for example, a sensor may monitor a patient's heartbeat – the trace on a screen is a graph, but no one could find an equation to give the heartbeat at any particular instant.

To plot a graph, we need to be able to record both $x$ and $f(x)$ for a range of values of $x$ in the same diagram. These two values we call the co-ordinates of a point; in the diagram the function is a series of points, linked to form a smooth curve – the graph of the function.

The basis of the diagram is two straight line axes at right-angles to each other crossing at a point we call the origin. These two lines are usually called the $x$-axis and the $y$-axis respectively – see the diagram in Figure 12.1.

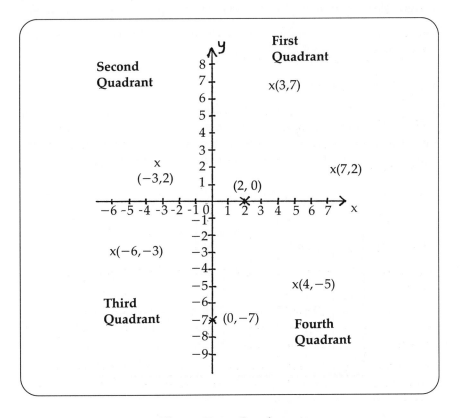

**Figure 12.1   Graph axes**

Points are marked along the (horizontal) $x$-axis, in equal steps, with 0 at the origin and positive values to the right, negative values to the left. Successive points must represent equal numeric intervals, so marking 0, 1, 2, 3, 4, etc is most common; intermediate values go to scale – so 1.5, although not marked, is half-way between the 1 and 2 values. In a similar manner, the (vertical) $y$-axis has positive values going upwards from 0 at the origin and negative values downwards.

The axes divide the area of the diagram into four quadrants; in the first quadrant all $x$-values and all $y$-values are positive (check by looking at the two parts of the axes which form the boundaries of the quadrant). In the second quadrant, all $x$-values are negative and all y-values are positive and so on in each quadrant.

We can now plot a point so as to reflect the graph's $x$ and $f(x)$ values. These are referred to as co-ordinates – to find the $x$, $f(x)$ position go to the $x$-value on the $x$-axis and then move vertically up or down to the value of $f(x)$ on the $y$-axis. In the diagram, seven points are plotted to illustrate the technique; for example by going to 3 on the $x$-axis and then moving straight up until level with 7 on the $y$-axis; point (3, 7) can be marked with a cross. Likewise (− 3, 2) is found by going to −3 on the $x$-axis and so on until level with 2 on the $y$-axis; please check the others.

Other axis systems with their own particular uses do exist, but these are not covered in this book.

### 12.3   TABLES OF VALUES

To be able to draw the graph of a function, you need to plot a set of points, this in turn means that for a range of values of $x$ you must find the values of $f(x)$. You can do this in a table or with a simple program. Figure 12.2 shows the table method for the function $f(x) = 3x^2 − 8x + 4$.

| x | −3 | −2 | −1 | 0 | 1 | 2 | 3 | 4 | 5 |
|---|---|---|---|---|---|---|---|---|---|
| $x^2$ | 9 | 4 | 1 | 0 | 1 | 4 | 9 | 16 | 25 |
| $3x^2$ | 27 | 12 | 3 | 0 | 3 | 12 | 27 | 48 | 75 |
| −8x | 24 | 16 | 8 | 0 | −8 | −16 | −24 | −32 | −40 |
| 4 | 4 | 4 | 4 | 4 | 4 | 4 | 4 | 4 | 4 |
| f(x) | 55 | 32 | 15 | 4 | −1 | 0 | 7 | 20 | 39 |

**Figure 12.2   Table of values**

In the table in Figure 12.2 the $x$ values from $-3$ to 5 appear along the top line to give a graph of $f(x)$ for that range of $x$ only. Since $f(x)$ includes a term in $x^2$, the $x^2$ values go on the second line. The "double-bar" separates lines 1 and 2 from lines 3, 4 and 5 – it is in these next three lines that we work out and list the various parts of $f(x)$.

The first line gives the values of $3x^2$ for each value of $x$, calculated all the more easily as the $x^2$ values are already known. The second line gives the equivalent values of $-8x$, and the third repeats the constant value $+4$. Since $f(x)$ is the sum of these three terms, we now add column by column, to give the $f(x)$ values on the bottom line; note that the $x$ and $x^2$ lines are not involved in this addition.

Thus, for each value of $x$ in the range, we have the $f(x)$ value. A computer could easily find the same values, using a simple program such as the three lines of Basic code which appear in Figure 12.3.

```
FOR X = −3 TO 5
     PRINT X, 3*X*X −8*X + 4
NEXT X
```

**Figure 12.3   Code in BASIC for values of $x$**

Now follows a second example in which the graph of $f(x) = \dfrac{2x + 3}{x + 6}$ is drawn for values of $x$ from $-4$ to 6 inclusive. Table 12.1 gives the values of $2x + 3$ and $x + 6$ and their quotient, the $f(x)$ line.

| $x$ | −4 | −3 | −2 | −1 | 0 | 1 | 2 | 3 | 4 | 5 | 6 |
|---|---|---|---|---|---|---|---|---|---|---|---|
| $2x + 3$ | −5 | −3 | −1 | 1 | 3 | 5 | 7 | 9 | 11 | 13 | 15 |
| $x + 6$ | 2 | 3 | 4 | 5 | 6 | 7 | 8 | 9 | 10 | 11 | 12 |
| $f(x)$ | −2.5 | −1 | −0.25 | 0.2 | 0.5 | 0.71 | 0.88 | 1 | 1.1 | 1.18 | 1.25 |

**Table 12.1   Tabulation to produce a graph of $f(x) = \dfrac{2x + 3}{x + 6}$**

Equally well this could have come from the Basic code:

```
FOR X = −4 TO 6
     PRINT X, (2* X + 3)/ (X + 6)
NEXT X
```

Finally, to produce a graph of $f(x) = 2x^3 - 7x^2 + 6x + 5$ for $x$ values from

−2 to 7 inclusive the table is as follows in Table 12.2. Can you write down the Basic code?

| x | −2 | −1 | 0 | 1 | 2 | 3 | 4 | 5 | 6 | 7 |
|---|---|---|---|---|---|---|---|---|---|---|
| $x^2$ | 4 | 1 | 0 | 1 | 4 | 9 | 16 | 25 | 36 | 49 |
| $x^3$ | −8 | −1 | 0 | 1 | 8 | 27 | 64 | 125 | 216 | 343 |
| $2x^3$ | −16 | −2 | 0 | 2 | 16 | 54 | 128 | 250 | 432 | 686 |
| $-7x^2$ | −28 | −7 | 0 | −7 | −28 | −63 | −112 | −175 | −252 | −343 |
| $+6x$ | −12 | −6 | 0 | 6 | 12 | 18 | 24 | 30 | 36 | 42 |
| $+5$ | 5 | 5 | 5 | 5 | 5 | 5 | 5 | 5 | 5 | 5 |
| $f(x)$ | −51 | −10 | 5 | 6 | 5 | 14 | 45 | 110 | 221 | 390 |

Table 12.2 Tabulation to produce the graph of
$$f(x) = 2x^3 - 7x^2 + 6x + 5$$

## 12.4 PLOTTING THE GRAPH

Once we have the table of values, we need to plot the points with co-ordinates $(x, f(x))$ on the axes. The scale and ranges on both axes depend on the ranges of $x$ and $f(x)$ values.

For $f(x) = 3x^2 - 8x + 4$ (See Figure 12.2) the x values go from −3 to 5 while the $f(x)$ values, which go on the y-axis, range from −1 to 55. Whilst a scale of 1cm per unit may suit the x-axis (as in Figure 12.4) the y-axis needs a scale of, for example, 1cm to 10 units so the graph can fit the space.

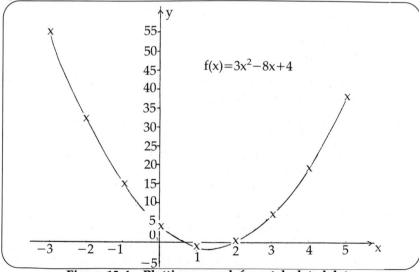

Figure 12.4 Plotting a graph from tabulated data

When the points have been plotted, draw a smooth curve through all the points; this is not always easy and you need a steady hand or sometimes the use of a flexible plastic curve.

The curve can now be used in the following ways:

(a) By going vertically upwards from the point 3.6 on the x-axis until the graph is cut we can find the value of $f(3.6)$ by reading horizontally onto the y-axis. Try it.

(b) By going horizontally from the point 25 on the y-axis to meet the graph (in two points, one to the left and other to the right), we can read vertically down onto the x-axis to read off the x-values which make $f(x) = 25$. This means that the x-values can be found for which $3x^2 - 8x + 4 = 25$ so providing the graphical solution of the quadratic equation $3x^2 - 8x - 21 = 0$. Try it.

(c) Other uses will be introduced in Chapter 13.

**NOW TRY THESE . . .**

1. Produce a table of values for $f(x) = 8x - 3$, for x from −4 to 5. Use it to plot the graph of $f(x)$.

2. Produce a table of values for $f(x) = 5 - 4x + 3x^2$ for x from −2 to 6. Plot the graph of the function.

3. Produce a table of values for the function $f(x) = x^3 - 7x^2 + 3x + 5$ for values of x from −3 to 7. Plot the function. Produce a second table of values for the function $g(x) = 3x + 4$ also for values of x from −3 to 7. Plot the graph of $g(x)$ on the same axes as for $f(x)$.

4. By finding any point(s) where the two graphs cross, give the value(s) of x for which $f(x) = g(x)$.

## 12.5  POLYNOMIALS

Different types of functions have different shaped graphs; it is worth looking at some of the more common ones.

A function $f(x)$ is a polynomial expression if you can write it in the form $f(x) = a + bx + cx^2 + dx^3 + ex^4 + \ldots$, where $a, b, c, d, e,$ etc are all constant. The different types of polynomial following have only a limited number of such terms. The simplest case is $f(x) = a + bx$ (so that $c = d = e = $ etc $= 0$ in the more general polynomial expression).

The expression $f(x) = a + bx$ is known as a linear function since its graph is a straight line. Such a function will always cross the y-axis (which measures $f(x)$) at the point $(0, b)$ and have a gradient (slope) of $a$. Thus the function $f(x) = 5x - 2$ has a gradient of 5 and will cross the y-axis at $(0, -2)$.

Gradient is the increase in the value of f(x) for a unit increase in the value of $x$; it is characteristic of a linear function that its gradient is the same at all points.

The graph of this particular function appears in Figure 12.5.

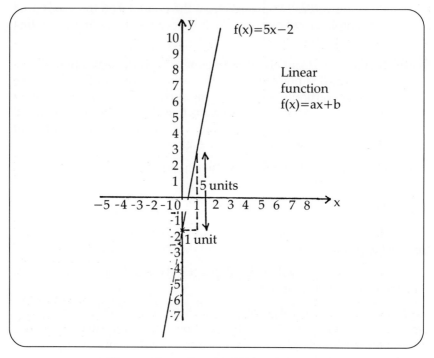

**Figure 12.5    Graph of linear function**

The second polynomial is the quadratic, in which $f(x) = ax^2 + bx + c$. The shape of the quadratic graph is a parabola, but with two alternative forms as Figure 12.6 shows: depending on whether $a$ is positive or negative.

If $a$ is positive, the parabola is "nose-down" and has a lowest point (minimum value), when $x = -b/2a$. If $a$ is negative, the parabola "points" up; its greatest (maximum) value is when $x = -b/2a$.

In either case the graph cuts the y-axis at $(0,c)$ and it cuts the x-axis at the two points which represent the solutions of the quadratic equation $ax^2 + bx + c = 0$ (Section 11.4). It is possible for the curve just to touch the x-axis, rather than cut it in two different points; this happens when the equation $ax^2 + bx + c = 0$ has two equal solutions; if however, the graph fails to cut the x-axis at all, the quadratic equation has no real solution at all. There is a close relationship between the quadratic function and its behaviour as seen from its graph and the solutions to a quadratic equation as described in Chapter 11.

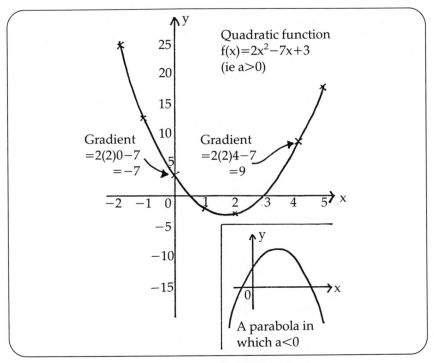

**Figure 12.6    Graph of quadratic function**

Note that in the case of a quadratic function the gradient (slope) of the graph changes with $x$; it is, however, always equal to $2ax + b$ at any point $(x, f(x))$ on the curve. In the main diagram of Figure 12.6, the gradient is positive from $x = 1.75$ upwards and the further to the right the steeper the gradient gets; if $x$ is less than 1.75 the gradient is negative.

The cubic function has $f(x) = ax^3 + bx^2 + cx + d$. Once again there are two characteristic shapes (as seen in Figure 12.7) – depending on the sign of $a$, the coefficient of $x^3$. In general, a cubic curve has one maximum and one minimum point, one "peak" and one "trough".

There's an infinite number of other possible polynomial functions, so we can't look at them all; the linear, quadratic and cubic are the most common. Note that the shapes are more complex as the number of terms in the polynomial increases.

One other function you may meet is that of $f(x) = \dfrac{1}{ax + b}$

The denominator is a linear function, but the shape is very much non-linear, as Figure 12.8 shows. There are two quite separate parts, and the function is not defined if $x = -b/a$; no value exists for $f(-b/a)$. This may appear rather strange at first; it stems from the fact that if $x = -b/a$, the denominator becomes zero – and dividing by zero has no meaning.

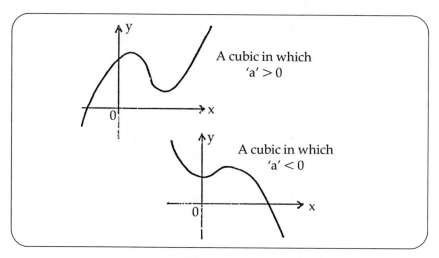

**Figure 12.7   Graphs of cubic functions**

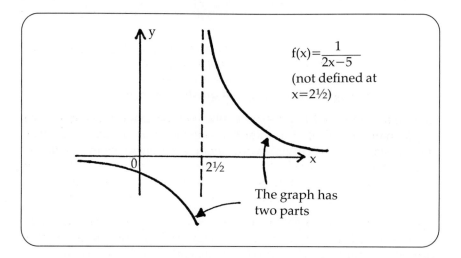

**Figure 12.8   Graph of a function which includes non-defined values**

## 12.6   EXPONENTIAL FUNCTIONS

We've met the word "exponent" before, eg in the context of the exponent form of floating-point representations in Chapter 5; it refers to the power to which a number is raised. Thus an exponential function is one in which $x$ is a power, as in $f(x) = 2^x$. The diagram in Figure 12.9 shows three different exponential functions in which $f(x) = 2^x$, $g(x) = 2.5^x$, and $h(x) = 3^x$.

All three curves have the same shape, as do all functions of the type $f(x) = a^x$, when a is positive. They all pass through the point (0,1) and lie completely above the $x$-axis; $f(x)$ can never be negative.

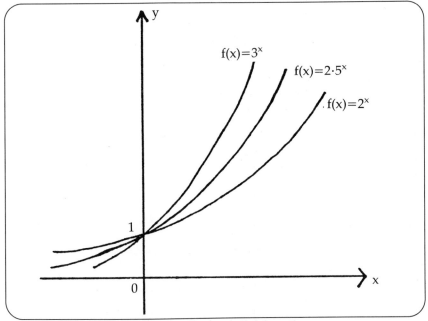

**Figure 12.9   Exponential functions**

## 12.7   SKETCHING CURVES

Plotting a curve requires a highly precise and accurate drawing – curve sketching requires only the essential shape of the function. That does not mean you can deliberately abandon accuracy – but sketching allows speed where accurate plotting is less important. In general, sketching gives the outline shape, and identifies such key features as the points where the curve crosses the axes and where it has "peaks" or "troughs".

Obviously, if a computer can produce an accurate curve as quickly as you can sketch by hand, it must be preferred – but it's not always convenient to use a machine, however accurate.

**Linear functions**
The general shape of a linear function $f(x) = ax + b$ is, of course, a straight line. Your sketch must show

— where it crosses the x-axis (ie when $f(x) = 0$)

— where it crosses the y-axis (ie when $x = 0$)

— that it is a straight line

You can also check the gradient is "about right" – at least, if it is positive ($a > 0$ in $f(x) = ax + b$) show the line sloping up from bottom left to top right.

The diagram in Figure 12.10 shows the sketch of $g(x) = 2x + 3$ and the stages taken to sketch it.

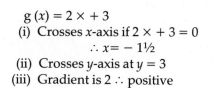

$g(x) = 2 \times + 3$
(i) Crosses x-axis if $2 \times + 3 = 0$
$\therefore x = -1\tfrac{1}{2}$
(ii) Crosses y-axis at $y = 3$
(iii) Gradient is 2 $\therefore$ positive

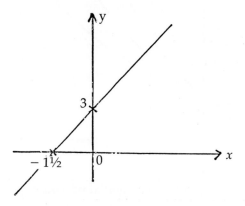

Note: No plotting of points except those
given above, ie $(-1\tfrac{1}{2},0)$ and $(0,3)$ and even
those are not measured, just marked in approximately.

**Figure 12.10    Sketching a linear function**

### Quadratic functions

You know the general shape of a quadratic is a parabola. We can deduce
at once, from the sign of the coefficient of $x^2$, whether it is "nose down"
or "nose up" (coefficient positive or negative respectively).

Use the following checklist – find:

— where it crosses the y-axis (ie when $x = 0$)

— the general shape, from the sign of the coefficient of $x^2$.

— (if possible) where it crosses the x-axis, by solving the equation
$f(x) = 0$; take care not to spend too much time on "formula".

— the maximum/minimum point when $2ax + b = 0$, ie at $x = -b/2a$
and $f(-b/2a)$.

Figure 12.11 shows the use of these stages in the case of a sketch of the
quadratic function $h(x) = x^2 - 3x - 10$.

$$h(x) = x^2 - 3x - 10$$

(i)   Crosses $y$-axis at $(0,-10)$

(ii)  Coefficient of $x^2$ is $+1$ ie,
      positive therefore "nose-down" parabola

(iii) $x = \dfrac{-(-3) \pm \sqrt{9 + 40}}{2}$

$\quad\quad = \dfrac{3 \pm 7}{2} = 5$ and $-2$

Hence it goes through $(5, 0)$ and $(-2, 0)$

*(iv)  Minimum value at $x = -(-3)/2(1)$

$$= 1\tfrac{1}{2}$$

$h(1\tfrac{1}{2}) = 2\tfrac{1}{4} - 4\tfrac{1}{2} - 10 = -12\tfrac{1}{4}$

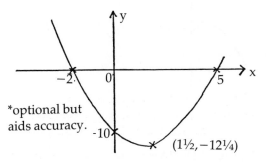

*optional but
aids accuracy.

**Figure 12.11   Sketching a quadratic**

### Cubic functions

We met the two "standard" forms of the cubic in figure 12.7. However, there are only two key points to get hold of:

— Find where it crosses the y-axis (ie when $x = 0$)

— Use the coefficient of $x^3$ to see which of the standard shapes is likely

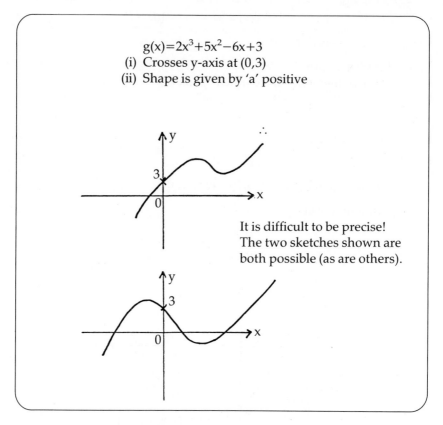

$g(x)=2x^3+5x^2-6x+3$
(i)  Crosses y-axis at (0,3)
(ii)  Shape is given by 'a' positive

It is difficult to be precise!
The two sketches shown are
both possible (as are others).

**Figure 12.12    Sketching a cubic function**

### Exponential functions

Here there is only one standard shape – the curve must go through (0,1) and the whole graph is bound to be above the x-axis. The only differences relate to gradient – the graph of $5^x$ goes up more steeply than that of $4^x$. Even so this factor is of importance only when you want to show two exponential functions in the same sketch. The general shape of $5^x$ appears in Figure 12.13.

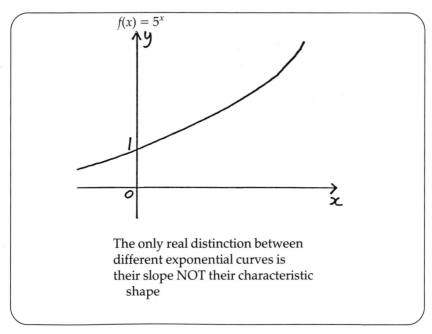

$f(x) = 5^x$

The only real distinction between different exponential curves is their slope NOT their characteristic shape

**Figure 12.13   Sketching an exponential function**

**NOW TRY THESE ...**

(1)  $f(x) = 3x + 4$

(2)  $g(x) = -2x - 3$

(3)  $f(x) = x^2 - 2x - 3$

(4)  $g(x) = x^2 - 5x$

(5)  $f(x) = 6 + x - x^2$

(6)  $h(x) = 4x^3 + 3x^2 - 7$

(7)  $f(x) = 7^x$

# 13 Using graphs for estimation

## OBJECTIVES

When you've worked through this Chapter, you should be able to:

— explain how interpolation and extrapolation differ

— interpolate and extrapolate values using graphs

— state what we mean by the gradient of a graph

— find the gradient of a graph at a given point

— note some uses of finding the area under a curve

— estimate area under a curve by square counting.

## INTRODUCTION

Now you can produce graphs of various functions accurately let's explore what we can do with them. I've already introduced some of the possibilities but, in this chapter, there are four other important areas to discuss.

Interpolation and extrapolation are used in forecasting methods. You also need to know how to estimate gradients (slopes) and measure areas under curves.

Note that in this chapter your only need for curve sketches is to obtain approximate shapes before accurate drawing.

## 13.1   WHAT ARE INTERPOLATION AND EXTRAPOLATION?

If you have a function defined on the lines of "$f(x) = \ldots$", you can obtain the value of $f(x)$ for any value of $x$ simply by substituting into the $f(x)$ equation. If, however, the function is given as a set of pairs of $x$ and $f(x)$ values, we do not know any $f(x)$ values for values of $x$ other than those in the set.

A good example follows from observing something at one minute intervals, eg, the speed of a car.

You may well know the speed after 7 minutes and also after 8 minutes, but not after 7.5 minutes as the value was not recorded. The same applies to a firm's trading profits as a function of time or a sensor output against steps of input voltage; we cannot determine intermediate values on the basis of what we know, but have to estimate values by interpolation.

Similarly, if you know your trading profits for the years 1980 to 1990 you can extend forwards, or extrapolate, to estimate for figures for 1991, indeed, perhaps even 1992. Extrapolation is particularly important to people who want to determine trends for the future on the basis of information about the past.

Let's look in detail first at interpolation. We use this when we know the discrete $(x, f(x))$ points on a graph, and want to estimate $f(x)$ for some $x$-value between two of those points. Clearly, if you know the formula "$f(x)=\ldots$", substitution will give the required value or if your automatic recording device gives values on a continuous basis (as in the case of a temperature sensor which moves a pen over a drum) it is simply a matter of reading off the value(s) required. Take a look at the following examples.

Table 31.1 shows two consecutive $x$-values and the corresponding $f(x)$ values.

| $x$ | $f(x)$ |
|-----|--------|
| 3.6 | 24.63  |
| 3.7 | 28.76  |

**Table 13.1   Data for worked example of interpolation**

How can we estimate the value of $f(3.68)$? In this case and with no further information it has to be assumed that there is a linear relationship between $x$ and $f(x)$ so that, since 3.68 is $8/10$ of the way between 3.6 and 3.7, we shall find that $f(3.68)$ is $8/10$ of the way between $f(3.6)$ and $f(3.7)$. Thus since the difference between the two $f(x)$ values is $28.76 - 24.63 = 4.13$ it follows that $8/10$ of this is 3.304. Thus $f(3.68) = 24.63 + 3.304$ or 27.93 to 2 dp as in Figure 13.1 (the same level of accuracy that was used previously for $f(x)$ values).

Assuming a linear relationship find $f(3.68)$
$f(3.68) = f(3.6) = 0.8 \times \{f(3.7) - f(3.6)\}$
$= 24.63 + 0.8 \times 4.13$
$= 24.63 + 3.304 = 27.934$

**Figure 13.1   Example of formula for interpolation**

However, if there are more than two pairs of values of $x$ and $f(x)$ then it may be possible to establish a more sophisticated relationship and so calculate an intermediate value with greater accuracy. Suppose you are given Table 13.2:

| x | f(x) |
|---|------|
| 4.7 | 12.94 |
| 4.8 | 15.31 |
| 4.9 | 16.25 |

**Table 13.2    Values for calculating $f(4.87)$**

and you wish to obtain $f(4.87)$ as accurately as possible. The method involves creating a table of differences as in Table 13.3:

| x | f (x) | Differences | |
|---|-------|-------------|---|
| | | 1st, $d_1$ | 2nd, $d_2$ |
| 4.7 | 12.94 | 2.37 | −1.43 |
| 4.8 | 15.31 | 0.94 | − |
| 4.9 | 16.25 | − | − |

**Table 13.3    Table of differences**

in which $d_1$ for $x = 4.7$ is $f(4.8) - f(4.7)$ and $d_1$ for $x = 4.8$ is $f(4.9) - f(4.8)$. We cannot find $d_1$ for $x = 4.9$ since the value of $f(5.0)$ is not known. Then the second difference $d_2$ for $x = 4.7$ is $d_1$ for $x = 4.8 - d_1$ for $x = 4.7$. It is not possible to calculate any other differences with the values available here. Next is a formula to lead us to $f(4.87)$ based on the fact that 4.7 is the 'base' value and that 4.87 is 0.17 above that base value. Furthermore for the purposes of the formula $x$ must be increasing in steps of 1 at a time and since in reality it has gone up in steps of 0.1, all $x$ values (and the differences between them) will be scaled up by a factor of 10, thus the 0.17 referred to as being the amount of 4.87 above the base value will be treated as 1.7 in fact. In the formula the quantity just defined as having a value of 1.7 will be generalised as $D$. The formula is:

$$f(4.87) = f(4.7) + D(d_1 \text{ at } x = 4.7) + \tfrac{1}{2}D(D - 1)\,(d_2 \text{ at } x = 4.7)$$

$$= 12.94 + 1.7(2.37) + \tfrac{1}{2}(1.7)(0.7)(-1.43)$$

$$= 12.94 + 4.029 - 1.7017$$

$$= 15.2673 \text{ or } 15.27 \text{ to the same level of accuracy used elsewhere for values of } f(x).$$

The formula introduced above has not been justified nor will any attempt be made to justify it; it is based upon more advanced mathematical ideas but it is important that it is *used* if one is to interpolate accurately. It uses a 'base' value of 4.7 since that is the lowest of the $x$-values in the original data and because both $d_1$ and $d_2$ can be worked out for this base value only. If we wanted instead to estimate the value of $f(4.74)$ then we have 0.04 above the base so that $D = 0.4$ (remembering the scaling factor) giving:

$$f(4.74) = f(4.7) + D(d_1 \text{ at } x = 4.7) + \tfrac{1}{2}D(D-1)(d_2 \text{ at } x = 4.7)$$

$$= 12.94 + 0.4(2.37) + \tfrac{1}{2}(0.4)(-0.6)(-1.43)$$

$$= 12.94 + 0.948 + 0.1716$$

$$= 14.0596 \text{ or } 14.06 \text{ to 2 dp.}$$

If presented with four pairs of values of $x$ and $f(x)$ rather than with three, then three difference values $d_1$, $d_2$ and $d_3$ will be required in addition to a revised formula. In the following example the $x$ values are given as 6.3, 6.4, 6.5 and 6.6 with the corresponding $f(x)$ values and we wish to estimate the value of $f(6.43)$. The table also sets out the differences required for the formula, which is now:

$$f(6.43) = f(6.3) + D(d_1 \text{ at } x = 6.3) + \tfrac{1}{2}D(D-1)(d_2 \text{ at } x = 6.3) + \tfrac{1}{6}D(D-1)(D-2)(d_3 \text{ at } x = 6.3).$$

The values are:

| $x$ | $f(x)$ | Differences | | |
| --- | --- | --- | --- | --- |
|     |        | 1st, $d_1$ | 2nd, $d_2$ | 3rd, $d_3$ |
| 6.3 | 202.867 | 9.957 | 0.344 | 0.006 |
| 6.4 | 212.824 | 10.301 | 0.350 | – |
| 6.5 | 223.125 | 10.651 | – | – |
| 6.6 | 233.776 | – | – | – |

**Table 13.4    Table of differences to obtain the value of $f(6.43)$**

Since $f(6.43)$ is to be estimated which is 0.13 above the base value and since we must scale up by 10, a $D$ value of 1.3 will be adopted.

Thus we shall have:

$f(6.43) = 202.867 + 1.3(9.957) + \frac{1}{2}(1.3)(0.3)(0.344)$
$\qquad + \frac{1}{6}(1.3)(0.3)(-0.7)(0.006)$

$\qquad = 202.867 + 12.9441 + 0.06708 - 0.000273 = 215.878$ to 3 dp.

## NOW TRY THESE . . .

(1)  $f(4.7) = 12.96$ and $f(4.8) = 17.31$  Estimate $f(4.72)$

(2)  $g(6.9) = 71$ and $g(7.0) = 64.3$  What is $g(6.97)$?

(3)  $f(3) = 215$, $f(4) = 227$ and $f(5) = 247$  Find $f(4.6)$

(4)  $f(3.16) = 49$, $f(3.17) = 51$ and $f(3.18) = 53$  Estimate $f(3.177)$

(5)  $f(12.6) = 93.1$, $f(12.7) = 94.7$, $f(12.8) = 97.3$ and $f(12.9) = 100.2$.
Interpolate to find the value of $f(12.76)$.

## 13.2  EXTRAPOLATION

Once again the concern is with finding values that were not included in the original set of values, but this time it is with values which lie *beyond* the range of those given. In the diagram shown in Figure 13.2, there are five points plotted $P_1$ to $P_5$. If we wanted to find the value of a point between $P_1$ and $P_5$ it would be possible to interpolate with some reasonable degree of accuracy, but if we wish to find $f(7.4)$ this is outside the given range and although the same techniques may be employed, involving the creation of a difference table and a revised formula, the more movement to the right of $x = 7$ or indeed to the left of $x = 3$, the less reliable the estimate becomes.

Since the use of this approach is needed for forecasting purposes, it is worth noting that more sophisticated methods do exist to determine the reliability of the results although these are beyond the scope of this book. In the example given here there are five pairs of $x$, $f(x)$ values so the formula becomes:

$f(7.4) = f(3) + D(d_1$ at $x = 3) + \frac{1}{2}D(D-1)(d_2$ at $x = 3)$
$\qquad + \frac{1}{6}D(D-1)(D-2)(d_3$ at $x = 3)$
$\qquad + \frac{1}{24}D(D-1)(D-2)(D-3)(d_4$ at $x = 3)$

The table of values is shown in Table 13.5:

Here, since $x$ already goes up in steps of 1, no scaling is required so it is possible to regard $D$ as 4.4. Thus:

$f(7.4) = 7.3 + 4.4(0.3) + \frac{1}{2}(4.4)(3.4)(-0.2)$
$\qquad + \frac{1}{6}(4.4)(3.4)(2.4)(0.5)$
$\qquad + \frac{1}{24}(4.4)(3.4)(2.4)(1.4)(-0.1)$

$\qquad = 7.3 + 1.32 - 1.496 + 2.992 - 0.20944$

$\qquad = 9.90656$ or 9.9 to 1 dp.

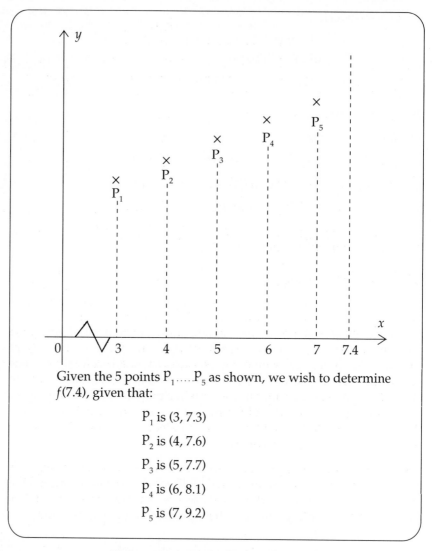

Given the 5 points $P_1 \ldots P_5$ as shown, we wish to determine $f(7.4)$, given that:

$P_1$ is (3, 7.3)

$P_2$ is (4, 7.6)

$P_3$ is (5, 7.7)

$P_4$ is (6, 8.1)

$P_5$ is (7, 9.2)

**Figure 13.2    Extrapolation diagram**

## 13.3    GRADIENTS

We met the gradient (slope) of a graph in the last chapter. Look at figure 13.3, the graph of a function $f$, containing a point $P$ with co-ordinates $(a, f(a))$. The gradient of a graph at a point is the change of $f(x)$ per unit change in the value of $x$ at that point. In the case of a straight line, the slope is constant; for all other functions (such as the one shown here), it changes from point to point. In this case, the graph is steeper as you move towards the right – so the gradient is getting larger.

Our method for finding the value of a gradient at a point is an estimate; its accuracy depends on the accuracy of the drawing. The method is

| x | f (x) | Differences | | | |
|---|---|---|---|---|---|
| | | 1st, $d_1$ | 2nd, $d_2$ | 3rd, $d_3$ | 4th, $d_4$ |
| 3 | 7.3 | 0.3 | − 0.2 | 0.5 | − 0.01 |
| 4 | 7.6 | 0.1 | 0.3 | 0.4 | – |
| 5 | 7.7 | 0.4 | 0.7 | – | – |
| 6 | 8.1 | 1.1 | – | – | – |
| 7 | 9.2 | – | – | – | – |

Table 13.5    Table of values for Figure 13.2

quite sound, as long as the slope is not changing too much around the point in question. Draw the tangent to the curve at P, as carefully as possible. It cuts the x-axis when $x = b$. The gradient is $f(a)$ divided by the length $(a - b)$. Note, in particular, that the values of $f(a)$ and $(a - b)$ are *not* the measured lengths on the drawing – but what these lengths stand for when you take account of the scales. Thus if $f(a) = 6$ and $(a - b) = 12$, the gradient is $6/12$ or $1/2$, no matter what the lengths of the two lines may actually be in the diagram.

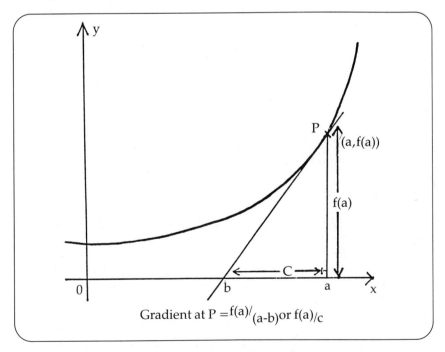

Figure 13.3    The gradient of a curve

## 13.4   THE AREA UNDER A CURVE

Sometimes we have to find the area under the graph of $f(x)$ between, for instance, $x = 2$ and $x = 10$, ie, the area shaded in Figure 13.4.

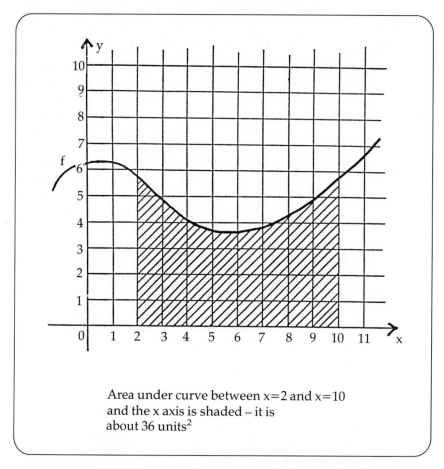

Area under curve between x=2 and x=10
and the x axis is shaded – it is
about 36 units$^2$

**Figure 13.4   Finding the area under a curve**

If the graph has been plotted accurately you can count the squares in the shaded area; we usually deal with a partial square by counting it if it is more than half shaded and ignoring it otherwise. The area of a square is not just 'one' – it depends on the scales on the two axes and what these axes stand for. If, for example the x axis shows time in seconds and the y axis speed in metres per second, the area represents time × speed, or distance in metres. Take special care if the time axis is in minutes and the speed in metres per second (for instance) then the squares are 60 metres each, but still of course represent distance.

Counting squares is rather crude. Other methods give better results – but it is not necessary for you to know these right now.

## 13.5   THE TRAPEZIUM RULE

If an estimate of the area under the curve is required between the $x$-axis and the ordinates at $x = 2$ and at $x = 18$, this can be done by subdividing the area into an *even* number of vertical strips, each of width $w$. If we use $y_0$ and $y_n$ as the heights of the first and the last ordinates then it is possible to add together the areas of all the strips, (each of which is a trapezium in shape), to yield the formula quoted in Figure 13.5.

In Figure 13.5 the strips are accorded dotted boundaries and it is easy to see that whilst areas such as ABCD produce an underestimate of the true area under the curve, these are compensated for by areas such as the one with ordinates of 5.8 and 5.6 which gives an overestimate of the true area. If we were to increase the number of strips then the width $w$ is reduced, so bringing the trapezia closer and closer to the 'true' area under the curve, allowing such a process to yield as accurate a result as may be desired, by choice of a sufficiently large number of strips. The heights of the ordinates may be determined by the '$f(x) = \ldots$' formula or derived from values observed, for example, in an experiment. Note, however, the necessity for there to be an *even* number of strips.

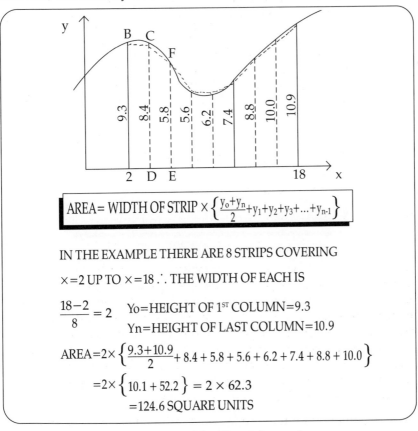

$$\text{AREA} = \text{WIDTH OF STRIP} \times \left\{ \tfrac{y_0 + y_n}{2} + y_1 + y_2 + y_3 + \ldots + y_{n-1} \right\}$$

IN THE EXAMPLE THERE ARE 8 STRIPS COVERING

$x = 2$ UP TO $x = 18$ $\therefore$ THE WIDTH OF EACH IS

$\dfrac{18-2}{8} = 2$    $Y_0 =$ HEIGHT OF 1ST COLUMN $= 9.3$

$Y_n =$ HEIGHT OF LAST COLUMN $= 10.9$

$$\text{AREA} = 2 \times \left\{ \tfrac{9.3 + 10.9}{2} + 8.4 + 5.8 + 5.6 + 6.2 + 7.4 + 8.8 + 10.0 \right\}$$

$$= 2 \times \left\{ 10.1 + 52.2 \right\} = 2 \times 62.3$$

$$= 124.6 \text{ SQUARE UNITS}$$

**Figure 13.5   The Trapezium rule**

## 13.6   SIMPSON'S RULE

This is a rather more sophisticated method than the Trapezium Rule but again requires the subdivision of the area into an even number of strips. This time, however, whilst it still requires a knowledge of the heights of the first and the last ordinates $y_0$ and $y_n$ respectively, it also subdivides the rest of the ordinates into 'odd' ones such as $y_1$, $y_3$, $y_5$, etc as well as the 'even' ones such as $y_2$, $y_4$, $y_6$, etc.

This is no more difficult a method to use than the Trapezium Rule and, like it, it is capable of a high degree of accuracy by increasing the number of strips. Using the same number of strips it is slightly more accurate a method than is the Trapezium Rule. Do note however, the absolute necessity for referring to the first ordinate as $y_0$ and *not* as $y_1$. That apart, its use is quite straightforward. In Figure 13.6 Simpson's Rule is used to estimate the area under the curve as shown; it has been drawn with 14 strips and covers the area contained between the curve, the $x$-axis and the ordinates at $x = 5$ and at $x = 26$.

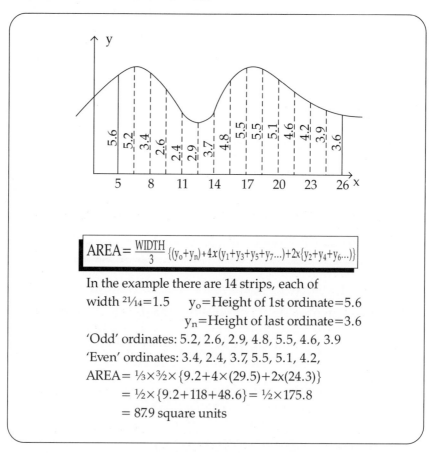

$$AREA = \frac{WIDTH}{3}\{(y_0+y_n)+4x(y_1+y_3+y_5+y_7...)+2x(y_2+y_4+y_6...)\}$$

In the example there are 14 strips, each of
width $21/14=1.5$    $y_0$=Height of 1st ordinate=5.6
                     $y_n$=Height of last ordinate=3.6
'Odd' ordinates: 5.2, 2.6, 2.9, 4.8, 5.5, 4.6, 3.9
'Even' ordinates: 3.4, 2.4, 3.7, 5.5, 5.1, 4.2,
AREA= ⅓×³⁄₂×{9.2+4×(29.5)+2x(24.3)}
    = ½×{9.2+118+48.6}= ½×175.8
    = 87.9 square units

**Figure 13.6   Simpson's rule**

**NOW TRY THESE . . .**

(1) Draw the graph of $f(x) = x^2 - 4x + 7$ as accurately as you can between $x = -3$ and $x = 5$. Draw tangents to the graph for $x = 1$, $x = 2$ and $x = 4$ to estimate the gradient of the curve at each point.

(2) A train starts from a station at 10.00 am exactly. It accelerates steadily and a minute later has a speed of 40 m/s (metres per second). Draw a (straight line) graph of speed against time and count squares to find how far the train goes in that minute.

(3) Draw the graph $f(x) = 3x^2 - 7x + 9$ as accurately as you can between $x = -2$ and $x = 4$. Estimate the area under the curve between these $x$-values using the 'counting squares' method.

(4) Plot this graph and find the area under it between $x = 3$ and $x = 11$

| $x$ | 3 | 4 | 5 | 6 | 7 | 8 | 9 | 10 | 11 |
|------|----|----|---|---|---|---|----|----|----|
| $f(x)$ | 13 | 11 | 9 | 7 | 7 | 8 | 12 | 14 | 18 |

**REVISION EXERCISES C**

This revision section concentrates on Chapters 10 to 13, on the mainly algebraic parts of the text.

**First example**

Two manufacturers make digital cassettes. Manufacturing COSTS consist of a FIXED COST and a PRODUCTION COST for each cassette (ie COSTS = $P^*n + F$).

(a) It costs MANUFACTURER X $500 to make 1000 cassettes, and $1000 to make 3500 cassettes.

MANUFACTURER Y has a FIXED COST of only ⅓ that for manufacturer X, but the PRODUCTION COST per cassette is 40% higher.

   (i)   Derive an equation for the manufacturing COSTS for manufacturer X in terms of the number of cassettes produced.

   (ii)  Derive a similar equation for the manufacturing COSTS for manufacturer Y.

   (iii) Determine the number of cassettes made by each manufacturer when their COSTS are the SAME.

(b) Manufacturer X fixes a SELLING PRICE which will give a profit of 40% of COSTS when they sell 6000 cassettes.

   (iv)  What should be this SELLING PRICE?

(v)   What will be the PERCENTAGE PROFIT for manufacturer Y if they sell 6000 at this same price? (Give answer to NEAREST WHOLE NUMBER).

(iv)  Why can manufacturer Y never make 40% PROFIT over COSTS no matter how many cassettes are sold at this price?

## Solution

*Part (a)*

One of the early problems when undertaking algebraic questions is to decide what symbols to use (and even which quantities to represent by symbols). In this case, the early references to $P$, $n$ and $F$ considerably reduce the problem – clearly $P$ is the production cost for each cassette and $n$ is the number of cassettes made, while $F$ must refer to the fixed cost.

Next we are given some information which links together costs and numbers of cassettes manufactured by X in two cases. This allows us to use the equation given in each case. Using COSTS $= P^*n + F$ we can replace $n$ by 1000 and COSTS by 500 in the first case, and $n$ by 3500 and COSTS by 1000 in the second.

$$500 = 1000P + F \quad \text{(i) and}$$
$$1000 = 3500P + F \quad \text{(ii)}$$

These are two simultaneous equations, which we may now solve for $P$ and $F$. Subtract equation (i) from equation (ii): $500 = 2500P$.

Divide both sides by 2500 giving $0.2 = P$

Therefore the production cost per cassette is $0.2. Next, substitute $P = 0.2$ into either equation (i) or equation (ii) in order to find $F$. I have selected equation (i):

$$500 = 1000^*0.2 + F$$

This leads to $500 = 200 + F$

and $F = 500 - 200 = 300$, therefore the fixed costs for X must be $300.

Next we must check that these values fit equation (ii) (the one we did not use in the substitution earlier on). If we substitute $F = 300$ and $P = 0.2$ into the two sides of equation (ii), the right side becomes $3500^*0.2 + 300 = 700 + 300 = 1000$ – the same as the left side. Thus we can state with confidence that for manufacturer X, the equation is:

$$\text{COSTS} = 0.2^*n + 300$$

In dealing with part (ii) we do not need to go through any more simultaneous equations. This time we use the information given in the question that manufacturer Y has a fixed cost "of only ⅓ of that for manufacturer X", which means that the fixed cost for Y must be $300 ×

⅓ = $100. Also we are told that "the production cost for each cassette is 40% higher" for Y than for X; therefore the production cost for Y must be a 40% increase on $0.2, or $0.2 × 140/100 = $0.28.

So, for manufacturer Y the corresponding equation is:

$$COSTS = 0.28^*n + 100$$

Part (iii) involves the COSTS being the same – so make them the same, by putting them equal to each other, leading to:

$$0.2^*n + 300 = 0.28^*n + 100$$

This is a straightforward linear equation in $n$ alone – solve it, and the value of $n$ that results must be the number of cassettes manufactured for which the costs are the same. This leads to:

$$300 - 100 = 0.28^*n - 0.20^*n$$

or,        $200 = 0.08^*n$

from which    $200 = 8n/100$

giving        $8n = 100 × 200 = 20000$

therefore    $n = 20000/8 = 2500$

*Part (b)*

The costs are the same when each manufacturer produces 2500 cassettes.

Part (b) gives additional information which we must use straight away. When X makes 6000 cassettes, COSTS = $0.2^* 6000 + 300 = $1200 + 300 = $1500. The profit is 40% of COSTS, ie $0.4 × 1500 = $600.

(iv) This means that X must obtain a total of $1500 + 600 or $2100 when selling 6000 cassettes – the selling price must be $2100/6000, or $0.35 each.

(v)  Now, if Y sells 6000 cassettes at this same 0.35 dollars each, their total costs will be $0.28^*6000 + 100 = $1680 + 100 = $1780; their total income from the sale is $2100 dollars as for X. If Y's sales value is $2100 dollars and manufacturing cost is $1780, Y's profit must be $2100 - 1780 = $320.

Expressing this profit as a percentage of the manufacturing COSTS gives a percentage profit of

$$\frac{320 × 100}{1780} = 17.977$$

or 18% to the nearest whole number.

(vi) To answer this part takes a little thought. In order to make 40% profit, with a selling price set at $0.35 dollars, we should consider the production cost *for each cassette made*, which is $0.28. A profit of 40% means we increase this to $0.28 × 1.40 = $0.392, in order to make a profit of 40% on the production costs alone, it would have to be still greater if we are to cover fixed costs as well. However, the selling price has already been set at $0.35 – so to achieve a 40% profit would require a selling price well in excess of that already set. Thus it is not possible to achieve a 40% profit level.

To extend the ideas behind this last part (though not asked for by the question) note that with a figure of $0.28 dollars to make each cassette, a selling price of $0.35 implies a profit of $0.07 dollars (or 25%) – but even this fails to cover the fixed costs. It follows that Y can never achieve a 25% profit level, and certainly there can be no hope at all of doing better than this.

### Second Example

(a) Rearrange the following equation into a quadratic and solve it, by factorising, for $x$

$$\frac{2x}{5x + 3} = \frac{1}{x + 2}$$

(b) The speed of an object is given by the equation $v = t^2 + 1$ where $v$ stands for the speed in metres per second and $t$ is the time in seconds since the start.

   (i)   Plot a graph of the object's speed between times $t = 0$ and $t = 4$, using intervals of half a second

   (ii)  The distance covered in this time is given by the area under the curve.

        Use the trapezium rule (with eight strips) to estimate this distance. The trapezium rule is given by:

        area = width of strip × $[(Y_0 + Y_8)/2 + Y_1 + Y_2\ldots . + Y_6 + Y_7]$
        where $Y_0$ = Height of first ordinate
              $Y_8$ = Height of last ordinate

   (iii) Show that the speed of this object will never be zero

### Solution
*Part (a)*

Part (a) is straightforward algebraic manipulation. Since it involves fractions with algebraic expressions top and bottom, the best thing to do is to get rid of the fractions altogether by "cross-multiplying", leading to

$$2x(x + 2) = (5x + 3)$$

Then multiply out the brackets: $2x^2 + 4x = 5x + 3$

This leads to $2x^2 + 4x - 5x - 3 = 0$

or $2x^2 - x - 3 = 0$

This is the quadratic equation required.

Now, since we are clearly told that we must solve by factorisation, we know that we must not use the formula method. Hence we need to find the factors of 2 times -3, ie of -6. These are (1, -6), (-1, 6), (2, -3), (-2, 3) – these are the only ones. We need to find the right pair of factors which add to give -1 (the coefficient of x) – the required pair is 2 and -3.

Thus we can rewrite the quadratic as

$$2x^2 + 2x - 3x - 3 = 0$$

From this we get $2x(x + 1) - 3(x + 1) = 0$ which leads to:

$$(2x - 3)(x + 1) = 0$$

If the product of these two linear factors is zero, then either of them may be itself zero – hence either $2x - 3 = 0$ or $x + 1 = 0$. In the first case this leads to $2x = 3$, or $x = 1\frac{1}{2}$; in the second case we get $x = -1$. The solutions are that $x = -1$ or $1\frac{1}{2}$.

To do part (b) section (i) we use the formula given for $v$ and a set of values of $t$ from 0 to 4 "using intervals of half a second" – to create a table of values of $v$ for various values of $t$. Here is the table.

| $t$ | 0 | $\frac{1}{2}$ | 1 | $1\frac{1}{2}$ | 2 | $2\frac{1}{2}$ | 3 | $3\frac{1}{2}$ | 4 |
|---|---|---|---|---|---|---|---|---|---|
| $v$ | 1 | $1\frac{1}{4}$ | 2 | $3\frac{1}{4}$ | 5 | $7\frac{1}{4}$ | 10 | $13\frac{1}{4}$ | 17 |

On the basis of this table, now draw a graph showing how $v$ varies with $t$.

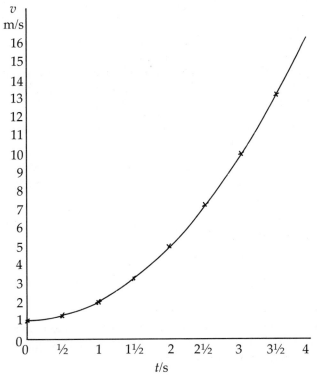

*Part (b)*

Part (b) requires an application of the trapezium rule – conveniently the question not only tells us the formula for the trapezium rule but also makes it immediately appropriate for our needs in this very question. The width of each strip is ½ second and we also need $Y_0 = 1$ and $Y_8 = 17$ as well as the other $Y$ values from the table. Therefore

area = ½ × [ (1+17)/2+1.25+2+3.25+5+7.25+10+13.25]m which is
0.5 × [(9+42)]m = 0.5 × 51m = 25.5 metres

To answer part (c), note that the speed is given (for *all* values of $t$) by the expression $t^2 + 1$; now $t^2$ must always be a non-negative quantity, whose smallest value is zero – hence $t^2 + 1$ can never be smaller than zero + 1 – ie can never be less than 1. Hence the speed can never be negative – in fact we can prove the rather more powerful statement, that it can in fact never be less than 1, even if this was not asked for.

**NOW TRY THESE . . .**

**Further exercises C**

1. (a) A company employs staff at three grades of pay, according to the table below

| Grade | Yearly salary ($) |
|-------|-------------------|
| 1 | 8000 |
| 2 | 16000 |
| 3 | 24000 |

The number of employees at each grade is in the ratio 7:2:1, where the highest number of employees is at Grade 1, the next highest is at Grade 2, and the lowest is at Grade 3.

The total number of employees is 480. Calculate the total salary bill for this company.

The employees at Grade 1 receive a pay rise of 4% plus $1000 per year. The other two grades receive pay rises of 5% each.

Calculate

(i) the new salaries for each grade

(ii) the new total salary bill

(iii) the percentage increase in the total salary bill

(b) The company advertises its goods on radio and television. In the equations below $T$ is the cost of a television advertisement and $R$ that of a radio advertisement.

$$5T + 2R = 5400$$
$$2T + 4R = 2800$$

Find the cost of a television advertisement and the cost of a radio advertisement.

(c) (i)   The amounts spent on television and radio are in the ratio 5:3. Find the ratio of the number of television advertisements to that of radio advertisements.

(ii)   Every television advertisement increases sales by $1500 and every radio advert increases sales by $210. Express these increases as percentages of their respective costs.

(iii)   The efficiency of each method of advertising is measured as the ratio of increased sales : cost of adverts. Calculate the efficiency of both means of advertising.

2. (a) Sketch the curve $y = 3x^2 + 2x + 1$
   and the line $y = 14x - 8$
   In both cases take values of $x$ from $x = 0$ to $x = 4$

   (b) Use your graphs to determine the points of intersection of the curve and the line

   (c) Confirm that you have the correct points of intersection by algebraic methods

   (d) Use Simpson's rule, with four strips, to determine the approximate area enclosed by the line and the curve.

   (The formula for Simpson's rule for the area under a curve with four strips is:
   Area $\frac{h}{3}(y_0 + y_4 + 4(y_1 + y_3) + 2(y_2))$  where h is the width of the strip and $y_0 \ldots y_4$ are the lengths of the sides of the strips.

3. (a) Produce a table of values for the curve
   $$y = 2x(2 - x)(14 - 5x)$$
   for $x = 0$ to $x = 2$ at intervals of 0.2

   (b) Sketch the curve from $x = 0$ to $x = 2$ using as large a scale as possible on your graph paper

   (c) Find from your graph the values of $x$ between 0 and 2, where $y = 9.75$

   (d) By counting squares, or by drawing trapezia, estimate the area enclosed between the curve and the x-axis from $x = 0$ to $x = 2$.

4. (a) Produce a table of values for the curve: $y = 4x^3 - 4x^2 - 13x - 5$
   for $x$ between $-2$ and $+3$ at half unit intervals.

   (b) Plot the graph, clearly marking the y values from the table.

   (c) Using the formula below, estimate the area between the curve and the $x$ axis between $x = -\frac{1}{2}$ and $x = 2\frac{1}{2}$, using strips of half unit width. An estimate for the area for $n$ strips, each of width $h$, is:

$$\text{area} = \frac{h}{3} \; (y_0 + y_n + 4*(y_1 + y_3 + \cdots) + 2*(y_2 + y_4 + \cdots))$$

5. (a) Plot the graphs of $y = x^3 - 3x^2 - x + 3$ and $y = 1 - x$
    for $-1 \leqslant x \leqslant +3$ in half unit intervals

   (b) Use your graphs to estimate the three values of $x$ for which
    $$1 - x = x^3 - 3x^2 - x + 3$$

   (c) Calculate the area between the curve and the $x$ axis between
    $x = -1$ and $x = +1$ using four strips of width $h = \frac{1}{2}$

   $$\text{area} = h * ((_y0 + _{y4})/2 + _{y1} + _{y2} + _{y3})$$

6. (a) An experiment relating time in seconds $(s)$ and temperature $(t)$
    gives the following formula: $t = s(s + 1)(2s + 1)$

   (i) Plot the curve between $s = 0$ and $s = 4$

   (ii) Use the curve to show how to estimate the length of time it
    takes for the temperature to rise from 70 to 150.

   (b) The following readings were taken in a different experiment
    relating time $s$ and temperature $t$. See table.

   | $s$ | $t$ |
   | --- | --- |
   | 0 | 0 |
   | 2 | 16 |
   | 6 | 192 |

   It is believed that a relationship of the form

   $$t = A(s - 2)^3 - Bs + C$$

   exists between $s$ and $t$.

   (i) Find A, B and C such that the recorded readings fit this
    relationship.

   (ii) Show that after four seconds the temperature would be 32,
    if the relationship is justified.

   (iii) Use the relationship to determine the temperatures ex-
    pected when $s = 3$ and $s = 7$.

# 14 Sets and Venn diagrams

## OBJECTIVES

When you've worked through this Chapter, you should be able to:

— state what we mean by a set and its elements (members)

— define subset, universal set, union, intersection, empty set, complement, disjoint sets

— list the members of these in various contexts

— use Venn diagrams to show these in various contexts

— relate Venn diagrams to NOT, AND, and OR operations.

## INTRODUCTION

Set languages gives us a very useful means of classification. It is also of great importance in the study of logic, the reason for looking at it here. Logic, as far as a computer is concerned, is not just a philosophy; it is directly involved in the physical make-up of the machine and how program statements are executed.

## 14.1 SET BASICS

In its simplest form a set is no more than a collection of objects, for instance, numbers, the names of people, colours, or the products of a software house. The most important point is that the members of the set have a common feature, which links them in some way. Perhaps the numbers are all divisible by 5, the people all work in the same department, the colours are those offered by a monitor, and so on.

Any one object, or item, in a set is an element of the set. We identify specific sets either by giving them names or, more conveniently, by using capital letters. So A may be the set of numbers divisible by 3 between 1 and 25 – its elements are

$$A = \{3, 6, 9, 12, 15, 18, 21, 24\}$$

We've seen two ways to describe set A – (note the curly brackets/braces), the first by defining it in words and the second by listing its elements. Often the second method is the more useful for processing. Note, however, that if you list the elements, the order has absolutely no significance. Thus A above could just as easily appear as

$$A = \{9, 18, 24, 3, 6, 15, 21, 12\}$$

Next, we need a symbol to show that a particular object is an element of a set. To show that 3 is an element of A we write

$$6 \in A$$

To show that 5 is *not* an element of set A, we write

$$5 \notin A$$

Thus if M is the set of computer manufacturers, Honeywell $\in$ M and Dunlop $\notin$ M.

It is also common to speak of subsets. Set B is a subset of A if every element of B is also included in A. Thus if A is the set of all people who work for a particular firm, and B is the people in the firm's data processing department, B is a subset of A; we write this as B $\subset$ A. As before, if D is *not* a subset of A, we write D $\not\subset$ A.

The last basic point is that if an element occurs more than once in a set, we list it only once. Thus the set of factors of 120 (which is $2\times2\times2\times3\times5$) is $\{2, 3, 5\}$.

Again, we might find that in a programming department, the C experts are Stephen, Lakbir, Mohammed and Anna, and those very competent in Cobol are Lakbir, Anna, Sean and Amarjit; the set of people good with either C or with Cobol is {Stephen, Lakbir, Mohammed, Anna, Sean, Amarjit}.

Note once more that the order does not matter.

## 14.2   THE UNIVERSAL SET

In any one situation, no matter what sets are used and what elements exist within these sets, there will be one set called the universal set. Represented by $\mathscr{E}$, this contains every element in each of the other sets, so every set in a problem is a subset of the universal set. Unfortunately, there is likely to be a different universal set for each situation, despite the title; in other words, a set is universal only for a particular situation.

The universal set therefore determines the "boundaries" of the situation – though sometimes it provides wider boundaries than the problem needs.

Consider the staff of the data processing department of Carblaze Bank. We may list as set W all the female employees of that department, as M all the male employees, as O all the operators, as S all the analysts (male or female) and so on. Thus there are many different sets, M, W, O, S, etc but each must be a subset of the department's staff. So that staff list is the Universal Set: $\mathscr{E}$ is the set of all people working in the data processing department of Carblaze.

It is possible to consider using the set of all employees of Carblaze as $\mathscr{E}$, whether or not they work in data processing; this would be quite feasible – but would provide far wider boundaries than we may need. Clearly, however, if we extend the problem to involve staff in other departments, we'd need a more appropriate universal set.

## NOW TRY THESE . . .

$\mathscr{E}$ = {red, blue, black, green, yellow, pink, orange}; A = {red, blue, green}; B = {yellow, pink, blue}; and C = {black, blue, red, green, yellow}. Decide whether these statements are true or false.

| | |
|---|---|
| (i)  Blue ∈ A | (vii)  {Red, Green} ⊂ A |
| (ii)  A ⊂ C | (viii)  {Green, Red} ⊂ B |
| (iii)  B ⊄ A | (ix)  {Blue, Yellow} ⊄ A |
| (iv)  Green ∉ B | (x)  Yellow ∉ A |
| (v)  Red ∈ B | (xi)  Yellow ∈ C |
| (vi)  C ⊂ A | (xii)  Orange ∈ C |

## 14.3   UNION AND INTERSECTION

The union of two sets A and B (written as A ∪ B) is the set of elements which occur either in set A or in set B or in both. We write elements which occur in both sets only once in the union.

So, if A = {a, b, c, d} and B = {c, d, e, f}, A ∪ B = {a, b, c, d, e, f}. Similarly, if P = {3, 6, 9, 12, 15} and Q = {6, 12, 18, 24}, P ∪ Q = {3, 6, 9, 12, 15, 18, 24}.

Figure 14.1 shows more examples.

A = {3, 6, 9, 12, 15, 18}

B = {5, 10, 15, 20}

A ∪ B = {3, 5, 6, 9, 10, 12, 15, 18, 20}

A = {e, x, a, m}

B = {t, r, i, a, l}

C = {s, t, r, a, i, n}

A ∪ B ∪ C = {a, e, i, l, m, n, r, s, t, x}

Don't forget: the order of elements in a set doesn't matter

**Figure 14.1   The union of sets**

It is easy to extend this concept to three or more sets; thus, if P = {Cobol, RPG11, Algol}, Q = {Algol, Fortran, Pascal, Ada} and R = {Basic, Algol, Cobol, Pascal}, then

P ∪ Q ∪ R = {Cobol, RPG11, Algol, Fortran, Pascal, Ada, Basic}.

Next, meet intersection. The intersection of two sets A and B, written as A ∩ B, contains those elements which exist both in set A and also in set B. Thus, if A = {2, 5, 8, 11, 14, 17, 20} and B = {5, 10, 15, 20, 25, 30}, the intersection, A ∩ B = {5,20}. Again we can extend to three or more sets – A ∩ B ∩ C is the set of elements found in A, also in B and also in C, as in Figure 14.2.

A = {3, 6, 9, 12, 15, 18}

B = {5, 10, 15, 20}

A ∩ B = {15}

A = {e, x, a, m}

B = {t, r, i, a, l}

C = {s, t, r, a, i, n}

A ∩ B ∩ C = {a}

**Figure 14.2    Examples of intersecting sets**

We call a set which contains no elements at all an empty set (or sometimes a null set). We write it as {} (or ∅). Empty sets may arise at the intersection of two sets with no elements in common; eg if A = {7, 14, 21, 28} and B = {5, 10, 15, 20, 25, 30}, A ∩ B = {}. Again, the set of people able to write a 1000-line program in half an hour might very well be an empty set.

## 14.4    COMPLEMENTS

As we are able to define a set A, we can also define A′, the set of elements which exist in ℰ but not in A. A′ is the complement of A.

Thus, if ℰ = {all integers between 1 and 15 inclusive} and A = {all even numbers}, A = {2, 4, 6, 8, 10, 12, 14} and A′ = {1, 3, 5, 7, 9, 11, 13, 15}.

It follows at once that A′ and A make up the Universal Set, and also that A ∩ A′ = {}. There is no reason why we can't extend the idea of a complement to a set such as A ∩ B – then we have (A ∩ B)′.

It is interesting to note that (A ∩ B)′ is the same as A′ ∪ B′. Also (A ∪ B)′ = A′ ∩ B′. You may like to check these now, or when we discuss Venn diagrams, later in this chapter.

Now examine Figure 14.3 anyway. Note here, a new shorter way to describe a set. A = {x:x is a multiple of 3} reads as "A is the set of x-values where each x is a multiple of 3" (or we could express this as A = {multiples of 3}). You may think this rather more complicated, but it has advantages, especially where the description in words is cumbersome. Compare, for example, the Universal Set definition given in Figure 14.3 and $\mathscr{E}$ = {whole numbers between 1 and 20 inclusive}.

$$\mathscr{E} = \{x : 1 \leqslant x \leqslant 20, x \text{ integral}\}$$
to define the Universal Set.

$$A = \{x : x \text{ is a multiple of 3}\}$$
$$B = \{x : x \text{ is an even number}\}$$

$$\therefore A' = \{1,2,4,5,7,8,10,11,13,14,16,17,19,20\}$$
$$B' = \{1,3,5,7,9,11,13,15,17,19\}$$

or

$$B' = \{x : x \text{ is an odd number}\}$$

$$A \cup B = \{2,3,4,6,8,9,10,12,14,15,16,18,20\}$$

$$\therefore (A \cup B)' = \{1,5,7,11,13,17,19\}$$

**Figure 14.3   Universal set and complements**

Using this example, and referring back to the earlier statement that $(A \cup B)' = A' \cap B'$ consider both A' and B' and list $A' \cap B'$; the result will be found to be given by {1, 5, 7, 11, 13, 17, 19}. It is not a coincidence that this is the same as the stated result for $(A \cup B)'$.

**NOW TRY THESE . . .**

1. $\mathscr{E}$ = {whole numbers between 3 and 19 inclusive}, A = {multiples of 3}, and B = {multiples of 7}. List the sets

(i) A

(ii) B

(iii) A ∪ B

(iv) A ∩ B

(v) A'

(vi) B'

(vii) (A ∪ B)'

(viii) (A ∩ B)'

2. $\mathscr{E} = \{x:5 \leqslant x \leqslant 26, x \text{ integral}\}$:

A = {x:x is a multiple of 5}

B = {x:x is a prime number}

C = {9, 16, 25}

(i) Describe C in words.

List each of the following.

(ii)  A

(iii)  B

(iv)  A ∩ C

(v)  A ∩ B

(vi)  B ∩ C

(vii) A ∪ B

(viii)  (A ∩ C)'

(ix)  (A ∪ B)'

(x)  (B ∪ C)'

(xi)  (B ∩ C)'

(xii)  A'

(xiii)  B'

(xiv)  C'

(xv)  A' ∩ B'

(xvi)  B' ∪ C'

(xvii)  A' ∩ B' ∩ C'

## 14.5  VENN DIAGRAMS

Venn diagrams are pictures that show sets and how they relate. They are often much more convenient than giving descriptions in words, and can sometimes be more convenient than listing elements. Figure 14.4 is a Venn diagram of A ∪ B.

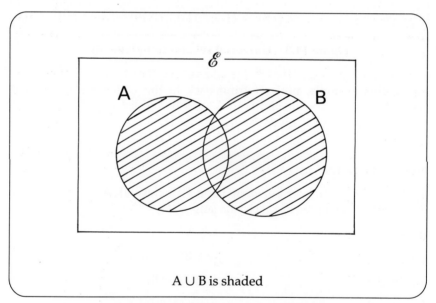

A ∪ B is shaded

**Figure 14.4   Venn diagram of A ∪ B**

From a Venn diagram, we can list the elements in various sets. If we examine Figure 14.5 we can see that

$$A = \{3, 6, 9, 12, 15, 18\}$$
$$\text{and } B = \{2, 4, 6, 8, 10, 12, 14, 16, 18, 20\}.$$

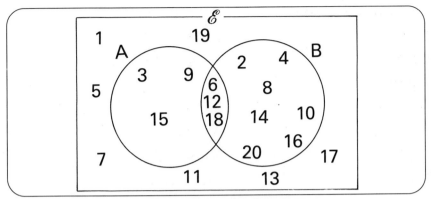

Elements may be shown

**Figure 14.5  Venn Diagram showing elements of a set**

We can also see the intersection A ∩ B – the set {6, 12, 18}. We can see too that (A ∪ B)' = {1,5,7,11,13,17,19}, and so on.

Note that the positions of the elements in a Venn diagram are critical only as far as they are in the correct region; the 6, 12, and 18 in A ∩ B could have been in any order – just as if we had listed A ∩ B. Also, the space given to each set has no significance – if one set appears larger it does not mean it contains a larger number of elements.

In a Venn diagram we often shade what is of interest – as in Figure 14.6, the intersection of the two sets P and Q.

Sometimes we may have two sets, A and B, for which A ∩ B = {}. Such sets are called disjoint – as in Figure 14.7.

Note how each Venn diagram clearly shows that the Universal Set contains the sets we are dealing with – it is a kind of "boundary" for the situation in question.

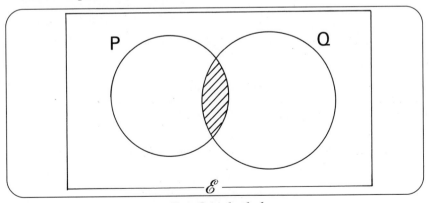

P ∩ Q is shaded

**Figure 14.6  Intersection of two sets**

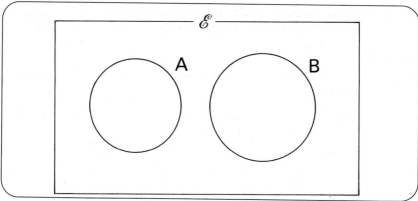

A and B are disjoint: A ∪ B = {}

**Figure 14.7   Disjoint sets**

The Venn diagrams of Figure 14.8 show how to shade complements. These are indicated in a Venn diagram in the case of two sets A and B; in the first A′ is shaded leaving A unshaded. In the second (A ∪ B)′ is

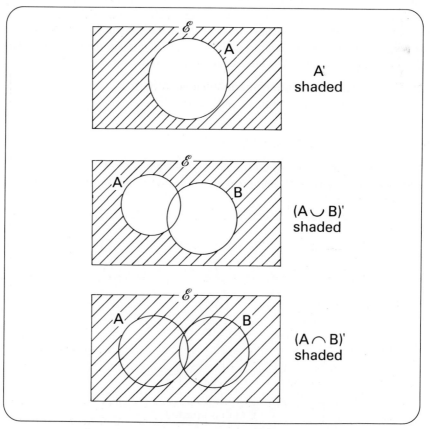

**Figure 14.8   Complements in Venn diagrams**

shaded and in the third (A ∩ B)'. In these diagrams the elements have not been included in order to show more clearly what is meant by the complement in each case.

Finally, study Figure 14.9. It shows three sets A, B and C, and all the unions and intersections.

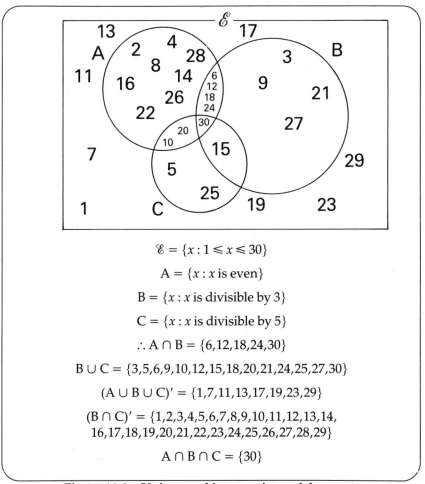

$$\mathcal{E} = \{x : 1 \leqslant x \leqslant 30\}$$

$$A = \{x : x \text{ is even}\}$$

$$B = \{x : x \text{ is divisible by 3}\}$$

$$C = \{x : x \text{ is divisible by 5}\}$$

$$\therefore A \cap B = \{6,12,18,24,30\}$$

$$B \cup C = \{3,5,6,9,10,12,15,18,20,21,24,25,27,30\}$$

$$(A \cup B \cup C)' = \{1,7,11,13,17,19,23,29\}$$

$$(B \cap C)' = \{1,2,3,4,5,6,7,8,9,10,11,12,13,14,$$
$$16,17,18,19,20,21,22,23,24,25,26,27,28,29\}$$

$$A \cap B \cap C = \{30\}$$

**Figure 14.9    Unions and intersections of three sets**

**NOW TRY THESE ...**

1. $\mathcal{E} = \{x:0<x<17,\ x\ \text{integral}\}$, $P = \{4,8,12,16\}$, and $Q = \{3,6,9,12,15\}$. Draw a Venn diagram to show these sets and their inter-relationships. Mark all elements in the correct regions of the diagram. From the diagram list $P \cap Q$ and $(P \cup Q)'$.

2. $\mathcal{E} = \{$Adam, Beryl, Chandrakant, Desmond, Elaine, Fearon, Guy, Henrietta, Idris, Jacqueta, Kathryn, Leo$\}$, the set of data processing staff; the set of Cobol programmers, $C = \{$Beryl, Desmond, Idris,

Kathryn, Leo}, and the set of Fortran programmers, F = {Adam, Beryl, Desmond, Guy, Jacquetta, Leo}. Show all this information in full detail using a Venn diagram with labels. Use this to answer the following questions.

(i)    How many people can program in Fortran?

(ii)   Who can program both in Cobol and in Fortran?

(iii)  Who can program in neither Cobol nor Fortran?

(iv)   How many people can program in Cobol but not in Fortran? (The set is $C \cap F'$).

(v)    How many people can program in Fortran but not in Cobol?

(vi)   List those who can program either in Cobol or in Fortran or in both.

3.  $\mathcal{E} = \{x : 12 < x < 29, x \text{ integral}\}$, P = {14, 21, 28}, Q = {18, 24}, and R = {16, 20, 24, 28}. Draw a Venn diagram to show these sets and their inter-relationships. Use the diagram to list the following.

(i) $P \cup Q$                          (v) $(P \cup Q \cup R)'$

(ii) $P \cap Q$                         (vi) $P \cap R$

(iii) $P \cap Q \cap R$                 (vii) $Q \cap R$

(iv) $(P \cap Q)'$                      (viii) $(P \cup R)'$

## 14.6   VENN DIAGRAMS AND LOGICAL OPERATIONS

The concepts of logic, as people used to describe many computer actions, are part of so called Boolean algebra (named after George Boole, who pioneered it). Any logical "proposition" consists of a statement which is either true or false, and never anything else. "You are sitting down" is such a statement – either it is true or it is false; there is no other answer. In the same way, "the sky is blue" is a logical proposition.

For convenience, we'll use a single letter such as p or q for any logical proposition; we shall also refer to the negation (opposite) of the proposition by p'. Thus if p is "It is raining", p' is "It is not raining". Clearly, if p is true, p' must be false, and vice versa.

People often use the concepts of Boolean algebra to describe the action of gates, the basic building blocks of circuits. These devices have one or more inputs and a single output. Chip designers use gates to create the half adders, full adders, flip-flops and other units which carry out calculations and exercise control in a processor. They can convert input decimal values into BCD, control hardware, and allow for interfacing.

We can show propositions, their negations and other related functions by Venn diagrams. See Figure 14.10.

(a) In the diagram, p' is shaded and p is unshaded – p and p' are equivalent to set A and its complement A'.

IF A < 25 OR B > 10 PERFORM A – CHECK

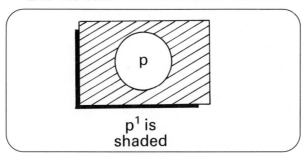

Figure 14.10   Venn diagram for a proposition

(b) Take two propositions p and q. The compound proposition p OR q means "either p is true or q is true or both are true". This compound proposition is common in programming conditional statements – such as the Cobol

The Venn diagram approach makes this equivalent to the union of the sets A and B – so that the shaded area in Figure 14.11 is p OR q (or A ∪ B).

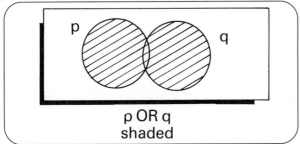

Figure 14.11   Venn diagram of proposition p OR q

(c) Now let's look at the compound proposition p AND q, meaning "both p is true and q is true". Again this often appears in programming. In the Venn diagram of Figure 14.12 the shaded area is p AND q equivalent to the intersection of two sets.

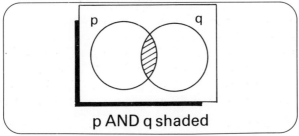

Figure 14.12   Venn diagram of p AND q

The similarity of Venn diagrams and therefore of the inter-relationships between sets with logical propositions will be further explained and we'll explore all this in more detail in Chapters 15 and 16.

# 15 Boolean algebra – the algebra of logic

## OBJECTIVES

When you've worked through this Chapter, you should be able to:

— explain what we mean by truth tables and discuss simple examples

— devise and use truth tables for NOT, AND and OR

— draw the symbols for NOT, AND and OR

— devise truth tables for simple logic circuits based on NOT, AND and OR

— describe the structure and use of the half adder circuit

— simplify logic statements using basic rules

— apply de Morgan's laws to simplify logic statements.

## INTRODUCTION

In the previous chapter, we first met logic by a proposition and its negation. We refer to a proposition as p (for instance), and to its negation as p', or as NOT p. In practice, you may need to analyse any logic circuit – given the inputs, find the output.

In the case of the very simple NOT circuit, there is just one input and one output. The input is the "value" of the proposition p – ie, whether it is true or false.

To carry out these tasks, we list in a table all the possible input values, and the output in each case. We call these tables "truth tables", and in them put 0 for false and 1 for true.

In this chapter we'll start with the NOT circuit as it is very simple.

## 15.1 TRUTH TABLES

Figure 15.1 shows the truth table, as defined above, for a NOT circuit.

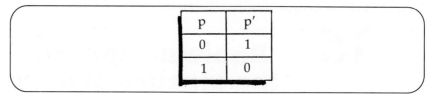

| p | p' |
|---|---|
| 0 | 1 |
| 1 | 0 |

**Figure 15.1   Truth table for NOT**

The truth table columns are for the input and output values, in this case p and NOT p (or p') respectively.

We also need to show NOT gates in diagrams. The symbol we use appears in Figure 15.2; the effect of such a gate is to invert an input signal (the value of p) to create the output signal. The NOT gate therefore inverts the input from "low" (0) to "high" (1) or vice versa.

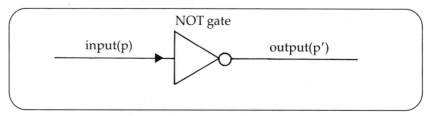

**Figure 15.2   NOT gate symbol**

We met the compound proposition OR in the previous chapter. Figure 15.3 shows the truth table for this, based on the various combinations of the values of the two inputs p and q. The only way this compound proposition can be false is if both input values are false.

**OR**

| p | q | p OR q |
|---|---|---|
| 0 | 0 | 0 |
| 0 | 1 | 1 |
| 1 | 0 | 1 |
| 1 | 1 | 1 |

**Figure 15.3   Truth table for OR**

It is worth taking note that the word OR is used here in its "inclusive" sense – p or q or both; a different logical operation also exists "exclusive OR", for p or q but not both although it is not developed any further here.

Figure 15.4 shows the symbol for an OR gate.

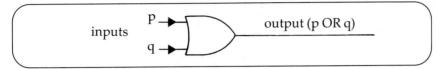

**Figure 15.4   OR symbol**

In practice, we can have three or more inputs to an OR gate. Figure 15.5 shows a three input circuit with the truth table which defines its effect. Once again the output is 0 only if all the inputs are 0.

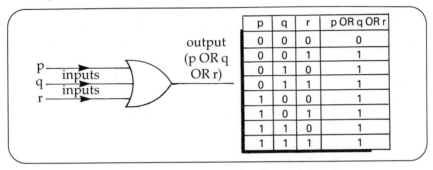

| p | q | r | p OR q OR r |
|---|---|---|---|
| 0 | 0 | 0 | 0 |
| 0 | 0 | 1 | 1 |
| 0 | 1 | 0 | 1 |
| 0 | 1 | 1 | 1 |
| 1 | 0 | 0 | 1 |
| 1 | 0 | 1 | 1 |
| 1 | 1 | 0 | 1 |
| 1 | 1 | 1 | 1 |

**Figure 15.5   "OR" circuit with truth table**

Note the way the various combinations of values of p, q and r are shown in the table, to ensure all combinations appear without duplication or exclusion. The third column, for r, shows alternate 0 and 1 etc; the preceding column, for q, shows alternately two 0s and two 1s etc; the column for p consists alternately of four 0s and four 1s. If there were four inputs, the next column to the left would have eight 0s and eight 1s, and so on.

The AND compound proposition appears in the truth table of Figure 15.6; this time the compound proposition is true only if both input propositions are true, and is false in all other cases.

| p | q | p AND q |
|---|---|---|
| 0 | 0 | 0 |
| 0 | 1 | 0 |
| 1 | 0 | 0 |
| 1 | 1 | 1 |

**Figure 15.6   AND truth table**

The AND gate symbol appears in Figure 15.7.

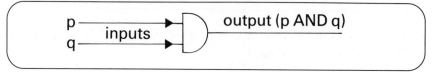

**Figure 15.7   AND symbol**

As with OR, there can be three or more inputs to an AND gate. Figure 15.8 shows the circuit and truth table. Again, the output is 1 only if all inputs are 1 and in no other case.

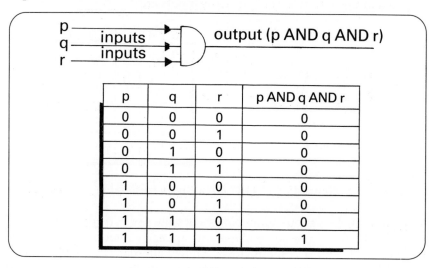

| p | q | r | p AND q AND r |
|---|---|---|---|
| 0 | 0 | 0 | 0 |
| 0 | 0 | 1 | 0 |
| 0 | 1 | 0 | 0 |
| 0 | 1 | 1 | 0 |
| 1 | 0 | 0 | 0 |
| 1 | 0 | 1 | 0 |
| 1 | 1 | 0 | 0 |
| 1 | 1 | 1 | 1 |

**Figure 15.8   Three-input AND**

## 15.2   COMBINING OPERATIONS

In practice circuits contain a mixture of the three basic gates, as in Figure 15.9.

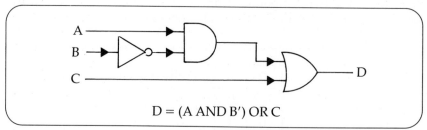

D = (A AND B') OR C

**Figure 15.9   Logic circuit with three gates**

Here the B input is into a NOT gate, with output NOT B (or B'). A and B' are inputs to an AND gate, with output A AND B'. Then the two inputs (A AND B') and C go into the OR gate – to produce (A AND B') OR C, ie the final output D. Note how we may draw the circuit as a diagram or describe it in (Booleaaan) algebra form.

To find the value of D, we need a truth table; this lists all possible values of inputs A, B and C, as in Figure 15.10.

| A | B | C | B' | A.B' | D |
|---|---|---|----|------|---|
| 0 | 0 | 0 | 1  | 0    | 0 |
| 0 | 0 | 1 | 1  | 0    | 1 |
| 0 | 1 | 0 | 0  | 0    | 0 |
| 0 | 1 | 1 | 0  | 0    | 1 |
| 1 | 0 | 0 | 1  | 1    | 1 |
| 1 | 0 | 1 | 1  | 1    | 1 |
| 1 | 1 | 0 | 0  | 0    | 0 |
| 1 | 1 | 1 | 0  | 0    | 1 |

**Figure 15.10    Truth table for Figure 15.9**

In the table, the extra columns between inputs and output are for the intermediate stages B' as it is an input to the AND gate and (A AND B') as it is an input to the OR gate. Finally having got (A AND B') and C, we can find D by using their values as inputs to the OR gate.

In practice, we usually want to design a logic circuit for a given effect. To do this we start with the Boolean algebra statement of the output. Maybe we can simplify that statement and design an easier circuit. In this case, we shall use de Morgan's laws (to be dealt with in section 15.4), though you may meet other methods later.

Computers use logic circuits for many tasks – including the control of input/output devices, access to storage, coders and decoders, arithmetic and other calculation processes, and in registers for control purposes. In hardware circuits, transistors provide the effect of logic gates; a number of such transistors may make up a solid-state integrated circuit ("chip" or IC) . An integrated circuit can combine a million or more gates, perhaps to form the low-cost micro-processors used in so many devices today; their advantages include reliability, small size and low power consumption.

Before we move on to simplifying logical statements, let's study a typical computer circuit, the "half adder", shown in Figure 15.11. The half adder has two inputs A and B and two outputs X and Y.

Note that the signal input at A goes into both the first AND gate and the OR gate; this does not imply any change of value – it can still be only 0 or 1. The same is true for B and marked on the circuit is the output from

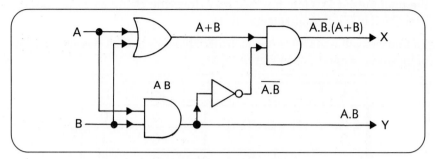

**Figure 15.11   Half adder**

each gate; thus the output from the OR gate is A OR B (expressed as A + B), and the output from the NOT gate ia (A AND B)' expressed as (A + B)'.

The first truth table in Figure 15.12 shows each of these intermediate values, so leading to the X and Y values. The second truth table is merely a summary of the first, giving only the two inputs and the two outputs.

| A | B | A+B | Y<br>A.B | $\overline{A.B}$ | X<br>$\overline{A.B}.(A+B)$ |
|---|---|-----|-----|-------|-----------|
|   |   |     |     |       |           |
|   |   |     |     |       |           |
|   |   |     |     |       |           |
|   |   |     |     |       |           |

Simplified truth table

| A | B | X | Y |
|---|---|---|---|
| 0 | 0 | 0 | 0 |
| 0 | 1 | 1 | 0 |
| 1 | 0 | 1 | 0 |
| 1 | 1 | 0 | 1 |

**Figure 15.12   Half adder truth tables**

The second truth table outputs may remind you of some earlier work, especially if you swap the X and Y columns. This circuit in fact gives us the rules for adding two binary digits (bits):

$$0 + 0 = 0$$
$$0 + 1 = 1$$
$$1 + 0 = 1$$
$$1 + 1 = 10 \text{ ie 0 with a "carry" of 1}$$

So, A and B are the two bits to add, with X their "sum" and Y the "carry" to the next column.

This circuit does not yet go far enough, since it does not cope with a "carry" from a previous column; all the same, it is an important circuit – we'll meet it again, as part of the full adder.

## 15.3   SIMPLIFYING BOOLEAN STATEMENTS

There is a large number of different simplifications we can apply to the algebraic (Boolean) statements of logic circuits. The first batch follows a single set A and its place in the universal set (Figure 15.13).

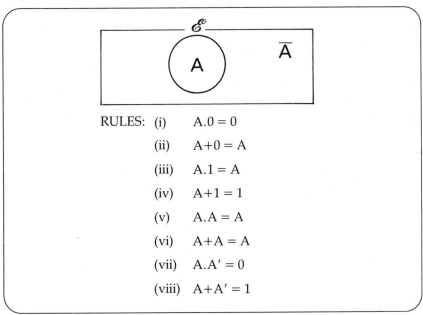

RULES: (i)    $A.0 = 0$

(ii)    $A+0 = A$

(iii)    $A.1 = A$

(iv)    $A+1 = 1$

(v)    $A.A = A$

(vi)    $A+A = A$

(vii)    $A.A' = 0$

(viii)    $A+A' = 1$

**Figure 15.13    Boolean Laws – universal set**

To appreciate these rules, take 1 for the universal set and 0 for the empty set. Also take intersection as AND and union as OR. Check each rule any way you wish.

Rule (i) – the intersection of the empty set with A is the empty set itself. In rule (ii), the union of A with the empty set is A. Rule (iii) considers the intersection of A with the universal set; the common ground between the two can only be A itself. In (vii) the intersection between A and its complement A' must be the empty set, whilst the union of these two (rule (viii)) is clearly seen to be the universal set.

Next, Figure 15.14 looks at two intersecting sets A and B and the four rules which emerge. For example rule (ix) states that the intersection of A with the union of A with B (that is the area common to both A and the union of A with B) must be just A; hence A. $(A+B) = A$. Similarly in (x)

A.B is the intersection of A with B; the union of this with A will just get A – and so on.

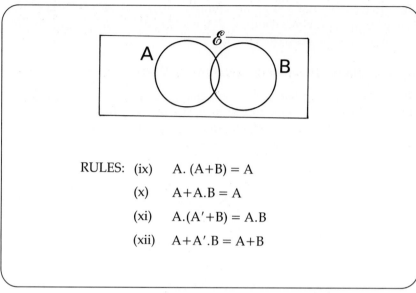

RULES: (ix)    A. (A+B) = A

(x)      A+A.B = A

(xi)     A.(A'+B) = A.B

(xii)    A+A'.B = A+B

**Figure 15.14    Boolean Laws – intersecting sets**

Next, the commutative laws shown in Figure 15.15 tell us that, when taking the union or the intersection of two sets, the order does not matter.

Commutative Laws:
$$\frac{A.B = B.A}{A+B = B+A}$$

**Figure 15.15    Commutative Laws**

The associative rules state that, when we have three propositions, it does not matter which two we combine first – so A.(B.C) and (A.B).C both provide equivalent ways of working out A.B.C. See Figure 15.16.

Associative rules:
$$\frac{A.B.C = A.(B.C) = (A.B).C}{\frac{A+B+C = A+(B+C) = (A+B)+C}{A+B+C+D = (A+B)+(C+D)}}$$

**Figure 15.16    Associative Laws**

The first distributive law tells us that we can work out A.(B+C) by getting rid of the brackets to produce A.B+A.C. This is like the convential rules of algebra we met in Chapter 10. The relationship A+B+C = 1 takes rather longer to deduce; it relies on earlier results and the reverse of the distributive law A.C+A.B = A.(C+B); then, since A+B+C = 1, it follows that B+C = A'.

Study Figure 15.17 where we write A.B as AB where there is no chance of confusion.

### Distributive Laws

$A(B+C) = AB+AC$

If $A+B+C = 1$ then

$$(A+B).(A+C) = AA+AC+BA+BC$$
$$= A+AC+AB+BC$$
$$= A+A(C+B)+BC$$
$$= A+AA'+BC$$
$$= A+0+BC$$
$$= A+BC$$

ie $(A+B)(A+C) = A+BC$

Double negatives $(A')' = A$

**Figure 15.17    Distributive Laws**

The "double negative" statement implies quite simply that the complement of the complement of A is A itself; this may seem obvious but is still warrants a mention.

## 15.4   DE MORGAN'S LAWS

Strictly, de Morgan's Laws are as much algebra as those we have just met. We deal with them separately and we apply them to a Boolean statement in three clearly defined steps. These are

(i)    change each AND to OR and each OR to AND

(ii)   negate all variables

(iii)  negate the whole expression

In Figure 15.18 these rules are applied to two different problems – proving, in the first case, that $(A+B)' = A'B'$, and, in the second case, the equivalent result that $(AB)' = A'+B'$.

The next example, Figure 15.19, is slightly more involved. Work through it with care.

Using de Morgan's rules on

(a)  (A+B)'

    Step (i)      (AB)'

    Step (ii)     (A'B')'

    Step (iii)    A'B'

    Therefore (A+B)' = A'B'

(b)  (AB)'

    Step (i)      (A+B)'

    Step (ii)     (A'+B')'

    Step (iii)    A'+B'

    Therefore (AB)' = A'+B'

**Figure 15.18   Using de Morgan's Laws**

(c)  (A+B)'.C'. First, use de Morgan's laws to convert (A+B)' to A'B' – we now have A'B'C'. Next, use de Morgan's laws on this result to give (A + B + C)'. Therefore (A + B)'C' = (A + B + C)'. In general, (A + B + C + D + ...)' = A'B'C'D' ...

**Figure 15.19   A more involved expression**

### 15.4.1  Karnaugh Maps

There are physical similarities between Karnaugh Maps and Venn diagrams, since they can both be used to represent Boolean expressions algebraically. It is possible to use Karnaugh Maps to simplify express-ions with as many as six variables although in this chapter they will be restricted to two- and three-variable cases, so dealing only with circuits

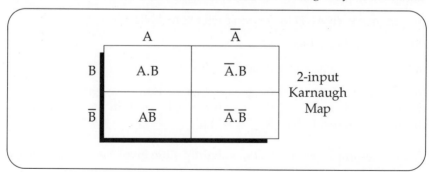

**Figure 15.20   2-input Karnaugh Map**

in which there are only two or three inputs. The process can however, be used to deal with far more complex simplifications.

The diagram in Figure 15.20 shows the two-input Karnaugh Map; with A and $\overline{A}$ along the top and B and $\overline{B}$ down the side, every one of the four cells is immediately defined by relation to the elements at the top and at the side hence as AB, $\overline{A}$B, A$\overline{B}$ and $\overline{A}\overline{B}$ respectively.

In the next diagram in Figure 15.21 the whole of A (ie AB + A$\overline{B}$) is shown shaded in the left-hand illustration and the whole of B (ie AB + $\overline{A}$B) can be seen shaded in the diagram on the right. It is possible to identify any one of the elements A, $\overline{A}$, B or $\overline{B}$ by reference to appropriate shading of components within this map.

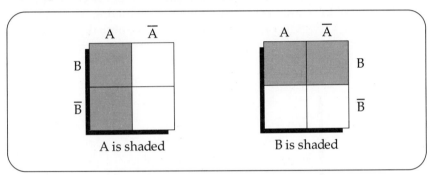

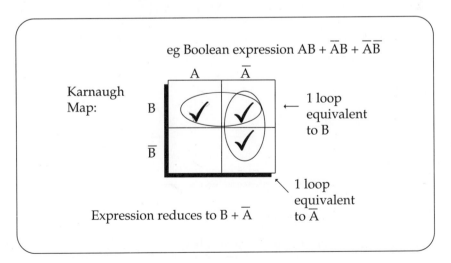

**Figure 15.21    Shaded Karnaugh Maps**

If given a Boolean expression such as AB + $\overline{A}$B + $\overline{A}\overline{B}$, as shown in Figure 15.22, each of the three constituent parts can be ticked on the Karnaugh Map. Next, loops are drawn around each pair of adjacent squares that are ticked, or any isolated square that is not so adjacent.

**Figure 15.22    Boolean expression as a Karnaugh Map**

Each loop now identifies the variable present in the simplification of the Boolean expression. In the diagram the loops identify B and $\bar{A}$ and the fact that the loops overlap is totally irrelevant; hence we find that AB + $\bar{A}$B + $\bar{A}\bar{B}$ is capable of simplification to B + $\bar{A}$ and this simpler form has exactly the same effect. Thus any circuit represented in this way could be simplified by another which does exactly the same but which requires far less circuitry.

It is now possible to proceed to the three-variable form of the Karnaugh Map. Since there can only be two sides to the rectangle drawn here we must let A and $\bar{A}$ go down one side whilst the top edge is made up of the four components BC, $\bar{B}$C, $\bar{B}\bar{C}$ and B$\bar{C}$ (which make up all the possible combinations of B and $\bar{B}$ with C and $\bar{C}$). Again, each of the eight squares identifies one of the eight possible combinations involving A or $\bar{A}$ with B or $\bar{B}$ with C or $\bar{C}$ (Figure 15.23). A itself can be identified as being the

|  | BC | $\bar{B}$C | $\bar{B}\bar{C}$ | B$\bar{C}$ |
|---|---|---|---|---|
| A | A.B.C. | A.$\bar{B}$.C. | A.$\bar{B}$.$\bar{C}$. | A.B.$\bar{C}$. |
| $\bar{A}$ | $\bar{A}$.B.C. | $\bar{A}$.$\bar{B}$.C. | $\bar{A}$.$\bar{B}$.$\bar{C}$. | $\bar{A}$.B.$\bar{C}$. |

3-input Karnaugh Map

**Figure 15.23    3-input Karnaugh Map**

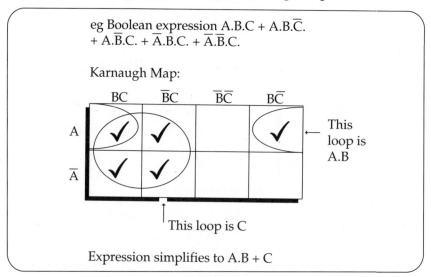

eg Boolean expression A.B.C + A.B.$\bar{C}$. + A.$\bar{B}$.C. + $\bar{A}$.B.C. + $\bar{A}$.$\bar{B}$.C.

Karnaugh Map:

Expression simplifies to A.B + C

**Figure 15.24    Boolean expression simplified using a Karnaugh Map**

whole of the top four squares whilst $\bar{A}$ is given by the bottom four. $\bar{B}$ is identifiable as being the central four squares since

$$(\bar{B}C + \bar{B}\bar{C})(A + \bar{A}) = \bar{B}(C+\bar{C}) = \bar{B}$$

and B is given by the two vertical squares on the left hand end combined with the two vertical squares at the right hand end. Likewise C could be identified as the left hand end block of four squares and C as the right hand end block of four. Other items can be defined by taking two squares at a time.

To simplify the Boolean expression

$$ABC + AB\bar{C} + A\bar{B}C + \bar{A}BC + \bar{A}\bar{B}C$$

the five units on the Karnaugh Map are ticked and loops of four squares or two squares are drawn as appropriate (Figure 15.24).

Since the left-hand end block of four squares is totally contained the presence of C in the simplification is easy to establish, but note also that $ABC + AB\bar{C}$ 'wraps round the back' to simplify to AB. Hence the whole expression reduces to AB + C, a considerable reduction from the original.

**NOW TRY THESE . . .**

1. Copy and complete the following truth table:

| A | B | A.B | A+B | (A+B).(A.B) |
|---|---|-----|-----|-------------|
| 0 | 0 |     |     |             |
| 0 | 1 |     |     |             |
| 1 | 0 |     |     |             |
| 1 | 1 |     |     |             |

2. Refer to the following circuit.

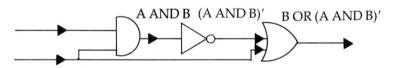

A AND B   (A AND B)'   B OR (A AND B)'

Copy and complete the truth table:

| A | B | A.B | (A.B)' | B + (A.B)' |
|---|---|-----|--------|------------|
| 0 | 0 |     |        |            |
| 0 | 1 |     |        |            |
| 1 | 0 |     |        |            |
| 1 | 1 |     |        |            |

3. Refer to this circuit:

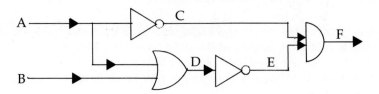

Write down the values at C, D, E and F, each in terms of A and B; produce a truth table for F for every combination of values of A and B.

4. Refer to this circuit:

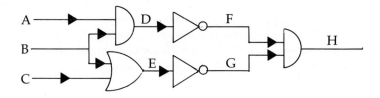

Write down the values at D, E, F, G and H, each in terms of A, B and C. Produce a truth table for F for every combination of values of A, B and C.

5. Use de Morgan's Laws to simplify each of the following.
   (i)     $A' + B' + C'$
   (ii)    $(A' + B').(B' + C')$
   (iii)   $A'.B' + B'.C'$
   (iv)    $(A.B)' + (B.C)' + (A.C)'$

6. Simplify each of the following using a Karnaugh Map.
   (i)     $A.B + A.B' + A'.B'$
   (ii)    $A.B + A'.B$
   (iii)   $A.B.C + A'.B.C' + A.B.C' + A'.B.C$
   (iv)    $A'.B'.C + A'.B'.C' + A.B.C' + A'.B.C'$
   (v)     $A.B'.C' + A.B.C' + A.B.C + A.B'.C + A'.B'.C$

# 16 More uses of logic

## OBJECTIVES

When you've worked through this Chapter, you should be able to:

— outline the structure, truth table and usage of the full adder circuit

— apply truth table concepts to simple circuits and systems

— give symbols and truth tables for NAND and NOR gates

— state the importance of NAND and NOR gates in circuit design

— give examples of the use of logical concepts in program statements.

## INTRODUCTION

Working with logic, often called Boolean algebra, is important in many areas of computing. We've seen how we may apply the basic ideas to gates, the simple building blocks of computer processor circuits, and the half adder, which is a more arithmetic circuit.

Now we'll take these ideas a little further by looking at the full adder circuit. This is more complex still than the half adder – but the half adder is of no real value as such, while the full adder circuit is in very wide use. We are also going to study the logic of a multi-switch lamp control, together with a closer look at NAND and NOR gates. In this way, we will be able to see how logic is of as much value (if not more) in programming as in circuit design.

## 16.1 THE FULL ADDER

When we discussed the half adder in Chapter 15, it was noted that it has limited use on its own as it cannot handle a "carry" from a previous addition. The solution is the full adder; by combining two half adders and an OR gate, this can cope with those inputs, including a "carry", and produce a "sum" and a "carry" forward. Figure 16.1 shows the full adder.

Note how the half adders appear only as blocks; as circuits get more involved, we draw standard elements (components), such as the half adder, this way to reduce the complexity of the diagram. Refer to Figure 15.11 for the half adder circuit.

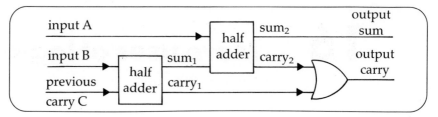

**Figure 16.1   Full adder**

The truth table in Figure 16.2 shows the "sum" and "carry" outputs from the full adder for the three inputs A, B, and previous carry C.

| Full Adder | | | | |
|---|---|---|---|---|
| Inputs | | | Outputs | |
| A | B | C | sum | carry |
| 0 | 0 | 0 | 0 | 0 |
| 0 | 0 | 1 | 1 | 0 |
| 0 | 1 | 0 | 1 | 0 |
| 0 | 1 | 1 | 0 | 1 |
| 1 | 0 | 0 | 1 | 0 |
| 1 | 0 | 1 | 0 | 1 |
| 1 | 1 | 0 | 0 | 1 |
| 1 | 1 | 1 | 1 | 1 |

**Figure 16.2   Full adder truth table**

In the same way, we can see (for interest) in Figure 16.3 how to use two full adders to add two two-bit numbers. Note again how the full adder is replaced in its turn, by a block component in the diagram. The (first) full adder at the right-hand side adds the "units" bits, and requires a zero carry from the previous (non-existent) operation. However, the (second) full adder at the left, which adds the $2^1$ bits, takes in the carry from the first adder. The carry from this second adder acts as the $2^2$ bit in the result, 101.

If we need to add two 12-bit numbers, we would link 12 full adders in much the same way. Can you produce a truth table for Figure 16.3?

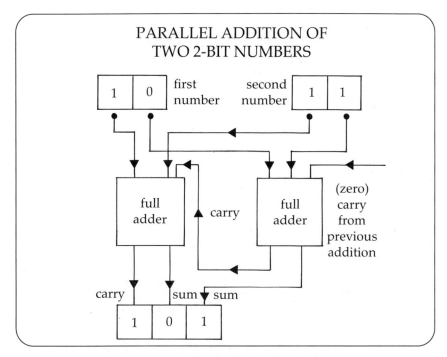

**Figure 16.3    Parallel addition of two two-bit numbers**

## 16.2    FLIP-FLOPS

This logic circuit is used for the purpose of data storage. There are two inputs R (for reset) and S (for set) and two outputs Q and $\bar{Q}$. For any given initial value of Q the values of R and/or S may cause Q to change. However, this change (if any), is also dependent upon the initial value of Q. It follows therefore that the output Q is fed back into the input side.

If Q is initially 0 (ie off) then *resetting* it (R = 1) can have no effect, but *setting* it (S = 1) must turn it on, giving it a value of 1. If Q is initially 1 (ie on) then setting it (S = 1) can have no effect since it is already set but resetting it (R = 1) will change it back to 0. It is not possible to both set *and* reset the input Q at the same time so we get the two 'not feasible' entries in the truth table in Figure 16.4.

Note carefully in the circuit diagram that both Q and $\bar{Q}$ are used to re-input into the OR-gates. This reset-set flip-flop is also referred to as a *bistable*.

## 16.3    LIGHT SWITCHES

Next, we will look at a fairly common type of industrial use for a logic circuit. At three different places in an office there are three separate switches that control the same light; each switch may be off (0) or on (1).

### R.S. FLIP-FLOP OR BISTABLE

| R | S | Initially Q | Now Q |
|---|---|---|---|
| 0 | 0 | 0 | 0 |
| 1 | 0 | 0 | 0 |
| 0 | 1 | 0 | 1 |
| 1 | 1 | 0 | Not Feasible |
| 0 | 0 | 1 | 1 |
| 1 | 0 | 1 | 0 |
| 0 | 1 | 1 | **1** |
| 1 | 1 | 1 | Not Feasible |

N.B. Both Q and $\overline{Q}$ are required for outputs

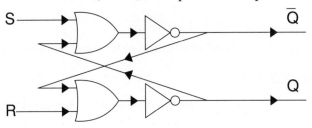

**Figure 16.4    Reset-set Flip-flop or bistable**

| A | B | C | output |
|---|---|---|--------|
| 0 | 0 | 0 | 0 |
| 0 | 0 | 1 | 1 |
| 0 | 1 | 0 | 1 |
| 0 | 1 | 1 | 0 |
| 1 | 0 | 0 | 1 |
| 1 | 0 | 1 | 0 |
| 1 | 1 | 0 | 0 |
| 1 | 1 | 1 | 1 |

**Figure 16.5    Light switch truth table**

The light will be on (1) if there are an odd number of switches on, and off (0) otherwise. Clearly, if the light is already on, nobody would touch a switch unless they wanted to turn the light off. The truth table in Figure 16.4 describes the possible values of the three switches A, B and C and the output (the light) in each case.

Study the table. Do you agree that there is an output? (ie the light is on) if A = 0, B = 0 and C = 1 or if A = 0, B = 1, C = 0, etc. The four cases are A'B'C, A'BC', AB'C' and ABC so we can describe the output with the Boolean expression A'B'C + A'BC' + AB'C' + ABC. This is next illustrated on the Karnaugh Map in Figure 16.6 which indicates that there is no possibility of simplification:

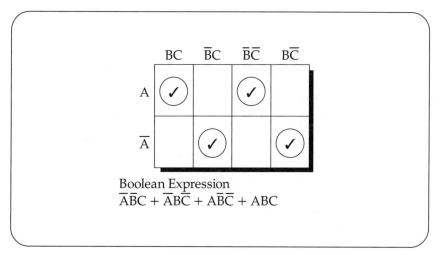

Boolean Expression
$\overline{A}\overline{B}C + \overline{A}B\overline{C} + A\overline{B}\overline{C} + ABC$

**Figure 16.6   Boolean expression of light switch truth table simplified into a Karnaugh Map**

Now we know the nature of the circuit, we can design it. Check that the drawing in Figure 16.7 meets our needs.

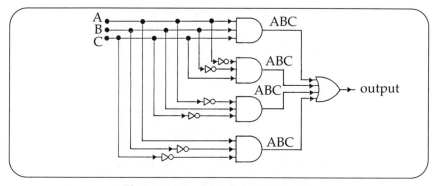

**Figure 16.7   Four-input OR gate**

The example above illustrates how we can design a circuit from a knowledge of the output(s) required for various states of the inputs. In the same way, we can design other more involved circuits.

## 16.4   NAND AND NOR GATES

Often people use other gates to build logic circuits; two of the most common are NAND and NOR.

The NAND gate in effect consists of an AND gate with a NOT gate after it to invert its output. The symbol and the truth tables in Figure 16.7 reflects this.

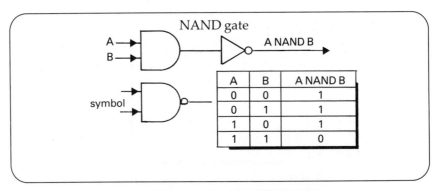

| A | B | A NAND B |
|---|---|----------|
| 0 | 0 | 1 |
| 0 | 1 | 1 |
| 1 | 0 | 1 |
| 1 | 1 | 0 |

**Figure 16.8   The NAND gate**

In the same way, the NOR gate is, in effect, an OR gate with a NOT gate after it to invert its output. The symbol and the truth table appear in Figure 16.9.

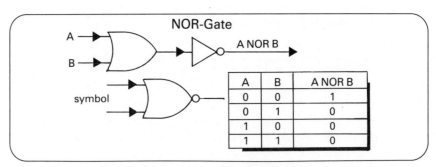

| A | B | A NOR B |
|---|---|---------|
| 0 | 0 | 1 |
| 0 | 1 | 0 |
| 1 | 0 | 0 |
| 1 | 1 | 0 |

**Figure 16.9   The NOR gate**

Anything you can build from AND, OR and NOT gates can just as well be designed to use NAND or NOR gates only – and more cheaply. You may like to study Figure 16.10 – it shows a half adder which uses NAND gates only.

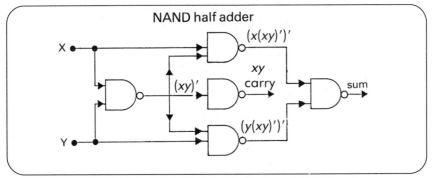

**Figure 16.10   Half adder built from NAND gate**

## 16.5   LOGICAL PROGRAMMING

All the examples so far on the use of logic have concerned the hardware aspects of computing. This is by no means the only use; indeed, logic circuits are of little interest to many people.

The use of logic in programming, both at high level and in machine code, is of much more general importance. We'll work in Cobol; the principles are the same in any language. Consider a compound conditional statement such as

IF TAX-VAL > 25 AND CODE-X NUMERIC OR

GROSS-TOTAL NEGATIVE PERFORM X-PARA

Here there are three elementary conditions – TAX-VAL > 25, CODE-X NUMERIC and GROSS-TOTAL NEGATIVE. Let's call these c-1, c-2 and c-3 respectively; the statement becomes

IF c-1 AND c-2 OR c-3 PERFORM X-PARA

The program's task is to decide whether the compound condition c-1 AND c-2 OR c-3 is true or false (so that it carries out X-PARA or not). This in turn depends on whether each of the three elementary conditions are true or false.

In this respect, we can think of three inputs c-1, c-2 and c-3 to a logic circuit. Check that Figure 16.11 meets our needs.

Many other such situations exist in programming, and require a knowledge of how to design and process conditional statements. Even the use of NOT to invert a condition is common practice in programming.

Likewise when working at machine-code level situations may be encountered in which the bit-patterns held in two storage locations have to be compared for the purpose of carrying out logical operations upon them. We may wish to mask out a portion of a word so that attention can be focused on, for example, a specific field within a program instruction.

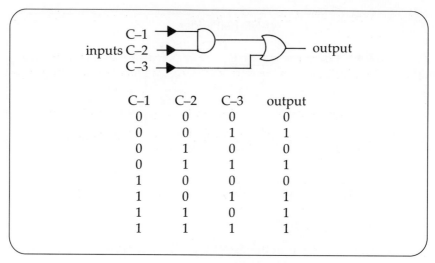

| C–1 | C–2 | C–3 | output |
|-----|-----|-----|--------|
| 0 | 0 | 0 | 0 |
| 0 | 0 | 1 | 1 |
| 0 | 1 | 0 | 0 |
| 0 | 1 | 1 | 1 |
| 1 | 0 | 0 | 0 |
| 1 | 0 | 1 | 1 |
| 1 | 1 | 0 | 1 |
| 1 | 1 | 1 | 1 |

**Figure 16.11   Logical programming**

Alternatively we may wish to set or to reset certain bits in a word, acting as switches, a task achieved by the use of logic operations. Sometimes we may need to ensure that the value of a particular word oscillates between two alternative values, again by the imposition of some logical process upon the bits.

Logic is therefore not solely the province of the hardware designer; it has a large number of important programming applications. We do not dwell on them here in depth as the subject belongs to courses in programming.

**NOW TRY THESE . . .**

1. The company safe has three locks. The keys are held, one each, by the manager and the two assistant managers. Devise a logic circuit to allow the safe to open (=1) only if the manager and one or both assistants use their keys.

Hint: draw up a truth table listing the eight possible combinations of the presence (=1) or the absence (=0) of each of the three keys; simplify the result before drawing the circuit.

2. Design a circuit to control the starting (=1) of a data recording device, which requires all three of the following to make it work.

   (i)   data recording device is switched on (=1)

   (ii)  it is connected to the modem (=1)

   (iii) the program asks for data recording (=1).

3. Three people at a meeting can each vote by pressing a button (=1) or not pressing it (=0); the latter implies a vote against. A decision is

taken in favour (=1) if any two or more buttons are pressed. Design a circuit to do this.

4. Four inputs represent binary 1, $2^1$, $2^2$, $2^3$. Design a circuit which will allow output (=1) only if the inputs stand for a decimal digit in the range 0 to 9 only.

5. Design a logic circuit to stand for this Basic program statement.

IF NOT SEX = "M" AND AGE < 10 OR AGE > 60 THEN ISSUE-PASS.

# 17 Arrays

## OBJECTIVES

When you've worked through this Chapter, you should be able to:

— explain the nature of an array in one, two and three dimensions

— understand how we refer to elements of an array

— outline program structures to insert data values into one - and two-dimensional arrays

— outline program structures for simple array processing

— add and subtract arrays and find scalar and array products.

## INTRODUCTION

People often use arrays in programming and when using a number of standard packages, notably spreadsheets. They are of value in office work, for holding a reference table, for example containing a range of commission rates or delivery charges; or they may hold a small file of data which needs processing in some way, perhaps sorting it into some sequence.

In scientific computing too, arrays are common, usually containing numeric data, in which case some people call them matrices (plural for "matrix").

Arrays may also appear when a machine processes instructions or handles remote enquiries, eg when storing data in stacks or queues, (which may very conveniently be represented by arrays).

## 17.1 WHAT IS AN ARRAY?

Here is a list of customer account numbers:

P328   A714   F305   A286   P394   R113   F219   A664   F317

We can define a specific value by its position in the list – eg, we could refer to item 4 rather than to A286. If the whole list (of nine items) has a name, say C, we can refer to each item by the name (C) and position – thus C(6) stands for R113.

This is an example of a list or one-dimensional array (sometimes called a linear array); we call C(6) *a subscripted variable*, 6 being the subscript. In this particular example it makes sense, of course, only if the subscript is a whole number in the range 1 to 9 inclusive.

The value of this approach is great. First, it reduces the number of different variables (and names) we need in a problem – C in the example caters for all the customer account numbers, with no need for nine different names. This point may not seem important in the abstract, but certain program languages possess a very restricted set of variable names.

The second advantage is far more significant; the subscripted array allows you to group a set of inter-related data values, and to manipulate them. The grouping may be the account numbers for thousands of customers, or it might be a set of fields relating to the same record.

We can extend this concept to the two-dimensional array, as shown in Figure 17.1. In this case, we may call the array a table (or a matrix if it contains numeric data only); we can think of it being made up of rows and columns. Now, to identify a specific box in the table, we refer to both row and column, as well as to the name given to the table. The name of the table in Figure 17.1 is T; it consists of 5 rows and 7 columns, so can hold 35 values. I've referred to some values specifically, such as T(5,6) – the item in row number 5, column number 6 of table T; this has the value 8, ie T(5,6) = 8.

| 6 | 5 | 13 | 0 | 8 | −3 | 6 | ← T(2,5) |
|---|---|---|---|---|---|---|---|
| 2.9 | 4 | 8 | −1 | (2) | 8.1 | −4 | |
| 18 | 15 | −3.7 | 2 | 2 | 3.8 | 6 | |
| −8 | 0 | (14) | 5 | 3.8 | 2.9 | −2 | ← T(5,6) |
| 3 | 8.1 | 6 | 3 | 17 | (8) | 4.7 | |

T(4,3)

**Figure 17.1   A two-dimensional array (table), T**

A 2,5

| SPRITE | 1300 | RED | 21564 | 2900 |
|---|---|---|---|---|
| MUSTANG | 2600 | WHITE | 49630 | (3500) |
| GOLF | 1500 | (RED) | 38050 | 2650 |
| (CAPRI) | 1700 | BLUE | 15063 | 4800 |

A 4,1           A 3,3

**Figure 17.2   Two-dimensional array, A**

In the second case, Figure 17.2, table A contains a mixture of numeric
and string data, but the reference system is exactly the same, with A(2,5)
for the value 3500.

Again, we can extend the concept, into three or more dimensions. The
diagram in Figure 17.3 shows a three-dimensional case, with the third
subscript for the "depth" in the structure; thus T(1,5,5) identifies the
element in row 1, column 5, and 5 "deep".

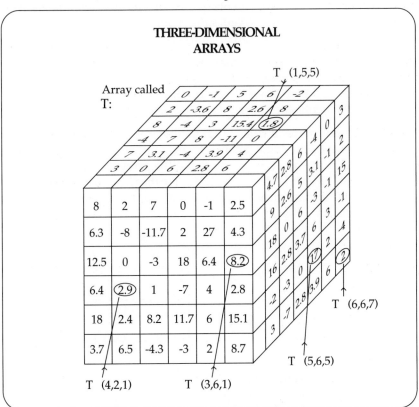

**Figure 17.3   Three-dimensional array T**

A three-dimensional array though not too hard to picture, is not much
fun to draw. Many languages allow more than three dimensions, but we
can't easily show these in a drawing.

I must stress that, though we may call arrays two- or three-dimensional,
this is the way in which people view them; it is not the way a machine
stores them. Thus, most machines store a 5 row by 7 column array as a
linear storage of 35 cells – the second row may in fact be items 8 to 14 in
that set. This makes no difference from the point of view of the
programmer, who can continue to picture the array as two-dimensional
and allow the software to convert between stored data and the picture.
In practice, we can also use variables for subscripts; thus we may refer to
P(X,Y). This lets us assign values X and Y during processing.

In the case of our 9-element list C, whose elements are C(1), C(2), . . . .,
we can refer to the general element as C(x), where x may take the values
from 1 to 9, eg within a program loop, to identify each element in turn.

## 17.2   BUILDING ARRAYS FROM RAW DATA

An array is, of course, not for holding a set of disorganised data. It
possesses a definable structure, and, in the one-dimensional case, is
most likely to have all the elements of the same type; they might each be
an examination mark in a given subject for a candidate, the age of a
person in a group, or the length of time between consecutive interrupts.

The order of items in the list may be the natural order in which they
have been selected or in which they occur as functions of time, or just by
chance. Later we may wish to re-structure the array by, for instance,
sorting the elements into order.

Figure 17.4 shows how a Basic program may read data and store it into
an array. It shows the array before and after the program carries out the
instructions. However, it is possible that the array may not have been
empty at first, but held other data. Note also that (of more importance to
programmers) the array may well possess a zero-th element (A (0)) as
well as the others.

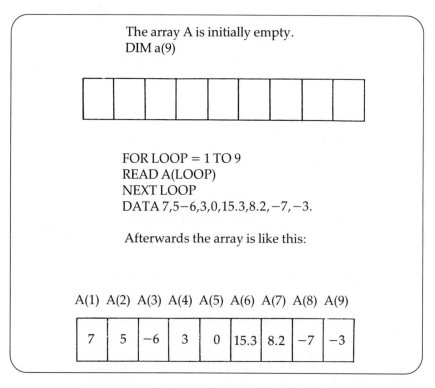

Figure 17.4   Building an array from raw data

In the two-dimensional case we may need to pay more regard to the way data goes in – it is more than likely to involve a mixture of data. Typically, it could be that each row identifies an individual record (an employee for example), and each element in that row is a field relating to that employee such as name, date of birth, pay to date, tax to date, and so on. Hence, any one column holds a set of fields for all the staff. It is quite possible that the data will be a mixture of numbers and strings, though this can be quite a problem with some program languages. Cobol readily accepts such a mixture, whereas many dialects of Basic require that the whole array contains either numbers or strings. (In such a case, convert the numbers into strings with STR$, so making the whole array alphanumeric; then use VAL to convert the strings back to numeric values as appropriate later.)

In Figure 17.5 a two-dimensional array holds the exam results of six students; it also shows two distinct ways to read the data into the array. In the first, data enters one student record at a time (ie on a "row by row" basis), in the second, it enters on a "column by column" basis, thus dealing with each subject in turn. The method used depends upon circumstances – the former is often the more natural.

| STUDENT NUMBER | MATHEMATICS | ENGLISH | SCIENCE |
|---|---|---|---|
| 1307 | 46 | 58 | 49 |
| 1314 | 71 | 42 | 83 |
| 1318 | 24 | 17 | 19 |
| 1321 | 83 | 46 | 78 |
| 1327 | 75 | 58 | 88 |
| 1334 | 40 | 32 | 47 |

```
DIM RESULT (6,4)
FOR ROW = 1 TO 6
    FOR COL = 1 TO 4
        READ RESULT (ROW, COL)
    NEXT COL
NEXT ROW
DATA 1307,46,58,49,1314,71,42, etc

DIM RESULT (6,4)
FOR COL = 1 TO 4
    FOR ROW = 1 TO 6
        READ RESULT (ROW, COL)
    NEXT ROW
NEXT COL
DATA 1307,1314,1318,1321,1327,1334,46,71, etc
```

Figure 17.5   Loading data into a two-dimensional array

We can work with more involved arrays such as the three-dimensional in just the same way. The coding is slightly more involved, but the principles are just the same. For the exam result case, we can picture the 6-row by 3-column structure (deleting the student number column) with values going "into" the paper for the marks for each question on each exam paper.

Rather than "reading in" a set of data into an array, we can assign specific values to the elements.

Figure 17.6 shows the coding of three different cases. In the first we need to "zeroise" each of the 15 elements in the linear array; as with other examples, using READ . . . DATA . . . – but the coding used here is far more efficient for the purpose. The third example is to remind us that we may wish to assign values to certain elements only, rather than to them all.

1. *Assign 0 to each item in the 15-element 1-D array L.*

   DIM L(15)

   FOR LOOP = 1 to 15

   LET L (LOOP) = 0

   NEXT LOOP

2. *Assign 1 . . .30 to the elements of 30-element 1-D array M.*

   DIM M(30)

   FOR LOOP = 1 TO 30

   LET M (LOOP) = LOOP

   NEXT LOOP

3. *Assign $x^3 - x^2 + 1$, for $x = 2$ to 17, to all but the first element of 1-D array N.*

   DIM N(17)
   FOR LOOP = 2 TO 17
   LET N (LOOP) = LOOP ↑ 3 − LOOP ↑ 2 + 1
   NEXT LOOP

**Figure 17.6    Assignment of values**

**NOW TRY THESE . . . . . .**

1 Refer to the following list, NUM.

   17.1 12.3 6.8 9.7 5.4 7.8 5.3 11.1 9.6 10.4 Give the values of

   (i)    NUM (3)

(ii)  NUM (7)

(iii)  NUM (11)

2.  Refer to the following 2-D array, T.

| Fred | Nancy | Liang | Lakbir | Suzanne | Li | David |
| Andrew | Rukshini | Scott | Gina | Fatima | Jan | Ho |
| Harriet | Sukinder | Ong | Suzie | Danielle | Sharjah | Maria |
| Uppal | Danipal | Tony | Petra | Franz | Ram | Drogo |
| Anna | Zsu-Zsu | Yola | Philip | Atwal | Hannah | Hong |

Write down the values of (i)   T(2,6)

(ii)  T(3,1)

(iii)  T(1,3)

(iv)  T(5,4)

How may we refer to (v)  Daipal?

(vi)  Franz?

## 17.3   ADDING ROWS OR COLUMNS

When we process an array, we often need to add the elements in a given row or column.

Consider the earlier example of exam results; if we add the elements in column 4 and divide the result by 6, we obtain the mean mark for science. Similarly, if we add the elements in row 5, columns 2 to 4 only, and then divide by 3, we get the mean mark of candidate 1327. The coding in Basic for both cases appears in Figure 17.7.

A point to note, however, is that this is only sensible if it involves adding like with like – so the result is itself sensible. We may agree to sum the candidate numbers to obtain a hash total for batch control purposes, but it would not be sensible to add a candidate's number to the marks in the exam – the result has no meaning.

## 17.4   ARRAY ARITHMETIC

Just as it is possible to do arithmetic with single numbers (scalars), we can work with numeric arrays, structured sets of scalar values. However, the result must be sensible; just as we would not expect to add with meaning someone's tax paid to date and the cost of an order from client, we must take care when working with arrays.

When we have to add or subtract arrays, they must be of exactly the same format; you can add two arrays only if they have the same number of rows and columns.

*The average science mark:*

 LET SUM = 0

 FOR STUDENT = 1 TO 6

 LET SUM = SUM + RESULT (STUDENT, 4)

 NEXT STUDENT

 PRINT "MEAN SCIENCE MARK:"; SUM/6

With the data used, this will result in

 MEAN SCIENCE MARK : 36.5

*The mean mark for candidate 1327:*

 C = 0

 FOR J = 2 TO 5

 C = C + R(5,J)

 NEXT J

 PRINT "CANDIDATE"; R(5,1); "AVERAGED"; C/4

With the data used, this will result in

CANDIDATE 1327 AVERAGED 70.75

**Figure 17.7 Processing an array in Basic**

Figure 17.8 shows how to add two arrays, of 4 rows and 3 columns. To achieve this, add each element in the first array to the corresponding element in the second, to produce a similar element in the result; thus in row 1 column 1, $7 + 4 = 11$.

$$
\begin{pmatrix} 7 & 5 & 9 \\ 4 & 0 & 6 \\ -3 & 2 & 5 \\ 1 & 4 & 2 \end{pmatrix}
+
\begin{pmatrix} 4 & 9 & 6 \\ 2 & 8 & -4 \\ 0 & 6 & 9 \\ -3 & 1 & 3 \end{pmatrix}
$$

$$
=
\begin{pmatrix} 11 & 14 & 15 \\ 6 & 8 & 2 \\ -3 & 8 & 14 \\ -2 & 5 & 5 \end{pmatrix}
$$

**Figure 17.8 Adding arrays**

Figure 17.9 shows we can subtract two arrays in just the same way – thus in row 3 column 2, $6 - 0 = 6$.

$$\begin{pmatrix} 3 & 7 \\ 4 & 1 \\ -2 & 6 \\ 5 & 4 \end{pmatrix} - \begin{pmatrix} 9 & 7 \\ 3 & 4 \\ -1 & 0 \\ 2 & 6 \end{pmatrix}$$

$$= \begin{pmatrix} -6 & 0 \\ 1 & -3 \\ -1 & 6 \\ 3 & -2 \end{pmatrix}$$

**Figure 17.9   Subtracting arrays**

Adding and subtracting arrays is straight-forward. What about multiplying, then? Again, no problem – except there are two kinds of array multiplication. One kind is "scalar" multiplication.

If you add an array to itself, the result is a new array in which every element is twice what it was before; we multiply the whole array by the (scalar) number 2. We can do this for any scalar number. The (scalar) product with 5 is an array with the same number of rows and columns, but whose elements are all five times larger. Figure 17.10 shows the product of an array M and 4. M is two dimensional – but just the same ideas apply to arrays of any number of dimensions.

$$M = \begin{pmatrix} 6 & 3 & 8 & 7 & 5 \\ 2 & -1 & 0 & 4{\cdot}1 & 3 \\ 9 & 5 & -7 & 2.1 & 6 \\ 4 & -3 & 0 & 2 & 8{\cdot}5 \end{pmatrix}$$

$$\therefore 4M = \begin{pmatrix} 24 & 12 & 32 & 28 & 20 \\ 8 & -4 & 0 & 16.4 & 12 \\ 36 & 20 & -28 & 8.4 & 24 \\ 16 & -12 & 0 & 8 & 34 \end{pmatrix}$$

**Figure 17.10   Scalar product of an array**

Figure 17.11 shows how we can combine scalar multiplication and addition. Of course, the result has just the same format as each of the two arrays.

$$6 \begin{pmatrix} 3 & 2 & 1 \\ 5 & 1 & -3 \end{pmatrix} \qquad +4 \begin{pmatrix} 3 & 1 & -2 \\ -4 & 0 & 6 \end{pmatrix}$$

$$= \begin{pmatrix} 18 & 12 & 6 \\ 30 & 6 & -18 \end{pmatrix} \quad + \quad \begin{pmatrix} 12 & 4 & -8 \\ -16 & 0 & 24 \end{pmatrix}$$

$$= \begin{pmatrix} 30 & 16 & -2 \\ 14 & 6 & 6 \end{pmatrix}$$

**Figure 17.11   Scalar multiplication with addition**

We can also multiply two arrays. However, in order to multiply arrays A and B the number of columns in A must equal the number of rows in B. Otherwise AB has no meaning.

An important outcome of this is that the order of multiplication is of vital importance, (not the case with numbers such as 7 and 58, as $7 \times 58$ is the same as $58 \times 7$).

If A is a 5 row by 4 column array and B is 4 by 3, AB exists – and will have 5 rows and 3 columns. On the other hand, BA has no meaning, as the number of columns in B (3) is not the same as the number of rows in A (5). Again, if A is $2 \times 3$ and B is $3 \times 2$, AB is a $2 \times 2$ array, and BA is $3 \times 3$. Hence, AB is not usually the same as BA in array multiplication.

How can we find the product AB? Study Figure 17.12. **Note**: In arrays, a point sign is used to denote multiplication.

$$A = \begin{pmatrix} 5 & 1 & 4 \\ -3 & 6 & 7 \end{pmatrix} \qquad B = \begin{pmatrix} 4 & 6 \\ 3 & 9 \\ -7 & 5 \end{pmatrix}$$

$$AB = \begin{pmatrix} 5.4 +1.3 +4.-7 & 5.6 +1.9 +4.5 \\ -3.4 +6.3 +7.-7 & -3.6 +6.9 +7.5 \end{pmatrix}$$

$$= \begin{pmatrix} 20 +3 -28 & 30 +9 +20 \\ -12 +18 -49 & -18 +54 +35 \end{pmatrix}$$

$$= \begin{pmatrix} -5 & 59 \\ -43 & 71 \end{pmatrix}$$

**Figure 17.12   Multiplying arrays**

To find the value for row 1 column 1, multiply the elements from row 1 of A by the elements of column 1 of B – leading to $5 \times 4 + 1 \times 3 + 4 \times -7$, then add the products $20 + 3 - 28$ to give $-5$. In the same way, to find the value in row 1 colum 2, multiply the elements from row 1 of A and the elements from column 2 of B – and so on. Figure 17.13 shows how to find the product BA. Please check it.

See Figure 17.2 for A and B

$$
\begin{aligned}
BA \quad = \quad &
\begin{pmatrix}
4.5 & +6.-3 & \quad & 4.1 & +6.6 & \quad & 4.4 & +6.7 \\
3.5 & +9.-3 & & 3.1 & +9.6 & & 3.4 & +9.7 \\
-7.5 & +5.-3 & & -7.1 & +5.6 & & -7.4 & +5.7
\end{pmatrix} \\[2mm]
= \quad &
\begin{pmatrix}
20 & -18 & \quad & 4 & +36 & \quad & 16 & +42 \\
15 & -27 & & 3 & +54 & & 12 & +63 \\
-35 & -15 & & -7 & +30 & & -28 & +35
\end{pmatrix} \\[2mm]
= \quad &
\begin{pmatrix}
2 & 40 & 58 \\
-12 & 57 & 75 \\
-50 & 23 & 7
\end{pmatrix}
\end{aligned}
$$

**Figure 17.13    Finding product BA**

Array multiplication is only valid if the result has meaning. In Figure 17.14, A is the number of each of the items ordered (7 of item 1, 6 of item 2, etc), while B gives the prices of the items ($16 for item 1, $8 for item 2, and so on). So AB gives the total cost of the order (7 articles at $16 each, plus ...); we can work out BA, but it has no meaning.

$$
A \quad = \quad
\begin{pmatrix} 7 & 6 & 12 & 2 \end{pmatrix}
$$

$$
B \quad = \quad
\begin{pmatrix} 16 \\ 8 \\ 5 \\ 9 \end{pmatrix}
$$

$$
\begin{aligned}
\therefore AB &= (7.16 + 6.8 + 12.5 + 2.9) \\
&= (112 + 48 + 60 + 18) \\
&= (238)
\end{aligned}
$$

*The cost of the order is $238*

**Figure 17.14    A meaningful array product**

**NOW TRY THESE ...**

$$A = \begin{pmatrix} 2 & 7 & 3 \\ 8 & 1 & 6 \end{pmatrix} \quad B = \begin{pmatrix} 4 & 0 & 5 \\ 1 & 3 & 7 \end{pmatrix} \quad \text{and} \quad C = \begin{pmatrix} 6 & -1 \\ 2 & 5 \\ 8 & 4 \end{pmatrix}$$

Work out each of the following:

(i)   A + B

(ii)  3A

(iii) 2A – B

(iv)  2B – A

(v)   AC

(vi)  CA

# 18 Using arrays

## OBJECTIVES

When you've worked through this Chapter, you should be able to:

— show how to use arrays for processing product orders and pricing

— outline the nature of a data structure, and the stack, queue and tree

— outline how to use an array to model a stack

— outline how to use an array to model a queue

— outline how to use an array to model a tree

— note some of the features of array (matrix) handling statements.

## INTRODUCTION

### 18.1 ARRAYS FOR PRICING

At the end of Chapter 17, we saw how the product of two arrays can produce the total cost of an order.

Figure 18.1 shows the product of two arrays S and P; each of the four rows of S contains details of the order placed by one customer for each of five products. List P arrays the prices of the five products. SP is the cost matrix C – it gives the cost of the order for each of the four customers, so that customer one has placed an order costing $195 and so on.

$$
\begin{pmatrix}
7 & 5 & 4 & 2 & 8 \\
4 & 3 & 7 & 12 & 2 \\
1 & 0 & 4 & 8 & 3 \\
3 & 8 & 19 & 0 & 2
\end{pmatrix}
\quad
\begin{pmatrix}
8 \\
13 \\
2 \\
9 \\
6
\end{pmatrix}
=
\begin{pmatrix}
1 & 9 & 5 \\
2 & 0 & 5 \\
1 & 0 & 6 \\
1 & 7 & 8
\end{pmatrix}
$$

$$
\text{S} \qquad\qquad \text{P} \;=\; \text{C}
$$

**Figure 18.1   Array multiplication for order costing**

We can extend this to a new array $P_1$ with three columns, each giving the prices of the products at different shops; item one costs $8 each at shop 1, $11 each at shop 2, and $6 each at shop 3. The product $SP_1$ – Figure 18.2 – now produces a 4 × 3 array $C_1$, the cost of each order at each shop; the first column gives the order value at shop 1, the second at shop 2, and so on.

We can see that all the customers get the best deals at shop 2; however, shop 1 is more expensive than shop 3 for the first three orders, but cheaper for customer 4.

$$
\begin{vmatrix}
7 & 5 & 4 & 2 & 8 \\
4 & 3 & 7 & 12 & 2 \\
1 & 0 & 4 & 8 & 3 \\
3 & 8 & 19 & 0 & 2
\end{vmatrix}
\quad
\begin{pmatrix}
8 & 11 & 6 \\
13 & 8 & 12 \\
2 & 3 & 5 \\
9 & 5 & 7 \\
6 & 4 & 5
\end{pmatrix}
\quad = \quad
\begin{pmatrix}
195 & 171 & 176 \\
205 & 157 & 189 \\
106 & 75 & 97 \\
178 & 162 & 219
\end{pmatrix}
$$
$$\phantom{xxxx}S\phantom{xxxxxxxxxxxxx}P_1\phantom{xxxxxxxxxxxxx}C_1$$

**Figure 18.2    Matrix multiplication – prices for three shops**

As people often store prices in table (array) form, the approaches here are quite common. Note once again that the order used for multiplication is critical; neither PS nor $P_1$ S has any meaning.

## 18.2 DATA STRUCTURES

A data structure is a way of holding data in a computer's store, to allow ease of processing. Various structures have advantages in different types of situation.

A stack is a common data structure. In systems software, a stack generally handles, for example, the stages of a calculation or data during processor interrupts; people also use it in translation programs, when evaluating expressions, or unscrambling source code, as well as when passing data from a main program to a sub-program or procedure and vice versa.

Physically a stack is a LIFO structure (last in first out) – it is like a pile of plates; staff add clean plates to the top of the pile and take plates off as required, also from the top. We do not generally take plates from the bottom of the pile because of the obvious physical difficulties, and for the same reason we do not add plates to the bottom either.

The simplest way to represent a stack is to use a one-dimensional array (or list) with two pointers; the first points to the base of the stack (usually fixed) and the second, the stack pointer, defines the address in store of the first available space in the stack. See Figure 18.3.

When we use a list to stand for a stack in this way, the base of the stack pointer will be fixed so as to point to the first element in the list; the stack pointer is free to move up or down (assuming the stack to be vertical) as data items go on to the top of the stack (a process called pushing) or leave the top of the stack (popping).

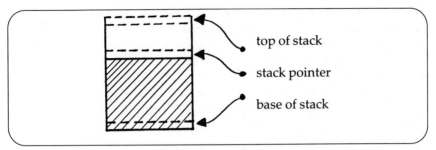

**Figure 18.3    A stack**

Figure 18.4 shows how to push data on to stacks in a program; it assumes that the stack can hold 50 data items, though this varies in practice. So the base of the stack is at S(1), and S(50) gives the top of the stack. Before we can add an item, eg E, to the stack, we must check the stack pointer P to make sure that space exists in the stack – if not, the program must take appropriate action. If space does exist, the item goes on to the stack and the pointer value changes.

Popping the stack in a program involves a similar code.

> Adding an item to the stack (pushing)
>
> NB: Before pushing is possible, the stack pointer must be checked to see if space is still available.
>
> 10   DIM S(50)
> ⋮
> 80  REM ** PUSHING SEQUENCE **
>
> 90   IF P < = 50 THEN 120        } Note: if P>50, the stack is full and the
> 100  PRINT 'STACK FULL'          program must act accordingly
> 110  STOP
> 120  LET S(P) = E                } E is the element being put onto the
> 130  LET P = P + 1               stack. P is incremented
> 140  ....
> ⋮

**Figure 18.4    Pushing data on to a stack**

The queue is another important data structure; it has a FIFO (first in first out) structure – it behaves like a shop queue; the first to join the queue is the first to leave it. In other words, new data items enter at the tail of the queue whereas popping takes place at the head. In a computer, the queue is used for real-time processing, for job scheduling in cases of multi-programming, and for applications such as data transfer.

As in the case of a stack, we can model a queue with a one-dimensional array, or list. As before, we need two pointers, the first to give the address of the front of the queue (the head pointer), and the second for the next available space at the back of the queue (the tail pointer). As items leave and enter the structure, the queue moves towards the end of the array; to prevent the tail pointer passing the end of the space available, the tail "wraps round" at the other end – so it appears to be chasing the head. I show both simple and wrapped round queues in Figure 18.5, with shading for the queue itself.

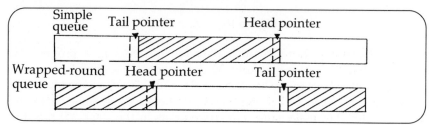

**Figure 18.5    The queue in a one-dimensional array**

Note that there must always be one open space between the tail and the head, so the system can distinguish between an empty and a full queue.

In the Basic coding of Figure 18.6 you can see the removal of a data item from the head of the queue – H and T are the head and tail pointers respectively; E is the item being popped. If H = T, the queue is empty, but if H = 1 (when H is not equal to T), this is a wrapped-round queue and the program must move the head pointer to the other end of the array.

```
Removing an item from the Queue
NB: Check first to see if the queue is empty.
10   DIM Q (50)
  :

200  REM ** REMOVAL SEQUENCE **
205  IF H <> T THEN 220
210  PRINT 'QUEUE EMPTY'
215  STOP
220  LET E = Q (H)
225  IF H = 1 THEN 240
230  LET H = H − 1
235  GO TO 245
240  LET H = 50
245  . . . . . . .
  :
```

**Figure 18.6    Popping an item from a queue array**

It is just as easy to add a data item to the tail of the queue when required.

## 18.3 TREES

The tree is a data structure used especially in system software translation programs and in storing complex data.

To look at a tree, see the structure of Figure 18.7 – it shows how a tree can represent an ordered set of data, numeric or (as in the example) textual.

The first data item (ie the text work "Tree") goes at the top, in the first node of the tree, the so called root node; to the left and to the right of the data item are the left and right pointers.

Since the second item ("diagrams") is alphabetically before the first, place it at a node on the left descendant from the root; to place the third item ("are"), start from the root node, go down left ("are" comes before "tree"), and down left again from "diagrams", since it occurs alphabetically before "diagrams".

In this way, we store all the values – always starting at the root and going down left or right (according to alphabetic sequence in this case) until finding the correct node. Any node with no descendants going down from it is a terminal node.

Having now established a tree structure and how to create a tree, the next stage is to see how to hold it as an array – see Figure 18.8. Each data item, in the order read in ("tree" first, so at node 1; "diagrams" second, so at node 2; etc) has three values associated with it. These values are its actual value (the data item itself), its left pointer (the number of the node to which it descends to the left), and its right pointer. Each node corresponds to the row with the same number in the 9 × 3 array T in Figure 18.8.

Each row holds the left pointer, the data item and the right pointer with −1 if there is no descendant.

For instance, node 4 has a value of "quite", it descends on the left to node 5 (which holds "easy"), and there is no right descendant; you can easily check this against the original tree structure.

However, we may want to create a rather more sophisticated 9 × 5 array A, with the same items in columns 1 to 3, plus a back pointer in column 4. The back pointer gives the address of the node from which the current node has come (its so called parent node). The trace pointer identifies the node whose value would follow the current value if all the data were to be arranged in alphabetic order.

To illustrate this, consider row 6 (for node number 6) in Figure 18.9. Since $A(6,1) = -1$ there is no left descendant; since $A(6,2) = 7$ the right descendant is node 7 ("you"); and $A(6,3) = $ "when", the value. Check

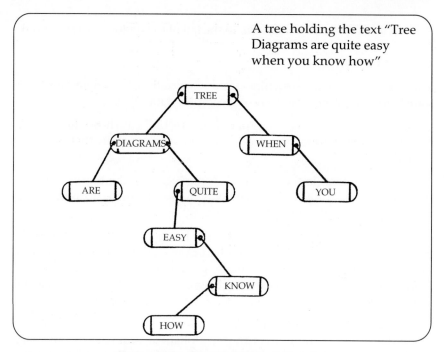

**Figure 18.7    Tree holding string data**

back with Figure 18.7. Now, since A(6,4) = 1, the parent node of
"when" is number 1, the root node itself – so "when" descends directly

| 2 | Tree | 6 |
|---|------|---|
| 3 | Diagrams | 4 |
| −1 | Are | −1 |
| 5 | Quite | −1 |
| −1 | Easy | 8 |
| −1 | When | 7 |
| −1 | You | −1 |
| 9 | Know | −1 |
| −1 | How | −1 |

T (4,1) = 5
etc:
tree held as
9 × 3 array
T

**Figure 18.8    Tree in a 9 × 3 array**

from "tree"; again you can easily check with the diagram.

Try the same checks for other nodes, such as 2 and 8. Note that the back
pointer for node 1 is −1 since it is the root node, and has no parent.

This new version of the tree array takes up more space but offers
additional facilities. Tree processing involves inserting and deleting data
items; it therefore involves adjusting all relevant pointers as well as
searching for specific values; programming such processes is an
interesting exercise.

| LEFT POINTER | RIGHT POINTER | VALUE | BACK POINTER | TRACE POINTER | |
|---|---|---|---|---|---|
| 2 | 6 | Tree | −1 | 6 | |
| 3 | 4 | Diagrams | 1 | 5 | |
| −1 | −1 | Are | 2 | 2 | Tree |
| 5 | −1 | Quite | 2 | 1 | held |
| −1 | 8 | Easy | 4 | 9 | as |
| −1 | 7 | When | 1 | 7 | 9 × 5 |
| −1 | −1 | You | 6 | −1 | array |
| 9 | −1 | Know | 5 | 4 | A |
| −1 | −1 | How | 8 | 8 | |

**Figure 18.9    Tree in a 9 × 4 array**

## NOW TRY THESE . . .

1. Produce a tree diagram to hold the following piece of text
   "Accounting packages include not only the software developed for users"

2. Use a 10 × 3 array to hold the information about the tree diagram of question 1, with left pointer, value, and right pointer in the three columns.

3. Extend this to a 10 × 5 array to show the pointers.

## 18.4 WORKING WITH ARRAYS

Techniques for processing arrays are dealt with fully in the programming book in this series "Programming Techniques and Practice". Here we therefore concentrate on the need for such processing, rather than how to carry it out.

After we have created an array, a requirement is to search it for certain information. This is not a very demanding task from a programming point of view; it consists of nothing more than examining every element in the array, eg on a column by column basis, until the program finds the element sought and can take appropriate action.

In some cases it may be best to use a binary chop if the data items are in some sequence. However, what is at least as important, is to know what you are seeking and why, and to understand the structure of the array and the information it carries.

The 5 column array used for the tree (Figure 18.9) gives some idea of how much information an array can store. Consider the problem of searching it for all terminal nodes; these have −1 for both left and right pointers. Thus the process of finding them involves statements of the form

IF A (ROW,1) = −1 AND A (ROW,2) = −1 THEN . . .

This will successfully carry out the action specified if the row contains a terminal node – and not otherwise.

Sorting an array is another standard process we often need. In the case of the tree array, we may need to list all the elements in order (alphabetically or numerically).

In the case of a queue holding details of the jobs run in a multi-programming system, we may need to sort the queue elements into a priority order, so implying that the system stores a priority level along with the details of each job in the queue.

Multiplying and adding 2-D arrays (matrices) is easy in those program languages with matrix facilities – we can find the product C of matrix A and matrix B by a statement like:

$$MAT\ C = MAT\ A\ *\ MAT\ B$$

This would automatically validate A and B to ensure that the system can multiply them at all; it would produce an appropriate error message in other cases. Other similar statements allow addition, subtraction, and scalar multiplication. In languages without these facilities, it is always possible to program round the difficulties to achieve what you need.

Other 1-D and 2-D array handling routines include merging, where, for instance, we may need to combine two or more lists into one. Again this is fairly easy to program.

In Section 18.1, dealing with product pricing applications, I noted that people don't always store prices in arrays; however, consider the commercial reality.

If you deal with only a small number of product lines, to hold the prices and descriptions in a table in main store provides the fastest possible means of accessing and using the information. On the other hand, a point of sales (POS) application in a supermarket, with many tens of thousands of product lines is more likely to hold the data on disk with high-speed access.

In these cases, the system holds data centrally to service the needs of a large number of checkout points; also we need to update prices and the list of available product lines on a daily basis; change is so dynamic in the retail world. Under such circumstances to hold all the data in a 2-D array would demand far too much central storage space (though some systems compromise between the use of arrays and disk access).

All the same, low-volume applications – such as the storage and use of discount rates, and so on – make extensive use of 2-D arrays.

# 19     Errors in data

## OBJECTIVES

When you've worked through this Chapter, you should be able to:

— list some common transcription and other data input errors

— explain how a fixed data word length can lead to errors in values

— explain, with examples, the nature of truncation, rounding and overflow errors

— work out absolute and relative errors in simple cases.

## INTRODUCTION

A lot of people believe that each value in computer output is 100 per cent accurate. Unfortunately, despite all the hype which surrounds computer sales, this is far from true; there are many reasons why errors appear.

However, not ALL output is inaccurate, of course, and we need to see the situation in perspective. The sources of errors can be controlled or reduced, but rarely can we get rid of them: but on the whole errors at the output stage are minor and can be ignored.

In commercial work, because of the way systems hold data, there tend to be fewer errors than in scientific work, but occasionally (fortunately rarely) a situation arises in which errors become capable of swamping the "true" values.

We can control many of the sources of error, even if we cannot completely remove them. In this chapter we'll look at some major sources of error; Chapter 20 deals with their control.

## 19.1 SOURCE ERRORS

In at least two situations people copy data from one medium to a second. These are:

(i)   at the source data creation stage in a user department

(ii) at the machine-readable form creation stage (data preparation)

Even the most accurate among us is likely to mis-copy occasionally, especially when working with numbers and when working under pressure; even if someone makes only one mistake for every 1000 characters typed (and that is exceptionally accurate), in the many millions of characters which exist in data files, just as many thousands of errors exist. Here are some forms of numerical typing errors. Just the same can occur in character strings.

(a) Single transposition, where one digit changes places with another: eg 237426 becomes 273426

(b) Double transposition, where three digits "move round": eg 963847 becomes 938647

(c) Inclusion of an extra digit: eg 21356 becomes 213456

(d) Loss of a digit: eg 9476305 becomes 946305

(e) Repeating a digit (a special case of (c)): eg 274889 becomes 2748889

(f) Other "random" errors: eg 28743 becomes 28643; 3824 becomes 37624

Other mistakes can occur in user departments. These include *actual* errors as distinct from copying errors, for example, putting down a wrong price (rather than mis-copying the correct one), or claiming to have worked for fewer hours in a week than is the case.

We can often prevent these latter mistakes (some of which may be deliberate) only by the design of the system as a whole – ensuring, for example, that a supervisor checks and countersigns all source documents when they relate to hours of work, or establishing a computerised control system with some sort of clocking on/clocking off routines so work is machine logged. System design has a great deal to do with the process of establishing controls to prevent potential abuse.

## 19.2 ERRORS FROM FINITE WORD LENGTH

In Chapters 3 and 4 we met the word as a unit of transfer and storage; and looked at some of the problems caused by fractional values. Let us now look at some of these problems in greater detail.

### 19.2.1 Truncation errors

Truncation, or "rounding down", involves removing any excess digits at the least significant end of a number so it can fit the space available. As the lost digits go from the less significant end of the number, the number stored is always less than or equal to the value before truncation took place.

If this happens with a single data value, the problem is unlikely to be serious. If, however, a large number of different truncations take place during a calculation, the effect might become cumulative and cause serious loss of accuracy.

Truncation will either decrease or increase the result of a calculation – depending on whether the quantity truncated is in the numerator or the denominator of a fraction, or whether it is added or subtracted.

To illustrate this, consider the expression $\dfrac{a+b}{c-d}$.

$a = 3.62841$, $b = 5.38634$, $c = 8.32174$ and $d = 8.31079$

The accurate result follows dividing 9.01475 by 0.01095, which is 823.26484. However, if the values of $a$, $b$, $c$ and $d$ are each truncated to three decimal places to fit a store, they would become $a = 3.628$, $b = 5.386$, $c = 8.321$ and $d = 8.310$; this time $\dfrac{a+b}{c-d}$ involves dividing 9.014 by 0.011, giving a solution of 819.454 (to 3 d.p.). This second result is 3.8102946 less than the exact value which indicates an error of well over 0.5%. The individual percentage errors in $a$, $b$, $c$ and $d$ are, respectively, 0.011%, 0.006%, 0.009% and 0.009%, but the effect of these relatively small errors, in total some 0.035%, is to produce an error in the result about fourteen times larger.

This type of error may be, in fact, much greater than you may think. Work through Figure 19.1, for instance. Here a possible error in one value of below 5% leads to an error in the result of well over 100%.

> Solve $105x + 100y = 305$
> $\qquad kx + 99y = 303$
> where $k = 105 \pm 5$
> (ie, the possible error in k is 4.76%).
> If k takes the central value 105, the solution is
> $x = 1$, $y = 2$.
> BUT, if $k = 100$ (its lower limit) we have
> $105x + 100y = 305$
> $100x + \ \ 99y = 303$
> This gives $x = -0.2658. \ldots$
> $y = 3.329 \ldots$
> Thus a 4.76% error in K gives an error of 126.58% in x and an error of 66.45% in y.

**Figure 19.1   Compounding an error**

### 19.2.2 Rounding errors

Rounding a number up will always tend to increase its value, just as rounding down (or truncation) always tends to reduce the value. The circumstances and the effects are much like those of truncation.

In general, however, we round off – rounding up if this causes the least change of value, and rounding down if that causes the least change. Proper rounding causes 7.325 to become 7.32 (to 2 decimal places) but 7.335 to become 7.34: (This is fairer than always rounding up to the nearest as is common). The rule is that if the last digit to be kept after rounding (in this case the second place of decimals) is even, we round the 5 down, whereas if it is odd we round the 5 up; in either case the last figure is even afterwards.

### 19.2.3 Overflow errors

Truncation and rounding errors both involve loss of accuracy at the least significant (right-hand) end of a number. However, overflow happens when a value becomes too large for the space available, then truncation occurs at the most significant (left-hand) end. For instance, if you declare a numeric field in a Cobol program to have a picture (maximum size) of 999 and try to store 2734 in it, the system will truncate the 2 and leave 734. Overflow errors are clearly very serious so control over them is vital.

Decimary (denary) to binary conversion has an effect too. Since numbers are held in a computer store in binary, when the system converts input decimal fractions to binary fractions, the conversion may not be exact, and, as a result, some truncation will occur. Using the truncated value in calculation will lead to a series of "knock-on" errors, and the output will not have the correct decimal value.

Thus if we have to store the exact decimal fraction 0.3 (which has a binary value of 0.0100 1100 1......) in six bits it will become 0.0100 11, whose decimal value is 0.296875 – a conversion error has occurred.

Sometimes we can carry out a calculation by two or more different methods, each essentially correct – yet one may produce a more accurate result than the other(s). We say that this method has a smaller algorithmic error; usually it involves a smaller number of stages; since rounding and truncation errors tend to build up at each stage, the process with the smallest number of stages is most likely to lead to the least error.

People often associate errors with fractions (except for overflow). However, integer values too can suffer truncation and rounding errors. Also the use of floating-point format can lead to error.

Consider the storage (in decimal) of the 27594 in a floating-point format with only four places for the mantissa. In such a case the value would become $+0.2759 \times 10^5$ – giving an immediate error, since 27594 is stored as though it were 27590.

### 19.3 RELATIVE AND ABSOLUTE ERRORS

Absolute error is the difference between the correct value of a number and the value used to store it.

In looking at conversion errors, we saw that 0.3 in binary may be really stored as 0.296875; in this case the absolute error is

$$\text{value stored} - \text{true value} = 0.296875 - 0.3$$
$$= -0.003125$$

We define relative error as absolute error/true value. The same example gives a relative error of $-0.003125/0.3 = -0.0104166 \ (-1.04166\%)$.

**NOW TRY THESE . . . .**

1. Check the forms of transcription error listed in 19.1. Identify the errors in:

   (a)  428714 becoming 42874

   (b)  7963528 becoming 7693528

   (c)  295374 becoming 2953174

   (d)  526317 becoming 563217

   (e)  73942 becoming 73742

2. (a) Calculate the value of $\dfrac{a + b}{c - d}$ as accurately as possible, when $a = 5.42365$, $b = 2.01437$, $c = 6.23915$, and $d = 6.23794$. Quote your answer correct to four significant figures.

   (b) Repeat the calculation in (a), but this time truncate the values of $a$, $b$, $c$ and $d$ to three decimal places each, before you evaluate the expression. Again quote the result correct to four significant figures.

   (c) Compare your answers to (a) and (b), and calculate the percentage error in (b) correct to three significant figures.

3. Express each of the following values (i) rounded up to two decimal places, (ii) to the nearest integer, (iii) truncated to one decimal place, and (iv) rounded off to two decimal places.

   (a)  4.3718

   (b)  3.9204

   (c)  8.0043

   (d)  7.0992

4. A COBOL data field has a picture of 999. State what it will contain if we attempt to store into it

   (a)  374.8

   (b)  729.17

   (c)  2147

   (d)  53916

5. (a) Express the decimal fraction 0.7 as a binary fraction, rounded off to six binary places.

(b)  Convert back to a decimal fraction the answer to part (a).

(c)  Express the error that results from this process, as a percentage correct to three decimal places.

# 20  Error control

## OBJECTIVES

When you've worked through this Chapter, you should be able to:

— explain the process of verification

— explain the process of validation, with simple examples

— state the nature and usage of check digits and work out simple examples

— note how to reduce rounding errors

— note how choice of algorithm can reduce errors in calculation.

## INTRODUCTION

In Chapter 19, we looked at some ways in which errors can occur in source documents, storage, and processing. Now we consider how we can control some of these errors. A number of the methods are aspects of total systems design, and most are quite straightforward and easy to understand and to implement.

## 20.1 TRANSCRIPTION ERRORS AND VERIFICATION

When a user department sends data to the computer area it is usually on source documents; these tend to get mislaid, so before they leave the department, it is normal practice to fill out a batch control slip for each batch of source documents.

On this control slip there may be two totals. The first may state how many documents are in the batch, while the second gives the result of summing a selected field on each document in the batch.

These totals allow the computing department to make an automatic check on receipt. The first value ensures that if any documents are mislaid, people know about it; the second is of value for checking data entry at the keyboarding stage.

The next stage is creating machine readable data in the data preparation area; then verification takes place to attempt to detect errors in transcription.

When all the data of the batch is entered, the values are checked in one of two ways, preferably by a second person (who is less likely to repeat any mistakes made by the first keyboard operator). The first way involves visually checking each record on screen against the source document; the second involves re-typing the data from the documents, but with the machine set to "verify" mode.

When the keys are pressed with the machine in "verify" mode, the system compares the values against the data already held. If it is not the same, the machine requests correction before going on.

In this way, most transcription errors are eliminated "off-line", before the file goes for processing. There is no guarantee that verification will find all errors – both operators might mis-read the source document in the same way, or an error may originate in the user department (which means that neither operator is likely to detect it).

Since most of these errors are "human", it is hard to do any better than eliminate most of them. Frustrating though it is, this is one area of computer accuracy in which we can achieve less than perfect control. It is important, therefore, not only to carry out verification, but also to design the whole system as carefully as possible to minimise the number of errors.

## 20.2 VALIDATION

Above, we dealt with checks that can reduce errors off-line.

Once data is in a machine-readable format, normally on disks or tape, program-controlled validation can check data on-line. Almost certainly there will be errors in the stored data; some of these could not have been detected by verification. (For instance, if a code number appeared wrongly on the source document, the operators can not be blamed for transcribing it as seen.)

Usually, batch systems include a full program for validation; this "data vet" program accepts as input the unchecked source data and outputs a file of checked, more error-free data plus a report of all records not output to that file because they contain errors. This gives staff the opportunity to correct reported errors.

Figure 20.1 is typical of a data vet carried out as part of a batch system.

In the case of interactive and real-time (non-batch) processing, the system must validate each record as it comes in, and return errors at once to the user, before processing.

Validation consists of establishing a series of criteria of "reasonableness" for each field; the criteria will vary for different situations – here are some examples.

— Data in a field must actually be present.

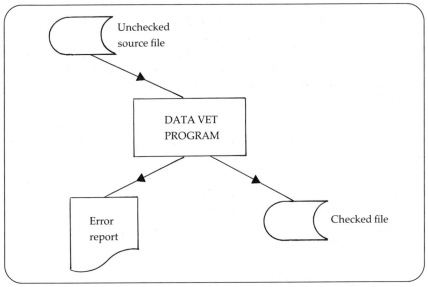

**Figure 20.1    Data vet in a batch system**

— Each character in a numeric field must be a digit, 0 to 9, or a point or a minus sign.

— A numeric field must lie within a certain range – for example, "number of hours worked in a week" may have to lie between 35 to 65.

— A field may have to contain a set number of characters – for example, an account number may be exactly six digits.

— To be valid a field may have to contain certain characters in given places.

— A reference (eg part) number may have to satisfy check-digit rules (see below).

— A date may have to appear in six-digit form, such as 420713 (yymmdd); where yy must lie between 00 and 99 in all cases, mm between 01 and 12, and dd between 01 and 31. More effective validation will pick up 420229 as impossible too.

Examples of some of these tests appear in Figure 20.3.

Once again – just because a data item satisfies all the programs validation tests, it still may not be correct. If a birthdate appears on a form as 420713 when the person's real birthdate is 370713, neither verification nor validation can pick up the error. In such cases, the only real checks which can succeed lie in the user department, and make up an important aspect of systems design.

Check digits are a type of validation system. If we create a six-digit customer account number, we must clearly guard against it being quoted incorrectly, to prevent the wrong customer being billed for an order.

One way to do this is to add a seventh digit – a check digit – according to some agreed algorithm. The method described here is not the only one – but the approach is typical

To each of the six digits we allocate a "weight" – seven (7) for the first, six (6) for the second, and so on, down to two (2) for the sixth, on a left to right basis. Next, multiply each digit by its weight and add the products to form a total. Divide this by 11 (chosen as the "modulus" for the system), and subtract the remainder from the modulus, 11. This gives the check digit, which now becomes the seventh digit of the account number. See Figure 20.2.

If the number has four digits instead of six, we'd use then weights of five (5), four (4), three (3) and two (2) and work out a fifth check digit as before. We can handle any length of number by a similar method.

Although 11 was chosen as the modulus, there are other possibilities such as 13, 17 and 19 – prime numbers of size 11 or greater. However, even using 11 as the modulus means the check digit might turn out to be 10; in such cases people often quote it as X to give a single "digit".

To obtain the check digit for 831405

Multiply each digit by its weighting
$$8 \times 7 = 56$$
$$3 \times 6 = 18$$
$$1 \times 5 = 5$$
$$4 \times 4 = 16$$
$$0 \times 3 = 0$$
$$5 \times 2 = 10$$
Sum of products 105
Divide sum by modulus:
$$105 \div 11 = 9, \text{ remainder } 6$$
Subtract remainder from modulus
$$11 - 6 = 5 \text{ Check digit is 5}$$
full number is 8314055

**Figure 20.2    Working out a check digit**

Having obtained a reference number with a check digit, it is easy for software to check that any input reference number matches the rules, this greatly helps reduce the problems of transposition of digits, etc.

In Figure 20.3 various common examples of validation systems are used starting with the check digit. Most apply to numeric fields; similar methods exist to validate input strings.

Validation examples

① Check digits (using modulus II and weightings
   of 5,4,3,2)
   The five-digit number 27103 (in which 3 is the
   check digit) is valid.
   The five-digit number 86043 is not valid.
② 39246 is numeric, but 39z64 is not.
③ For a field supposed to have six digits
   290156 is valid – 29156 is not.
④ If a rate of pay must lie between 5·50
   and 12·75, 6·38 is valid but 4·32 is not, nor is 13·65.
⑤ If a stock number must begin with
   A or B, followed by three digits, A805 is valid, as is B647 – but
   C926 is not, nor is A12.

**Figure 20.3    Examples of validation**

## 20.3 ROUNDING ERRORS

Although we can never completely eradicate rounding errors (Section
19.2), we can restrict their effects as follows.

— Never truncate or round up exclusively – both will distort results
   over time; instead, always round off. This will lead to fairly
   unbiased rounding and ensure that stored values are neither
   consistently low (the result of truncation) nor consistently high
   (that of rounding up all the time). Rounding off the parts of an
   answer tends to balance the errors with, in effect, about as many
   truncations as roundings up.

   (In binary, rounding off is even easier than in decimal - to round
   off to five binary places, for instance, round down if the sixth place
   holds 0 and up if it holds 1).

— In floating-point arithmetic use the same rule of rounding. Note
   that in such cases, the errors are worse if they affect the value of
   the exponent.

— Minimise conversion errors in the same way.

— Always use the maximum space available for holding intermediate
   results, to keep absolute errors as small as possible and avoid the
   effects of error build-up. This applies even in cases where the final
   result has to be quoted to only one or two decimal places.

Add together 0·003574 + 0·002807
+ 0·019276 + 0·154308
① Exact value is 0·179965
② Add in descending order:
(a) 0·154308 + 0·019276 = 0.173584
= 0·174 (to 3s.f.)
(b) 0·174 + 0·003574 = 0.177574
= 0·178 (to 3s.f.)
(c) 0·178 + 0·002807 = 0·180807
= 0·181 (to 3s.f.)
③ Add in ascending order:
(a) 0·002807 + 0·003574 = 0·006381
= 0·00638 (to 3s.f.)
(b) 0·00638 + 0·019276 = 0·025656
= 0·0257 (to 3s.f.)
(c) 0·0257 + 0·154308   = 0·180008
= 0·180 (to 3s.f.)

**Figure 20.4    Order of operations – rounding techniques**

We can further reduce the effects of rounding errors if we add (or subtract) a set of values in ascending order of size. Figure 20.4 shows how to add four values of very different size in three different ways. The first way is exact; in this case the order doesn't matter. The second involves using the four quantities in descending order of magnitude, rounding at each stage to three significant figures (s.f.); the third method involves the same level of rounding, but this time handling the values in ascending sequence.

It is clear that the third result is closer to the true value. While the "descending order" approach is not *always* the worse, it is mostly safer to use the "ascending order" approach.

## 20.4 HANDLING ALGORITHMIC ERRORS

In Chapter 19, we saw that the choice of algorithm to solve a problem often influences the accuracy of the result – even if each algorithm is valid for the problem. If the algorithm involves working out fractions or other values in which rounding errors may occur, these errors may build up and lead to an unacceptable level of inaccuracy.

Consider a program loop with a loop counter X; this is to start at 0 and go up to 8 in steps of decimal 0.1. The arithmetic is to use six binary places, with rounding at each stage to correct the value to five places. The five-bit binary value for decimal 0.1 is 0.00011 – this already produces a sizeable error, since it equals decimal 0.09375 (rather than 0.1).

Look at the first two columns of Figure 20.5. You can see the effect on X of these errors at each step; by step 10, X ought to be exactly 1 (since it should be 0 + 10 × 0.1) – but in fact it is rather less. By step 20 it should be exactly 2 (binary 10), but it is in fact decimal 1.875. So if the program uses the values of X for calculations within the loop, there are likely to be considerable errors.

| | loop counter values | |
|---|---|---|
| STEP | FIRST METHOD | SECOND METHOD |
| 1 | 0.00011 | 0.00011 |
| 2 | 0.00110 | 0.00110 |
| 3 | 0.01001 | 0.01001 |
| 4 | 0.01100 | 0.01100 |
| 5 | 0.01111 | 0.01111 |
| 6 | 0.10010 | 0.10010 |
| 7 | 0.10101 | 0.10101 |
| 8 | 0.11000 | 0.11000 |
| 9 | 0.11011 | 0.11011 |
| 10 | 0.11110 | 1.00000 |
| 11 | 1.00001 | 1.00011 |
| 12 | 1.00100 | 1.00110 |
| 13 | 1.00111 | 1.01001 |
| 14 | 1.01010 | 1.01100 |
| 15 | 1.01101 | 1.01111 |
| 16 | 1.10000 | 1.10010 |
| 17 | 1.10011 | 1.10101 |
| 18 | 1.10110 | 1.11000 |
| 19 | 1.11001 | 1.11011 |
| 20 | 1.11100 | 10.00000 |
| 21 | 1.11111 | 10.00011 |
| 22 | 10.00010 | 10.00110 |

Figure 20.5   Program loop with cumulative errors

We could, however, control the loop with an integer counter C, going up in steps of 1 from 0 to 80 inclusive; then we can find X as C/10 at each stage. The third column of Figure 20.5 contains the values of X that result; they still contain some error, but by step 10 the error has vanished, and again at step 20. Hence, although the intermediate values may indeed not be exact, the second method can certainly produce far more accurate results from step 10 onwards. Whereas the error in the first method becomes progressively worse in absolute terms, the error in the second never exceeds the worst case (that at step 9).

One lesson to be learned from this is clearly to use as much integer calculation as possible, converting from integer to fractional value only when you need to.

## 20.5  NESTING METHODS

If we had to calculate the value of the polynomial expression $4x^3 - 7x^2 + 5x + 19$ for any given value of $x$, then there would be potentially several different calculations to be undertaken, each of which will contain a source of error if $x$ is non-integral, so the number of rounding errors could lead to a great deal of inaccuracy. This clearly would be compounded still further if the polynomial had to be evaluated for each one of a range of $x$-values.

In order to compensate for this it is possible to 'nest' the expression as follows:

$$4x^3 - 7x^2 + 5x + 19$$
$$= (4x^2 - 7x + 5) x + 19$$
$$= ((4x - 7) x + 5) x + 19$$

in which a linear expression $4x - 7$ is nested inside another and so on. The calculation is shown in Figure 20.6.

To evaluate $4x^3 - 7x^2 + 5x + 19$
for $x = 3.6$ use $((4x - 7) x + 5) x + 19$
and compute from $4x - 7$ outwards:
$((14.4 - 7) * 3.6 + 5) * 3.6 + 19$
$= (7.4 * 3.6 + 5) * 3.6 + 19$
$= (26.64 + 5) * 3.6 + 19$
$= 31.64 * 3.6 + 19$
$= 113.904 + 19$
$= 132.904$

To evaluate $8x^2 + 5x - 6$
Use $(8x + 5) x - 6$, etc.

To evaluate $9x^4 - 7x^3 + 4x^2 + 5x - 3$
Use $(((9x - 7) x + 4) x + 5) x - 3$
etc.

**Figure 20.6   Nesting methods**

This approach allows for a reduction in the number of calculations that have to be accomplished at each stage and so will tend to reduce the amount of error that may arise. Even if integral values of $x$ do not lead to error risks the nesting method does provide for a faster means of evaluating such polynomials in all cases. In particular, this method is valuable in cases where the expression has to be calculated within a loop for a large number of different $x$-values; apart from being less error-prone it is also faster and well-suited to calculator usage even if a computer is not being used.

## 20.6   TO CONCLUDE

Some errors, regrettably, are unavoidable – but the purpose of these two chapters is to identify areas in which errors are most likely to occur, and some methods to contain them.

Human errors will always be present in some measure, but good system design, and verification and validation can cut them down, if not make then vanish.

Errors cause by a computer's word size are also unavoidable; hand-held calculators suffer from the same drawback. Whenever you have a lengthy calculation to do, remember the value of algorithm design.

### NOW TRY THESE . . .

1. A stock-code is valid if it is six characters long, starts with an alphabetic character, and has the remaining characters numeric. Which of the following are valid stock-codes?
   (a) A7197
   (b) 123759
   (c) P26471
   (d) T328X6

2. Using a modulus of 13 and a weighting system in which the $N^{th}$ digit from the right has a weight of $N$ (eg weights of 5, 4, 3, 2, 1 respectively for a five-digit number), which of the following satisfy the check-digit criteria?
   (a) 90254
   (b) 7342
   (c) 60135
   (d) 58271

3. Using a modulus of 11 and the same weighting system as question 2, find suitable check digits to add on to each of the following:
   (a) 7539
   (b) 62817

4. A record contains three fields to be validated. Field A must be numeric and between 25 and 75 inclusive; field B must be six characters long (with both first and last alphabetic); and field C must

be a four digit numeric quantity that satisfies a modulus 17 check-digit routine using the weighting system of question 2. Decide which of the following records are fully valid.

| Record | Field A | Field B | Field C |
|--------|---------|---------|---------|
| P      | 84      | A3625X  | 5305    |
| Q      | 71      | A77396  | 7178    |
| R      | 34      | B2914A  | 2300    |
| S      | 5T      | D26114C | 6425    |

5. Round off each of the following binary fractions to four binary places:
   (a) 0.001101
   (b) 1.011010
   (c) 0.010110
   (d) 1.000101

6. Add 0.036284, 0.91738, 0.002596 and 0.007423, giving your answer correct to four decimal places. **Hint**: consider the order of addition.

7. Nest each of the following expressions:
   (a) $8x^2 - 7x + 5$
   (b) $4x^3 - 3x^2 + 7x + 2$
   (c) $4x^3 + 7x + 2$

8. Nest the expression $5x^3 - 7x^2 + 3x - 6$. Use the nested version to obtain the value of the expression when $x = 2.7$.

## REVISION EXERCISES D

This set of revision questions relates to the contents of chapters 14 to 20, and also sometimes requires techniques found in other parts of the text. Thus it serves to integrate the whole of the subject matter.

### First example

(a) A supplier of computer media sells two packs of materials for cleaning floppy disk drives. The economy pack contains one bottle of cleaning fluid, five tissue cleaners and one cleaning disk. The standard pack contains three bottles of fluid, 20 tissue cleaners and two cleaning disks.

   (i)   Express this information as a 2 × 3 array Q.

         A bottle of cleaning fluid costs $1.20, a tissue cleaner costs $0.50 and a cleaning disk costs $3.50.

   (ii)  Express this information as a column array P.

   (iii) Calculate the product QP.

   (iv)  What is the cost of four economy packs and three standard packs?

(b) (i)  You have three large numbers A, B and C. Explain why it is better to calculate A/B*C rather than A*C/B.

(ii)  Compare BCD arithmetic with floating point arithmetic with regard to space used, accuracy and speed.

(iii) Describe overflow. Show how overflow can occur in 8 bit integer arithmetic, using 120 + 64 as an example.

## Solution

Parts a) and b) refer to quite different parts of the course; treat them separately. Casting an eye straight ahead into sub-part (i), we see at once the key-word "array" – this alerts us to the essential subject of part (a). All we are told before (i) is a set of facts about the contents of each of two packs which contain three types of item in them – that shows the relevance of how the question describes the array Q. Perhaps the only other factor to recall is how a $2 \times 3$ array and a $3 \times 2$ array differ. Since Q is $2 \times 3$, it has 2 rows and 3 columns – remember this when setting out the data. Thus it is absolutely straightforward to write out Q like this:

$$Q = \begin{pmatrix} 1 & 5 & 1 \\ 3 & 20 & 2 \end{pmatrix}$$

The order of the elements *within* each row matches the order in which they appear in the text; in just the same way the order of the rows (economy size followed by standard size) matches the order given in the question.

Text inserted between parts of a question usually provides *additional* information; in this case ii) is about this extra information, while iii) uses the results of both i) and ii).

Part ii) asks for a column array – be sure, therefore, that what you offer is a column, and not a row array. The result is

$$P = \begin{pmatrix} 1.20 \\ 0.50 \\ 3.50 \end{pmatrix}$$

Here the order of the elements matches that of the *row* elements in Q as defined earlier – we keep the order of "fluid", "tissue", "disk" (if this were not the case, later calculations would have no meaning at all).

Part (iii) asks you to calculate the product QP. Remember first that we can have such a product only if the number of columns in Q is the same as the number of rows in P – in our example both figures are 3 so that the calculation can go ahead. (The product PQ is not defined: the number of columns in P is not the same as the number of rows in Q.) While this type of checking may seem a nuisance, it can save you from falling into quite simple traps.

Having checked that there is a definable result of the product QP, the next step is to carry out what is now quite straightforward arithmetic. We have :–

$$QP= \begin{pmatrix} 1 & 5 & 1 \\ 3 & 20 & 2 \end{pmatrix} \begin{pmatrix} 1.20 \\ 0.50 \\ 3.50 \end{pmatrix} = \begin{pmatrix} 1\times1.20+5\times0.50+1\times3.50 \\ 3\times1.20+20\times0.50+2\times3.50 \end{pmatrix} = \begin{pmatrix} 7.20 \\ 20.60 \end{pmatrix}$$

(Since we are finding the product of a 2 × 3 and a 3 × 1 matrix, we expect the result to be a 2 × 1 matrix, as indeed is the case.)

In order to answer (iv) the intention was for you to use the result of (iii), a "cost" array telling us that the economy pack costs $7.20 whilst the standard size pack comes at $20.60. We could express the data about the numbers of each pack as a row array (4 3) and multiply the cost array by this to produce:

$$\begin{pmatrix} 4 & 3 \end{pmatrix} \begin{pmatrix} 7.20 \\ 20.60 \end{pmatrix} = (4 \times 7.20 + 3 \times 20.60) = (90.60)$$

Again we should check first that such a product exists and also what 'shape' this product would have (the product of a 1 × 2 and a 2 × 1 is 1 × 1). The final result is a cost of $90.60.

However, some students may not think of how to use arrays to solve this part of the question; they may well find the cost of four of a $7.20 pack plus three of a $20.60 pack. This may not be what was wanted, but if it gives the correct answer it satisfies the needs of the question as set. On the other hand, if the question had said "use arrays to calculate the cost of four economy packs and three standard packs", no marks would follow finding the answer without their use.

Part (b) of the question is very different – it has nothing to do with arrays.

Part (i) deals with the order of doing calculations: clearly A/B$^*$C ought to have exactly the same value as A$^*$C/B. The problem relates to the finite size available for doing arithmetic within the computer. With A and C both large, the product will be very large – maybe too big to fit exactly inside the system. Then what goes into storage is not exactly A$^*$C, but an approximation to it; dividing by B will give an inaccurate value.

On the other hand, to work out A/B first is not likely to lead to an error of this kind; if A and B are both large, their quotient will not be particularly large, so the system can hold it with a reasonable level of accuracy, and multiplying by C will not lead to the same problem.

Thus, the A$^*$C/B calculation is more likely to create overflow and potentially serious errors than finding A/B$^*$C.

The BCD and floating point comparisons require a knowledge of each method and the difficulties it gives. Hence in answering (ii), refer to the following main points:

— BCD needs more bits than floating point

— BCD is exactly accurate and has no possible sources of error - floating point methods frequently involve approximations based on the space available for exponent and mantissa

— BCD arithmetic is always slower than floating point

— floating point is not *exact* when working, especially with decimal values; so leads to rounding errors.

Floating point arithmetic uses fewer bits for the same size quantity and so has a greater range of values within the same bit space than BCD can do.

Do note you need not attempt to decide which method is better – this depends on which factors are most relevant for the situation, and so on the advantages and disadvantages to decide that case on its merits.

To answer (iii) note that overflow is merely the situation which occurs when a calculation leads to a result too large for the storage space available. The calculation may be addition or multiplication but these are not the only processes which lead to overflow.

To illustrate this, consider adding 120 and 64 using 8 bits for each (and for the result). In binary, 120 is 0111 1000 and 64 is 0100 0000; thus

$$
\begin{array}{r}
0111\ 1000 \\
\underline{0100\ 0000} + \\
1011\ 1000
\end{array}
$$

1011 1000 is a negative value (the leading bit, the sign bit, is 1), in fact -72. Clearly this is not the correct sum of 120 and 64! With only eight bits available, the range of values the system can hold is -128 to +127 only; adding 120 and 64 leads to 184, which is outside this range, so cannot be handled in this way. Overflow has taken place.

### Second Example

(a) A company sells disks of type A and B, 3.5″ and 5.25″ diameter respectively, in boxes of ten. If five boxes of A and three boxes of B cost $66, while three boxes of A and four boxes of B cost $55, what is the cost of one box of each type?

(b) A 3″ disk, type C, is now offered. A group of 33 customers led to the following sales: 15 bought A, 18 bought B and 13 bought C, while one bought all three, five bought B and C, seven bought only A, and twice as many bought both A and B as bought both A and C. Represent this as a Venn diagram with all sets enumerated.

(c) One firm buys a total of 200 boxes of A, B and C in the ratios 2:3:5.

   (i)   How many boxes of each type do they buy?

   (ii)  The new prices of the disks are in the ratio 5:7:8 for A, B and
         C. If the cost of disks of type A is then cut by 10%, what will be
         the percentage reduction in the user's bill for the 200 boxes? Give
         your answer correct to one decimal place.

### Solution

Part (a) deals solely with solving a pair of simultaneous equations – there
are two unknowns (the costs of each of the two types of box), and two
sets of information about these two unknowns. First define the
unknowns as, perhaps, a and b – $a is the cost of a box of disks type A,
while $b is that of a box of type B. Now we convert the two sets of
information into equations (i) and (ii).

$$5a + 3b = 66 \quad \text{(i)}$$
$$3a + 4b = 55 \quad \text{(ii)}$$

There is no single way of going forward to eliminate either a or b from (i)
and (ii). Let us multiply (i) by 4 and (ii) by 3 – then after multiplication,
both equations have 12b terms in them. (We might, just as well, have
multiplied (i) by 3 and (ii) by 5, so that both equations would have a 15a
term.) The results are:–

$$20a + 12b = 264 \quad \text{(iii)}$$
$$9a + 12b = 165 \quad \text{(iv)}$$

Take (iv) from (iii) to get:

$$11a = 99$$

Division by 11 gives:

$$a = 9$$

Use this value to substitute into either (i) or (ii). Using (i) gives:

$$45 + 3b = 66$$

so that $\qquad 3b = 66 - 45 = 21$

and $\qquad b = 7$

Now we put a = 9 and b = 7 into equation (ii) as a check. (Do not use (i)
as that gave us b). In the check, the left-hand side gives $3 \times 9 + 4 \times 7 =$
$27 + 28 = 55$; since this is the same as the right-hand side, the solution
appears correct. Hence a box of type A costs $9 and a box of type B costs
$7.

Part b) introduces a third type of disk. However, the key to tackling the
question is in (b)(i), with the phrase 'represent . . . as a Venn diagram'.
Since there are three types of disk in use, and clients can choose A or B

or C or any mixture, we face a straight-forward triple intersection of three sets. It seems only sensible to call these A, B and C. The diagram includes all we know about the buying patterns listed:-

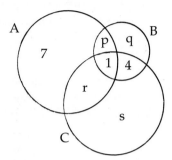

We cannot fill all seven of the zones in the Venn diagram, but three have data, and the others carry unknowns p, q, r and s. Now, 15 people bought type A, so that $7 + p + 1 + r = 15$, which leads to

　　　(i)　　$p + r = 7$

18 bought type B, so $p + q + 1 + 4 = 18$, which gives

　　　(ii)　$p + q = 13$

Also 13 bought type C, so $r + s + 1 + 4 = 13$, which leads to

　　　(iii) $r + s = 8$

Since "twice as many bought both A and B as bought A and C", it follows that

　　　(iv)　$p + 1 = 2(r + 1)$

or　　　　　$p + 1 = 2r + 2$

ie　　(v)　　$p = 2r + 1$

Using $p = 2r + 1$ in (i) leads us to

　　　　$2r + 1 + r = 7$

or　　　$3r = 6$, from which $r = 2$. Using this in equation (v) produces $p = 5$. Putting that in turn into (ii) gives

　　　$5 + q = 13$ or $q = 8$. Finally, using $r = 2$ in (iii) leads to $2 + s = 8$ or $s = 6$.

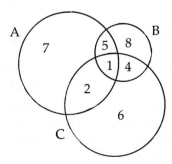

As a final check, put all the values into the Venn diagram and see if they total 33, as required.

To work on part c), we start with a straightforward problem on ratios – there are 2 + 3 + 5 = 10 parts totalling 200 which means that each part must be 20 boxes. Hence 40 boxes of type A, 60 of B and 100 of C are bought – all that is needed for (i).

To deal with (ii), we recognise that we know nothing about these new prices other than that they are in the ratios 5:7:8. If we take the new price of a box of type A to be $5x, the prices of B and C must of $7x and $8x respectively.

Thus the cost of the 200 boxes is

$$40 \times 5x + 60 \times 7x + 100 \times 8x$$

This comes to 200x + 420x + 800x or $1420x. If the price of type A goes down by 10%, the reduction is 10% of 200x dollars or 20x dollars. The percentage cut in the user's bill must now be $\frac{100 \times 20x}{1420x}$ % or $\frac{2000}{1420} = 1.4\%$

### Third example

The correct functioning of a machine is monitored by three lamps A, B and C. The machine is working if one of the following conditions holds

> all 3 bulbs are lit
> all 3 bulbs are out
> A is lit and ONE of B or C is out
> C is lit and A is out

i)   Produce a Boolean expression to represent when the machine is working.

ii)  Show that you can simplify this Boolean expression to $A.B + \bar{A}.\bar{B} + C$. It is now intended to automate the monitoring of the machine by producing an electronic component. Consisting of AND , OR and NOT logic, this will produce a signal when the machine is NOT working correctly.

iii) Produce a Logic network diagram for this component.

### Solution

The essence of nearly all questions of this type is to start off with the appropriate truth table (see below); A, B and C are the inputs in the process, and the correct working of the machine D is the output. We need a table to show all the possible combinations of values of A, B and C, and the relevant value of D for each

| A | B | C | D |
|---|---|---|---|
| 0 | 0 | 0 | 1 |
| 0 | 0 | 1 | 1 |
| 0 | 1 | 0 | 0 |
| 0 | 1 | 1 | 1 |
| 1 | 0 | 0 | 0 |
| 1 | 0 | 1 | 1 |
| 1 | 1 | 0 | 1 |
| 1 | 1 | 1 | 1 |

**Truth table**

This tells us $D = \bar{A}.\bar{B}.\bar{C} + \bar{A}.\bar{B}.C + \bar{A}.B.C + A.\bar{B}.C + A.B.\bar{C} + A.B.C$. This is the Boolean expression needed in (i).

To simplify this, we can write it as $A.C.(B + \bar{B}) + \bar{A}.C(B + \bar{B}) + \bar{A}.\bar{B}.\bar{C} + A.B.\bar{C}$; this becomes $A.C + \bar{A}.C + \bar{C}.(\bar{A}.\bar{B} + A.B)$, having noted that $B + B = 1$ etc. This in turn is $C.(A + \bar{A}) + \bar{C}(\bar{A}.\bar{B} + A.B)$, which becomes $C + \bar{C}.(\bar{A}.\bar{B} + A.B)$. This finally reduces to $C + \bar{A}.\bar{B} + A.B$, as required.

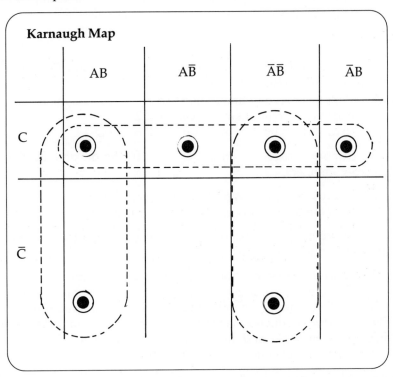

$D + \bar{A}.\bar{B}.C + \bar{A}.\bar{B}.C + \bar{A}.B.C + A.\bar{B}.C + A.B.\bar{C} + A.B.C = C + \bar{A}.\bar{B} + A.B$

Part (iii) involves merely translating the simplified expression into a diagram.

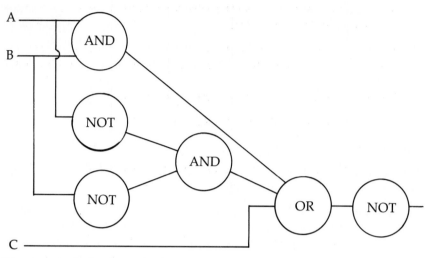

Note particularly the use of the final NOT. We need this as the original Boolean expression defined the correct working of the machine – but the aim of this circuit is to detect malfunction of the machine.

**Further Exercises D**

1. A company makes two microcomputers, Solar and Gem using three main components X, Y and Z.
   Solar uses three X components and two Y
   Gem uses two X components and three of Z
   i)      Express this information as a 2 by 3 array Q.

   The company receives an order for 100 Solar and 50 Gem micro-computers.

   ii)     Express the order as a row matrix (array) P.
   iii)    Find the product PQ, and interpret its meaning.

   It takes two hours to make one X component, 1 hour to make one Y and 3 hours to make a Z.

   iv)     Express the production time as a column array R.
   v)      Calculate the product PQR, and interpret its meaning.
   A second order for 50 Solar and 100 Gem microcomputers arrives. By then new production techniques have cut the time needed to produce X by 20%, and that to produce Z by a third. The time to produce Y has not changed.

   vi)     Use matrix (array) techniques to determine the component requirements for the second order.

   vii) How many hours are needed to produce the second order?

For the first order, labour costs were three units per hour; they rose by 10% for the second order.

viii) Are the labour costs for the second order greater or smaller than those for the first order?

2. A printer ribbon firm launches three new ribbons. A market research survey shows that the probability of any shop's selling the products is
Ribbon A: 0.75      Ribbon B: 0.50      Ribbon C: 0.80

   a) Find the probabilities that a shop will
     i)    sell all three ribbons
     ii)   sell A but NOT sell B and NOT sell C
     iii)  sell any two of the ribbons but NOT all three

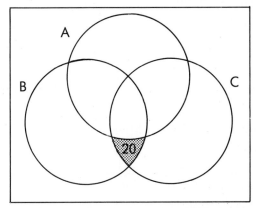

b) Assume that 200 shops sell the ribbons exactly as predicted. Complete the Venn diagram to show the numbers selling the different combinations of ribbons. For instance, the shaded area stands for the number of shops selling B and C but NOT selling A. This has a probability of
$0.5 \times 0.8 \times 0.25 = 0.1$. For 200 retailers, this is 20.

3. a) Calculate the twos complement form of every three bit code, by completing the table.

| CODE | | | COMPLEMENT | | |
|---|---|---|---|---|---|
| A | B | C | X | Y | Z |
| 0 | 0 | 0 | 0 | 0 | 0 |
| 0 | 0 | 1 | 1 | 1 | 1 |
| 0 | 1 | 0 | | | |
| 0 | 1 | 1 | | | |
| 1 | 0 | 0 | | | |
| 1 | 0 | 1 | | | |
| 1 | 1 | 0 | | | |
| 1 | 1 | 1 | | | |

b) Express *each* of X, Y and Z as a Boolean expression in terms of A, B and C.

c) Simplify each of these three expressions (if not already simplified).

4. A firm makes two products A and B. Both products need machines X and Y during the process. To make one of product A needs two hours on machine X and four on Y; to make one of product B needs one hour on X and three on Y.

a) 200 hours are available on machine X, and 460 hours on Y.

 i)   Write down the two equations which express how many of A and B the firm can produce to use all the available hours on each machine.

 ii)  Express these two equations as an array (matrix) equation.

 iii) Pre-multiply both sides of this array equation by

$$\begin{pmatrix} 3/2 & -1/2 \\ -2 & 1 \end{pmatrix}$$

 iv)  Explain what the result means

b) The time available on machine X goes up by 16%, and that on Y by 10%. Work out how many of A and B the firm can now produce using all the available hours.

5. A very effective method of producing a valid code from a base number is to apply *consecutive* weights as follows. For base number 561, multiply the 1 by 2, the 6 by 3 and the 5 by 4. Adding these gives $1*2 + 6*3 + 5*4 = 40$. We must then add 4 to get the next number exactly divisible by 11. Then the check digit is 4 and the valid code is 561 4.

a) What is the code for each of these base numbers?
   i)  824        ii)  509

b) Make a transcription mistake in the code you obtained in (a) (ii); show that this error would be detected when the number is validated.

c) Make a transpositional mistake (ie, exchange two adjacent digits) in the code you obtained in part (a) (ii) and show that this error would also be detected by validation.

d) Exactly the same technique, with weights up to 10 gives each published book an unique identification code known as its ISBN (International Standard Book Number). This is a ten digit code (eg 0 85012 661 4). In this example the check digit is 4; this is the 661st book produced by publisher number 85012.

i)   Show that 0 85012 661 4 is a valid ISBN.

ii)  What would be the ISBN for the 685th book published by publisher 85012?

e) Measurements cannot have a check digit applied; they are also correct to only a certain precision.
Someone gives two lengths $x$ and $y$ as
$x = 6.0 \pm 0.4$ and $y = 2.0 \pm 0.2$ Find the upper and lower bounds for

i)   the area of the rectangle with sides $x$ and $y$;

ii)  the remaining length when two pieces of length $y$ are cut from a piece of wood of length $x$.

6. A computerised alarm system has a processor that depends on three inputs A, B and C. The alarm output ($x = 1$) is according to the table.

| Inputs | | | Output |
|---|---|---|---|
| A | B | C | X |
| 0 | 0 | 0 | 1 |
| 0 | 0 | 1 | 0 |
| 0 | 1 | 0 | 1 |
| 0 | 1 | 1 | 1 |
| 1 | 0 | 0 | 1 |
| 1 | 0 | 1 | 0 |
| 1 | 1 | 0 | 1 |
| 1 | 1 | 1 | 0 |

i)   Produce a Boolean expression for X in terms of A, B and C.

ii)  Simplify this as far as you can.

iii) Draw a logic network diagram for the processor.

The alarm signal, X, together with a signal Y from a keyswitch, are inputs to a logic component; this sounds the bell only if the two inputs are different. We would use a half adder for this purpose, if we ignore one of its outputs.

iv)  Draw the half adder circuit with X and Y as inputs; show which output would sound the alarm bell.

7. a) i)   Draw a Venn diagram to show the relationship between the following sets;

$\mathcal{E} = [\, x{:}x \text{ is an integer}, 1 \leqslant x \leqslant 30 \,]$
$C = [\, x{:}x \text{ is divisible by 4} \,]$

$B = [\, x{:}x^2 \leqslant 90\, \}$
$A = [\, 1, 2, 3, 5, 8, 13, 21\, \}$

ii)    What is the complement of a set?

iii)    List the elements in the set NOT (A OR B).

iv)    Evaluate the logical expression: $x = 8$ OR $x < 6$ AND $x = 1$ for $x = 8$ and for $x = 5$

b)   i)    Solve each of the following inequalities:
      $3(x\text{-}2) \leqslant 5 - 2(4-x)$      $4x + 7 > 3\,(x + 2)$

ii)    What range of values of $x$ satisfies both inequalities?

8. a)   Obtain a Boolean expression for the following logic circuit.

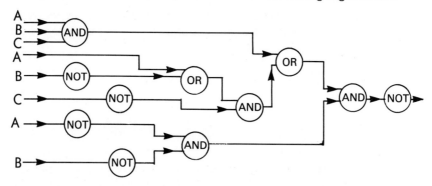

b)   Produce a truth table for this expression.

c)   Using the truth table, or by other means, show that we could simplify the circuit to use ONE three input gate.

9. a)   In a sample of 100 faulty printers, 16 had only electrical faults, 14 had only mechanical faults, and six had only assembly faults; 22 had both mechanical and electrical faults. Twice as many had both mechanical and assembly faults as had both electrical and assembly faults. There were two more with ALL three faults than had both mechanical and assembly faults.

i)    Express this information in the form of a Venn diagram.

ii)    From this, find how many printers had all three faults.

b)   A box contains 40 chips, of which six are faulty. Two are taken separately at random from the box, and not replaced. Find the probabilities that

i)    the first chip chosen is faulty;

ii)    both are faulty;

iii)   the first works but the second is faulty

Express your answers correct to two places of decimals.

c) If the probability that you can enter data into a spreadsheet is ¾, and the probability that the software loads correctly is 0.9, there are four possible results when you try to use the spreadsheet. Draw the appropriate probability tree to illustrate this situation, and find the probability of each of the four possible outcomes.

10. a) A supplier of computer stationery distributes two packs of stationery for printers. The smaller pack contains eight boxes of single paper, five boxes of triplicate paper and one box of labels. The larger pack contains 18 boxes of single paper, 12 boxes of triplicate paper and two boxes of labels.

   i)    Express this information as a 2 by 3 array X.

   A box of single paper costs $3, a box of triplicate paper costs $10, and a box of labels costs $15.

   ii)   Express this information as a column matrix (array) Y.

   iii)  Calculate the product XY, and interpret its meaning.

   iv)   What is the total cost of four smaller packs and two larger packs?

   b) The cost of a box of single paper increases by 12% and a box of triplicate paper by 8% – but the cost of a box of labels falls by 5%.

   i)    Express the new costs as a column matrix (array) Z.

   ii)   Calculate the product XZ.

   iii)  What is now the total cost of four small and two large packs?

   iv)   Express this total cost as a percentage of the original cost of four small and two large packs (to 1 decimal place).

11. a) Computers sometimes use numbers which contain errors. Give five examples of how such errors may have arisen.

   b) A computer is used to solve the following pair of simultaneous equations:
   $105x + 100y = 310$
   $Ax + 95y = 295$
   The coefficient A in the second equation is recorded as equal to 100, but would be up to $\pm 1\%$ in error.

   i)    Using $A = 100$ what solution would the computer obtain?

   ii)   Show that $x = 30$, $y = -28.4$ could possibly be a correct solution.

   iii)  Briefly explain why the results obtained by the computer differ so widely from other possible solutions.

c) If you were asked to add together a set of numbers using a calculator which holds numbers only correct to six significant figures, should you use any particular approach regarding the order in which you add the numbers?

12. A motor is controlled by a one bit signal M; M = 1 implies motor on, and M = 0 implies motor off. Three control signals A, B and C are used, but A overrides the other two unless BOTH B and C are zero – in which case the motor comes on.

    a) i)    Construct a truth table to show M for all possible states of A B and C.

    ii)    Write down the Boolean expression for M in terms of A, B and C, and simplify it.

    iii)    Draw a logic circuit to accept the inputs A, B and C and output M.

    b) A state sensor Y sends a one bit signal if the motor is already on. This signal is combined with M, so that the motor starts only if it is off, and stops only if it is on. Draw a diagram of a half adder to combine Y with M, and mark the output to use.

13. Three binary signals are A, B and C; a decoder M relates to these signals thus
A is a control signal, and BC is a two digit binary number.
M = 1 when A = 1 and BC is non-zero.
M = 1 when A = 0 and BC is an odd number.
In all other cases, M = 0.

    a) Produce a truth table for M, and express M as an *unsimplified* Boolean expression.

    b) Simplify the Boolean expression for M, and produce a logic circuit for this simplified expression.

    c) Show that an equivalent expression for M is $E = \bar{C}.(\overline{\bar{A}.\bar{B}})$.

    d) Explain the significance of E as an expression for producing a circuit for the decoder.

14. A company supplies boxes of five types of diode to computer manufacturers. During one month they receive the following orders from four manufacturers:

Manufacturer 1:  6 boxes of diode type A, 10 boxes of type B, 4 boxes of type C, 10 boxes of D and 8 boxes of E.

Manufacturer 2:  4 boxes of type B, 8 boxes of D, 12 boxes of C, 10 boxes of E and 6 of A.

Manufacturer 3: 8 boxes of E, 4 boxes of C, 8 of D, 4 of A and 10 of B.

Manufacturer 4: 4 boxes of C, 4 of E and 6 of D.

a) Draw up an array containing the details of the orders; put manufacturers on the rows, and types of diode on the columns.

b) What information is held in row 2 of the array?

c) The charges for the boxes are
   $8.5 for type A
   $9.0 for type B
   $9.5 for type C
   $10.0 for type D
   $10.5 for type E
   Write down these prices in a suitable array; then use array multiplication to find the amount to charge each manufacturer.

d) The following percentage increases now apply to the costs of the boxes:-
   Type A: 5%; B: 10%; C: 20%; D: 10%, E:12%;

   i)    What would now be the charge for manufacturer 2?

   ii)   Find the percentage increase to manufacturer 2. Give your answer correct to the nearest percentage.

15. a) Here is a pair of simultaneous equations:
   $$x + y = 5$$
   $$Ax + y = 4.95$$

   i)    Obtain expressions for $x$ and $y$, each in terms of A.

   ii)   If $A = 0.94 \pm 0.04$, show that possible solutions of the equations are $x = 0.5$, $y = 4.5$ and $x = 2.5$, $y = 2.5$.

   iii)  What does this indicate regarding the maximum relative errors in the solution to the simultaneous equations?

   iv)   What do we call simultaneous equations which have this problem?

b) A computer holds the values $x$ and $y$, known to be approximations to the exact values $X$ and $Y$, with errors $a$ and $b$ respectively. The absolute values of both $a$ and $b$ are each less than $e$, where $e$ is small.

   i)    Briefly explain why a computer ALWAYS holds SOME numbers which are inaccurate.

   ii)   What do you understand by the maximum RELATIVE ERROR?

   iii)  What is the maximum RELATIVE ERROR when $x$ and $y$ are subtracted?

# Appendix 1

## Answers to questions

**CHAPTER 1**

**1.1**

| | | | | | | | |
|---|---|---|---|---|---|---|---|
| (a) | 120 | (h) | −9 | (o) | 27 | (v) | −126 |
| (b) | 21 | (i) | −8 | (p) | 20 | (w) | 35 |
| (c) | −104 | (j) | −5 | (q) | 6 | (x) | 19 |
| (d) | −102 | (k) | 10 | (r) | 5 | (y) | 8 |
| (e) | −198 | (l) | 12 | (s) | 23 | (z) | 11 |
| (f) | 12 | (m) | 9 | (t) | 5 | | |
| (g) | 5 | (n) | 21 | (u) | 24 | | |

**1.2**
1. 74 000
2. 121
3. 18
4. 68
5. 4368
6. (a) 1 362 500  (b) 637 500  (c) 411 422

**1.3**
1. (a) $\frac{4}{5}$  (b) $1\frac{15}{28}$  (c) $5\frac{17}{72}$  (d) $\frac{3}{8}$  (e) $3\frac{1}{6}$  (f) $\frac{11}{28}$
   (g) $\frac{1}{12}$  (h) $\frac{9}{20}$  (i) $1\frac{1}{3}$  (j) $1\frac{1}{2}$  (k) $\frac{1}{4}$  (l) $1\frac{1}{3}$
2. 96
3. 24
4. 8
5. (i) 108  (ii) 72  (iii) 5.2 secs
6. (i) 4.5 h  (ii) 38 250  41 400  44 100

**1.4**
1. 2003.167
2. 47.57
3. 44.814
4. 12.9
5. $187.25
6. (i) 7.205 MB  (ii) 2.795 MB
7. (i) 7  (ii) 5

**1.5**
1. 10
2. 7:3
3. $204
4. 25
5. 36
6. 76 square metres

**CHAPTER 2**

**2.2**  1. $90
   2. $5940
   3. $1581
   4. (i) $530   (ii) $561.80   (iii) $595.51
   5. $185
   6. 19.44%
   7. (i) $1 144 000   (ii) $1 006 720
   8. (i) 68.25 KB   (ii) 71.6625 KB – (71.663 KB to the nearest byte)
   9. 7½%
   10. 18.75%
   11. 4.17%
   12. 22.62%

**2.3**  1. (a) $4^5=1024$   (b) $2^8=256$   (c) $5^4=625$
      (d) $3^7=2187$
   2. (a) 1   (b) ⅑   (c) ¼   (d) 2   (e) 5   (f) 2

**2.4**  1. (i), (iii) direct;   (ii), (iv), (v) inverse
   2. (i) a third of a second
      (ii) 3 minutes 40 seconds
   3. (i) 30 pages
      (ii) 60 pages
      (iii) 15 pages
      (iv) 180 characters

**CHAPTER 3**

**3.2**  1. (i) 6   (ii) 9   (iii) 29   (iv) 13   (v) 19   (vi) 50
      (vii) 26   (viii) 115   (ix) 205   (x) 150
   2. (i) 15   (ii) 21   (iii) 35   (iv) 110   (v) 132
      (vi) 242   (vii) 263   (viii) 459   (ix) 862   (x) 1485
   3. (i) 20   (ii) 35   (iii) 27   (iv) 60   (v) 125
      (vi) 162   (vii) 2739   (viii) 2821   (ix) 4013
      (x) 62,014
   4. (i) 1.25   (ii) 6.625   (iii) 0.1875   (iv) 2.296875
      (v) 5.109375   (vi) 8.453125   (vii) 3.6875
      (viii) 25.14453125

**3.3**  1. (i) 1101   (ii) 11001   (iii) 11101   (iv) 1000000
      (v) 1001001   (vi) 1111111   (vii) 1100111
      (viii) 10101111   (ix) 11101100   (x) 11000111
      (xi) 100010010   (xii) 111101101
   2. (i) 11   (ii) 21   (iii) 27   (iv) 47   (v) 57
      (vi) 123   (vii) 140   (viii) 144   (ix) 177   (x) 455
      (xi) 1024   (xii) 1436

3.  (i) 17   (ii) 1D   (iii) 23   (iv) 2A   (v) 3B
    (vi) 4F   (vii) 61   (viii) 8C   (ix) FE   (x) 104
    (xi) 1FD   (xii) 219   (xiii) 50F   (xiv) 7CE
    (xv) ABC   (xvi) 2F0F

**3.5**   1. (i) 0.10000111   (ii) 0.11101000   (iii) 0.01001011
   2. 0.310550
   3. 0.33F7C
   4. (i) 556   (ii) 614   (iii) 33   (iv) 26   (v) 0.65
      (vi) 0.54   (vii) 3.2   (viii) 13.54
   5. (i) 111010101   (ii) 101011110   (iii) 10011.1
      (iv) 1000110.101011
   6. (i) D3   (ii) 25   (iii) 0.E   (iv) 5.8
   7. (i) 101011   (ii) 111111000111   (iii) 1000.11
      (iv) 111101.1110001

**3.8**   (1) 10 0100   (2) 11 0001   (3) 11 0010   (4) 110 1000
   (5) 10 1110   (6) 100 0101   (7) 1111 1101   (8) 1 0111
   (9) 10 0100   (10) 10 1110

## CHAPTER 4

**4.1**   1. 0010 1101 1001             7. $-820$
   2. 0110 0001                   8. 1100 0111
   3. 0.0101 111                  9. $-61$
   4. 0.0101 1110 1001 110       10. $-512$ to $+511$
   5. 001 0010.1110 0           11. 11.671 875
   6. 1110 1110 1101            12. 10 1111 0001

**4.2**   1. (i) 0010 0010$_2$ ($34_{10}$)   (ii) 0100 1111$_2$ ($79_{10}$)
   2. (i) 0001 0000 0001$_2$ ($257_{10}$)   (ii) 0101 1001 0011$_2$ ($1427_{10}$)
      (iii) 0010 1010 0010$_2$ ($674_{10}$)

**4.3**   1. 0000 0110 0001, ie $1552_{10}$
   2. 6
   3. 0010 0001 1001   (i) 67   (ii) 67
   4. 0100 1101 1011   (i) 38   (ii) 39

**4.4**   1. 0001 0101 0010 0110
   2. 0010 0101 0011
     + 0100 0010 0110
     ───────────────
      0110 0111 1001 = $679_{10}$
     ───────────────
   3. 0001 0011 0101 0110
     +      0010 0110 0111
     ───────────────────
      0001 0110 0010 0011 = $1623_{10}$
     ───────────────────

**4.5**   1. 0010 0101 0000
   2. 1110 1110 1100
   3. 1|0001 0011 1100 = $316_{10}$

4. 0.1011 1100 0010
5. 0000 1100 0011.0110 1101 0100
6. −786
7. 53
8. 0000 1010 1100   (i) 5   (ii) 5
9. 0000 0010 0101$_2$   0100 1010 0000$_2$ = 1184$_{10}$
10. 0111 1001 and 0101 0011 0110 giving 0110 0001 0101, or 615$_{10}$

## CHAPTER 5

**5.1**   (i)    $0.74 \times 10^7$; 0.74; 7; 0.74E7
         (ii)   $0.256 \times 10^{10}$; 0.256; 10; 0.256E10
         (iii)  $0.628 \times 10^{-4}$; 0.628; −4; 0.628E−4
         (iv)   $0.153 \times 10^{-9}$; 0.153; −9; 0.153E−9
         (v)    $-0.82 \times 10^7$; −0.82; 7; −0.82E7
         (vi)   $-0.554 \times 10^{11}$; −0.554; 11; −0.554E11
         (vii)  $-0.27 \times 10^{-3}$; −0.27; −3; −0.27E−3
         (viii) $-0.79 \times 10^{-7}$; −0.79; −7; −0.79E−7

**5.2**   1.   (i) 0001 1011 1011   (ii) 0111 1110 1101   (iii) 1001 1010 0111
              (iv) 1111 1110 0001
         2.   −127 to −0.000 030 518 and +0.000 030 518 to +127
         3.   −2 143 289 300 to $-4.547\ 47 + 10^{-13}$ and $+4.547\ 47 \times 10^{-13}$ to
              +2 143 289 300

**5.3**   1.   (i) 85   (ii) 255   (iii) 417   (iv) 4   (v) 1
              (vi) −2   (vii) −3   (viii) 4   (ix) 0   (x) −3
         2.   (i) $0.10011 \times 2^5$
              (ii) $0.10100 \times 2^6$
              (iii) $0.10100 \times 2^2$
         3.   (i) $0.10100 \times 2^2$
              (ii) $0.10011 \times 2^7$
              (iii) $0.10111 \times 2^3$
         4.   (i) $0.1100 \times 2^6$
              (ii) $0.1100 \times 2^9$
         5.   (i) $0.101 \times 2^3$
              (ii) $0.100 \times 2^8$
         6.   $(0.1010\ 10 \times 2^6) + (0.1001\ 01 \times 2^7)$ giving $0.1110\ 10 \times 2^7$ or
              0001 1111 1010

## Answers to Further Exercises A

1. (a) $625, $1250 and $3125

   (b)

| Year | Balance after sales and expenses | Interest | Balance c/f |
|------|----------------------------------|----------|-------------|
| 1 | 3 000 | 300 | 3 300 |
| 2 | 8 300 | 996 | 9 296 |
| 3 | 13 296 | 1 662 | 14˙958 |

|  4 | 19 958 | 2 195 | 22 153 |
|---|---|---|---|

(c)  $12 153 to be divided, so tax = $4051
(d)  $8102 to be shared, so they get $1012.75, $2025.50 and $5063.75
(e)  Sectors have angles of 45°, 90° and 225°
Sectors have angles of 120° (tax), 30°, 60° and 150°

2. (a)  (i)  −128 to +127
        (ii)  1001 1100
        (iii) 0101 0100
              1001 0000+
              ─────────
              1110 0100 which is −28
        (iv) 0110 0100 + 0011 0010 = 1001 0110
Since adding two positive values produces a negative total, overflow must have occurred.

   (a)  (i)  −32 to +31.75
        (ii)  Maximum absolute error is 0.125 (see chapter 19)
        (iii) (1)  0011 0010
              (2)  1110 1111
              (3)  0000 0111
        (iv) 3% (see chapter 19)

3. (a)  0001 1001 and 1110 0111
   (b)  −128 to +127
   (c)  0 100101 1010001001
   (d)  0.375
   (e)  0 101000 110101010
        relative error is 0% to nearest whole number (0.117% otherwise): see chapter 19

4. (a)  (i) A number has two separate parts, in the form $M \times 2^P$, where M is the mantissa and P the exponent. The range of the mantissa is given by $\frac{1}{2}.5 \leq M < 1$ and $-1 \leq M < -\frac{1}{2}.5$. Thus the mantissa is that part of the number which is multiplied by a power of 2, ie the binary representation with the "binary part removed" to give a normalised value. The exponent is the number of places the binary point must be moved to give a normalised mantissa. Twos-complement is a method of representing both positive and negative numbers with an implied sign incorporated into the number. It is based on modular arithmetic and means that there is no need for subtraction. Excess−32 form means that 32 is added to the representation – hence −32 is given by 0. The system can cater for a range of negative and

positive values without the need for treating negatives separately.

(b)    A is 68.75 and B is 3.3125

(c)    The exponent of B is increased to 7 with a shift of five places in the mantissa so that B becomes $0.000001101 \times 2^7$. Adding the mantissas leads to a sum of $0.100100000 \times 2^7$; this is stored as 0 100100000 100111.

(d)    The computed result of A + B is $1001000_2 = 72$ yet the correct value is $72\frac{1}{16}$. The difference is due to the truncation (or rounding) error introduced when the mantissa of B was shifted five places (see chapter 19).

## CHAPTER 6

**6.2**    1.    (a)  Quantitative, continuous
(b)  Quantitative, discrete
(c)  Qualitative
(d)  Quantitative, continuous
(e)  Quantitative, discrete
(f)  Quantitative, discrete
(g)  Quantitative, discrete
(h)  Qualitative
(i)  Quantitative, discrete
(j)  Quantitative, continuous

2.

| Salary | Tally | No of staff |
|---|---|---|
| 60– | /// | 3 |
| 80– | // | 2 |
| 100– | //// | 4 |
| 120– | / | 1 |
| 140– | ## //// | 9 |
| 160– | ## //// | 9 |
| 180– | ## | 5 |
| 200– | ## / | 6 |
| 220– | / | 1 |
| 240– | // | 2 |
| 260– | ## / | 6 |
| 280– | ## /// | 8 |
| 300– | ## | 5 |
| 320– | / | 1 |
| 340– | //// | 4 |
| 360– | /// | 3 |
| 380–399 | / | 1 |

3.

| Time/s | Tally | Frequency |
|---|---|---|
| 275– | ## / | 6 |
| 300– | ## / | 6 |
| 325– | /// | 3 |
| 350– | ## | 5 |

| 375– | // | 2 |
| 400– | //// //// | 8 |
| 425– | // | 2 |
| 450– | /// | 3 |
| 475– | //// | 4 |
| 500– | //// | 4 |
| 525– | /// | 3 |
| 550– | // | 2 |
| 575–599 | // | 2 |

**6.4**  1.  Pictogram using human figures probably, all of equal size – best if each stands for 25 people

2. (i) Pie chart angles: IBM 72°, ICL 42°, Unisys 24°, Tandem 30°, Honeywell 54°, Hewlett Packard 42°, DEC 84°, Data General 12°

   (ii) Lengths of bars proportional to frequencies; widths equal; order does not matter

3. Same as for 2(ii); did you remember the key?

4. For 1988 the angles are: industrial action 70°, hardware faults 81°, software faults 174° and human error 35°. For 1990, they are 15°, 37°, 249° and 59°; radius is 1.26 times that used in 1988.

5  Data is continuous; diagram follows as for Figure 6.11

6. Data is discrete; diagram follows as for Figure 6.12 but with a frequency polygon.

**6.7**  1

| Age, less than, | 20 | 25 | 30 | 35 | 40 | 45 | 50 | 55 | 60 | 65 |
|---|---|---|---|---|---|---|---|---|---|---|
| Cumulative frequency | 0 | 12 | 29 | 50 | 68 | 82 | 95 | 107 | 116 | 120 |

Roughly 41, 87, 46

2. Initial downwards trend, then rising quite sharply by end of period. Tuesday consistently better than other days.

3. There is some evidence of inverse correlation between $x$ and $y$.

4. There is no clear evidence of any pattern.

**CHAPTER 7**

**7.3**  1. (i) $\frac{1}{10}$  (ii) $\frac{7}{20}$  (iii) $\frac{1}{4}$  (iv) $\frac{9}{10}$  (v) $\frac{3}{10}$  (vi) 1  (vii) $\frac{9}{10}$

2. (i) $\frac{17}{30}$  (ii) $\frac{4}{15}$  (iii) $\frac{2}{15}$  (iv) $\frac{13}{30}$  (v) $\frac{1}{6}$  (vi) 0

**7.4**  (i) $\frac{4}{5}$  (ii) $\frac{1}{5}$  (iii) $\frac{8}{15}$  (iv) $\frac{3}{20}$  (v) $\frac{1}{60}$  (vi) $\frac{2}{5}$  (vii) $\frac{1}{25}$  (viii) $\frac{4}{125}$

**7.5**  1. (i) $\frac{11}{30}$  (ii) $\frac{4}{15}$  (iii) $\frac{3}{10}$  (iv) $\frac{7}{15}$  (v) $\frac{3}{5}$  (vi) $\frac{1}{300}$

2. (i) 0.8  (ii) 0.3  (iii) 0.7  (iv) 0.04  (v) 0.1

(vi) 0.3   (vii) 0.2   (viii) 0.2

**7.6**    1.

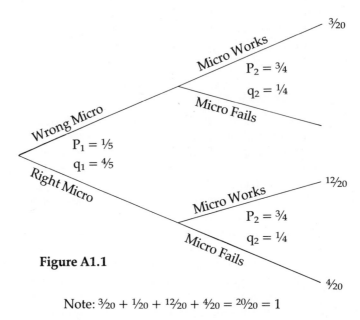

**Figure A1.1**

Note: $\frac{3}{20} + \frac{1}{20} + \frac{12}{20} + \frac{4}{20} = \frac{20}{20} = 1$

2. Add two branches at each right-hand point, for working disk ($p_3=\frac{2}{3}$) and for disk failure ($q_3=\frac{1}{3}$). The new right-hand probabilities are, in order, and in sixtieths 6, 3, 2, 1, 24, 12, 8, 4 (which add up to 60).

3. Using the data in order, my tree gave the probabilities in six-hundredths as 2, 1, 18, 9, 38, 19, 342, 171 (which add up to 600).

**CHAPTER 8**

**8.1**    1.   (a) $14\frac{5}{7}$   (b) 27 (to nearest day)

       2.   (a) 2.9 (to nearest 0.1 s)

           (b) 2.6 (to nearest 0.1 s)

           (c) 10.3%

       3.   6.3 years (to nearest 0.1 year; – <u>not</u> 6.1 years!

**8.2**    1.   23   26   28   29   29   32   35   37   38   41   42   49   51

          median – 35 years

       2.   28.5 minutes

**8.3**    1.   5

       2.   beige

**8.4**  1.  Here I choose the mode, 19, as the working mean.

| $x$ | $f$ | $d=x-19$ | $fd$ |
|---|---|---|---|
| 17 | 4 | $-2$ | $-8$ |
| 18 | 8 | $-1$ | $-8$ |
| 19 | 19 | 0 | 0 |
| 20 | 12 | 1 | 12 |
| 21 | 5 | 2 | 10 |
| 22 | 2 | 3 | 6 |

$$\Sigma f = 50 \qquad\qquad \Sigma fd = 12$$
$$\text{Mean} = 19 + {}^{12}\!/_{50} = 19.24 \text{ calls/day}$$

2.  76.3 pages/job
3.  Mean is 155 errors/hour (to nearest integer)
4.  $7255

**8.5**  1.  5

2.

| Salary less than | 4000 | 5000 | 6000 | 7000 | 8000 | 9000 | 10 000 | 11 000 | 12 000 |
|---|---|---|---|---|---|---|---|---|---|
| cf | 0 | 7 | 26 | 64 | 109 | 143 | 170 | 191 | 200 |

**8.6**  1.  95

2.  (ii) $35 + 5 \times \dfrac{7}{7+9} = 35 + \dfrac{35}{16} = 37.1875$, or 37.2 years

## CHAPTER 9

**9.2**  1.  Range 29; inter-quartile range 12
2.  (i) Increase to 32    (ii) no change at all
3.  65
4.  (i) 35  (ii) 15  (iii) 7.5
5.  (i) no change  (ii) 17  (iii) 8.5

**9.3**  1.  Mean 6.8 minutes
Deviations  $-0.7$  0.5  $-1.4$  0.1  1.9  $-1.5$  $-0.4$  1.5
Squared deviations  0.49  0.25  1.96  0.01  3.61  2.25  0.16  2.25
Sum of squared deviations  10.98
Mean of squared deviations  1.3725
Standard deviation  1.1715 minutes
Variance  1.3725 minutes$^2$

## Answers to Further Exercises B

1.  (i)

| Period 1 | cf | %cf | Period 2 | cf | %cf |
|---|---|---|---|---|---|
| 84 | 84 | 21 | 60 | 60 | 12 |
| 86 | 170 | 42.5 | 80 | 140 | 28 |
| 122 | 292 | 73 | 165 | 305 | 61 |
| 86 | 378 | 94.5 | 110 | 415 | 83 |
| 16 | 394 | 98.5 | 55 | 470 | 94 |
| 6 | 400 | 100 | 30 | 500 | 100 |

(ii)

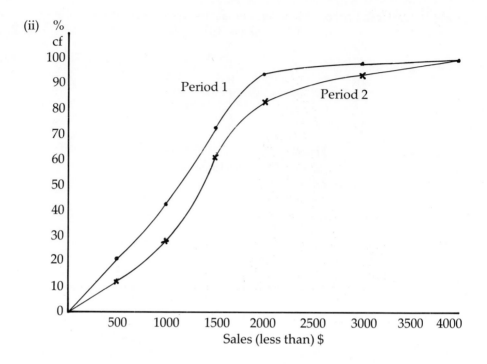

(iii) For Period 1, median = 1125 and inter-quartile range =
1550 − 625 = 925.
For Period 2, median = 1375 and inter-quartile range =
1750 − 925 = 825.

(iv) Although there was a 25% increase in the number of sales
staff employed during the second period this has NOT
resulted in a proportionately larger increase in the median
value. It has however, led to more sales with less
dispersion between the sales of different sales staff.

2.  (i)

| Class | f | cf | %cf |
|---|---|---|---|
| 1.5 to <1.6 | 1 | 1 | 2.5 |
| 1.6 to <1.7 | 2 | 3 | 7.5 |
| 1.7 to <1.8 | 1 | 4 | 10 |
| 1.8 to <1.9 | 6 | 10 | 25 |
| 1.9 to <2.0 | 9 | 19 | 47.5 |
| 2.0 to <2.1 | 10 | 29 | 72.5 |
| 2.1 to <2.2 | 7 | 36 | 90 |
| 2.2 to <2.3 | 2 | 38 | 95 |
| 2.3 to <2.4 | 0 | 38 | 95 |
| 2.4 to <2.5 | 2 | 40 | 100 |

(ii) Histogram:–

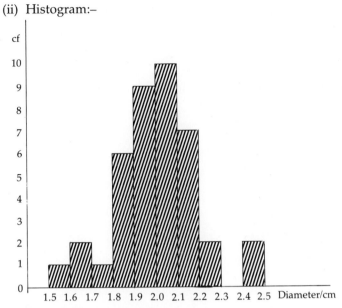

(iii) See solution to part (i).

(iv)

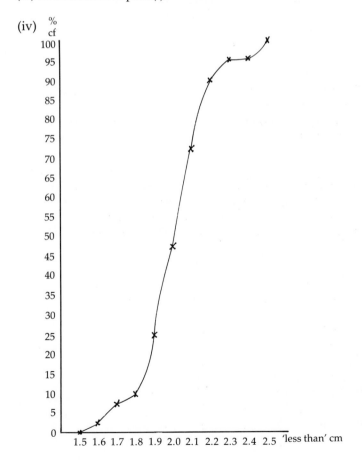

(v)  Median = 2.01 cm   Inter-quartile range = 2.11 − 1.9 = 0.21 cm

(vi) Reject 14% undersize and 17½% oversize, 31½% in all.

3.  (i)

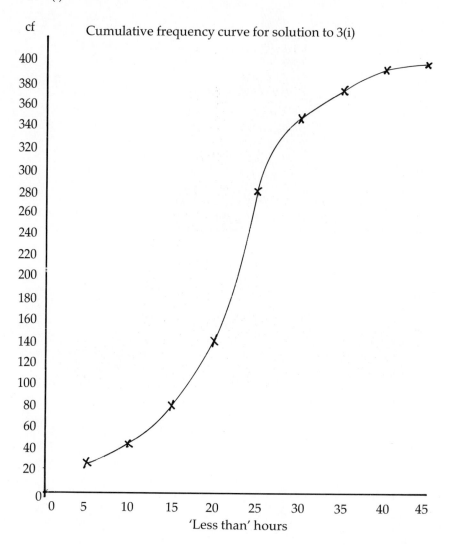

cf

Cumulative frequency curve for solution to 3(i)

'Less than' hours

(ii)  61

(iii) 37

(iv)  
| Class | Frequency |
| --- | --- |
| 0–5 | 28 |
| 5–10 | 17 |
| 10–15 | 36 |
| 15–20 | 62 |
| 20–25 | 137 |
| 25–30 | 69 |

|       |     |
|-------|-----|
| 30–35 | 25  |
| 35–40 | 21  |
| 40–45 | 5   |

Frequency          Histogram for solution to 3(iv)

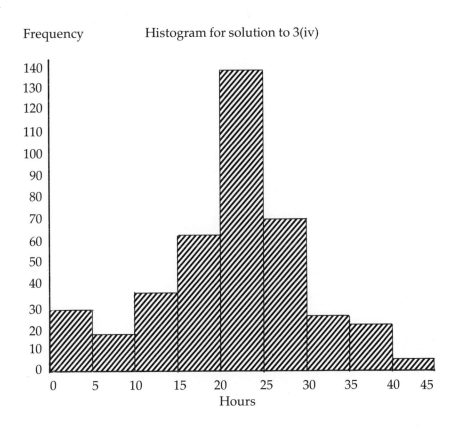

4.  (i)  Histogram for 4(i)

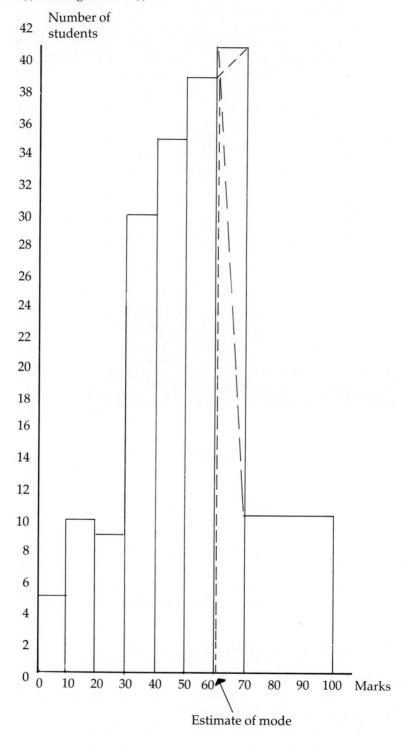

Number of students

Marks

Estimate of mode

(ii)  Mean = 51.9
      Standard deviation = 20.5
(iii) Mode is 60.1 – shown on histogram drawn in 4.(i)
(iv)  The mode is the only measure of central tendency that can
      be used with data which is qualitative – it is not affected
      by extreme values whereas the mean is.

2.

| $x$ | $x-200$ | $d=\dfrac{x-200}{50}$ | $f$ | $fd$ | $fd^2$ |
|---|---|---|---|---|---|
| 50 | −150 | −3 | 2 | −6 | 18 |
| 100 | −100 | −2 | 7 | −14 | 28 |
| 150 | −50 | −1 | 15 | −15 | 15 |
| 200 | 0 | 0 | 21 | 0 | 0 |
| 250 | 50 | 1 | 16 | 16 | 16 |
| 300 | 100 | 2 | 14 | 28 | 56 |
| 350 | 150 | 3 | 12 | 36 | 108 |
| 400 | 200 | 4 | 8 | 32 | 128 |
| 450 | 250 | 5 | 4 | 20 | 100 |
| 500 | 300 | 6 | 1 | 6 | 36 |

$$f = 100 \quad fd = 103 \quad fd^2 = 505$$

$$\text{Mean} = 200 + 50 \times \frac{103}{100} = 200 + 51.5 = 251.5: \text{mean is } \$251.5$$

$$\text{Standard deviation} = 50 \sqrt{\frac{505}{100} - \left(\frac{103}{100}\right)^2}$$

$$= 50 \sqrt{5.05 - 1.03^2}$$

$$= 50 \sqrt{5.05 - 1.0609}$$

$$= 50 \sqrt{3.9891} \quad = 50 \times 1.9973$$

$$= \$99.86$$

Variance 9972.75 dollars$^2$

3.  Mean 33.48 years; standard deviation 10.83 years

**CHAPTER 10**

**10.2**  1.  (a) 625  (b) 243  (c) 64  (d) 512  (e) 1
          (f) 17  (g) 5.29  (h) 1

2.  (a) $25x$   (b) $9a$   (c) $11x - 4y$   (d) $14ab$
    (e) $8a^2 - 2a$   (f) $10a^3$   (g) $12abc + 18bc$
3.  (a) 56   (b) 80   (c) 60   (d) 124   (e) 320
4.  (a) $30x^7$   (b) $24a^3b^3c$   (c) $4xy$   (d) $27y^4z^3/4$
    (e) $60a^3b^4c^2$   (f) $4b^5/c^4$
5.  (a) 39   (b) 15   (c) 2   (d) 58   (e) 1   (f) 76
6.  (a) $8x^2 - 12xy$   (b) $30a^2 + 15ab$   (c) $9a^2 + 3ab$
    (d) $2a^2 - 5ab - 3b^2$   (e) $8x^2 - 22x + 5$
    (f) $6x^2 + 17x + 5$   (g) $9x^2 - 24x + 16$   (h) $16x^2 - y^2$
    (i) $6a^2 - 5ab - 21b^2$   (j) $a^2 - ab + 4b^2$

**10.4**  1.  227
          2.  0.88
          3.  $-3.9168$

**10.5**  1.  Multiply by 7 then subtract 4.
              Therefore add 4 then divide by 7; hence $x = \dfrac{y + 4}{7}$

          2.  $u = \dfrac{s - 16t^2}{t}$

          3.  $4x - 7 = 1$
              $\quad\;\; 4x = 8$
              $\quad\;\;\;\; x = 2$
          4.  $9x = 56$
          5.  $x^2 - 2 = 0$

## CHAPTER 11
**11.1**      (1) 6   (2) 5   (3) 4   (4) $\frac{7}{16}$   (5) $-\frac{3}{5}$
              (6) $\frac{17}{7}$   (7) $\frac{3}{2}$   (8) 13   (9) 26   (10) $-4\frac{1}{2}$
              (11) 1   (12) $-97$
**11.3**  1.  (a) $x = 4,\quad y - 2$
              (b) $x = 5,\quad y = 2$
              (c) $x = 2,\quad y = -3$
          2.      $x = 2.5,\quad y = 1$

**11.4**  1.  (a) 3 or $-1$                    (d) 1.58 or 0.423
              (b) 0.275 or $-7.27$            (e) 1.72 or $-0.117$
              (c) 0.676 or $-5.18$

          2.  (a) no real solutions           (d) two different solutions
              (b) two equal solutions         (e) two equal solutions
              (c) two different solutions

## CHAPTER 12
**12.1**  1.  (i) 5   (ii) 13   (iii) 10
          2.  (i) $\frac{7}{3}$   (ii) $-\frac{1}{9}$

3. (i) $6x^2+4x+7$
   (ii) $6x^2-10x-3$
   (iii) $14x+10$

**12.4** 1.

| $x$ | $-4$ | $-3$ | $-2$ | $-1$ | 0 | 1 | 2 | 3 | 4 | 5 |
|---|---|---|---|---|---|---|---|---|---|---|
| $f(x)$ | $-35$ | $-27$ | $-19$ | $-11$ | $-3$ | 5 | 13 | 21 | 29 | 37 |

2.

| $x$ | $-2$ | $-1$ | 0 | 1 | 2 | 3 | 4 | 5 | 6 |
|---|---|---|---|---|---|---|---|---|---|
| $x^2$ | 4 | 1 | 0 | 1 | 4 | 9 | 16 | 25 | 36 |
| $3x^2$ | 12 | 3 | 0 | 3 | 12 | 27 | 48 | 75 | 108 |
| $-4x$ | 8 | 4 | 0 | $-4$ | $-8$ | $-12$ | $-16$ | $-20$ | $-24$ |
| 5 | 5 | 5 | 5 | 5 | 5 | 5 | 5 | 5 | 5 |
| $f(x)$ | 25 | 12 | 5 | 4 | 9 | 20 | 37 | 60 | 89 |

3.

| $x$ | $-3$ | $-2$ | $-1$ | 0 | 1 | 2 | 3 | 4 | 5 | 6 | 7 |
|---|---|---|---|---|---|---|---|---|---|---|---|
| $x^2$ | 9 | 4 | 1 | 0 | 1 | 4 | 9 | 16 | 25 | 36 | 49 |
| $x^3$ | $-27$ | $-8$ | $-1$ | 0 | 1 | 8 | 27 | 64 | 125 | 216 | 343 |
| $-7x^2$ | $-63$ | $-28$ | $-7$ | 0 | $-7$ | $-28$ | $-63$ | $-112$ | $-175$ | $-252$ | $-343$ |
| $3x$ | $-9$ | $-6$ | $-3$ | 0 | 3 | 6 | 9 | 12 | 15 | 18 | 21 |
| 5 | 5 | 5 | 5 | 5 | 5 | 5 | 5 | 5 | 5 | 5 | 5 |
| $f(x)$ | $-94$ | $-37$ | $-6$ | 5 | 2 | $-9$ | $-22$ | $-31$ | $-30$ | $-13$ | 26 |
| $q(x)$ | $-5$ | $-2$ | 1 | 4 | 7 | 10 | 13 | 16 | 19 | 22 | 25 |

## CHAPTER 13

**13.1** 1. 13.8
2. 66.3
3. 238
4. 52.4
5. 96

**13.4** 1. Gradients are $-6$, 0 and 14.
2. About 530m
3. 84 units$^2$
4. 83.5 units$^2$

## CHAPTER 14

**14.2** (i) true  (ii) true  (iii) true  (iv) true
(v) false  (vi) false  (vii) true  (viii) false
(ix) true  (x) true  (xi) true  (xii) false

**Answers to Further Exercises C**

1.  (a)  Salary bill is $5 376 000
         (i)  $9 320,   $16 800,   $25 200
         (ii)  $5 953 920
         (iii)  10.75%
    (b)  Cost of television advert is $1000 and that of a radio advert is $200.
    (c)  (i)  1:3
         (ii)  150% and 105%
         (iii)  3:2 and 21:20

2.  (a)  (See graph)
    (b)  (1,6) and (3,34)
    (c)  Solve $y = 3x^2 + 2x + 1$ and $y + 14x = 8$, leading to quadratic in $x$ with the solutions $x + 1$ and $x = 3$.
    (d)  4

3.  (a)

| $x$ | 0 | 0.2 | 0.4 | 0.6 | 0.8 | 1.0 | 1.2 | 1.4 | 1.6 | 1.8 | 2.0 |
|---|---|---|---|---|---|---|---|---|---|---|---|
| $y$ | 0 | 9.36 | 15.36 | 18.48 | 19.2 | 18.0 | 15.36 | 11.76 | 7.68 | 3.6 | 0 |

    (b)  (Graph follows)
    (c)  0.21 and 1.5
    (d)  24

4.  (a)

| $x$ | −2 | −1½ | −1 | −½ | 0 | ½ | 1 | 1½ | 2 | 2½ | 3 |
|---|---|---|---|---|---|---|---|---|---|---|---|
| $y$ | −27 | −8 | 0 | 0 | −5 | −12 | −18 | −20 | −15 | 0 | 28 |

    (b)  (Graph follows)
    (c)  36 square units below the $x$ axis (or −36)

Graph for 2(a)

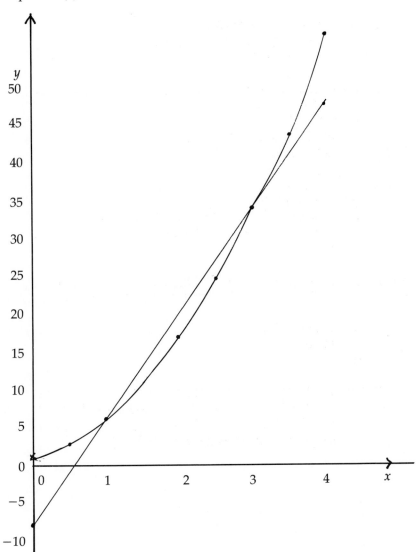

Graph for 3(b)

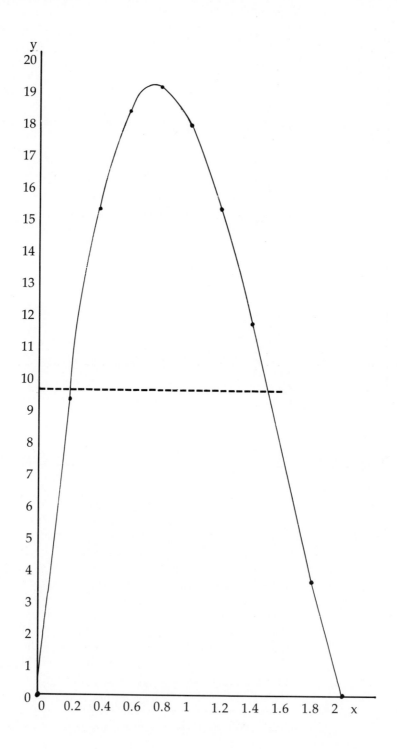

Graph for 4(b)

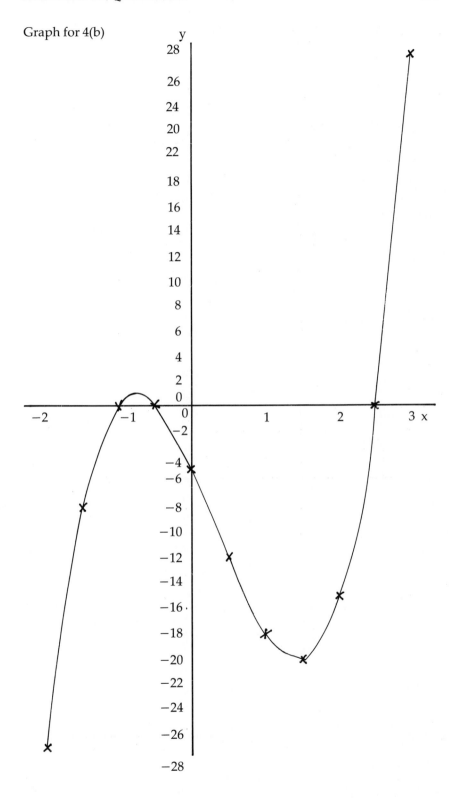

5.  (a)  (Graph follows)
    (b)  −0.8, 1, 2.75
    (c)  3.75 square units

6.  (a)  (Graph follows)
        (ii)  $3.8 - 2.8 = 1$ second
    (b)  (i)  A = 3, B = 4 and C = 24
        (ii)  If t = 4, $T = 3(2)^3 - 4(4) + 24 = 32$
        (iii)  If t = 3, temperature = 15
               If t = 7, temperature is 371

Graph for 5(a)

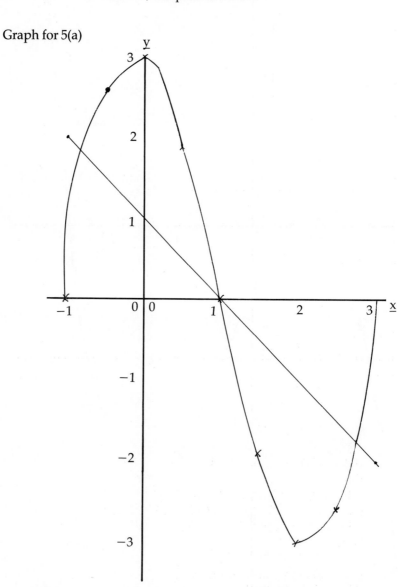

Graph for 6(a)

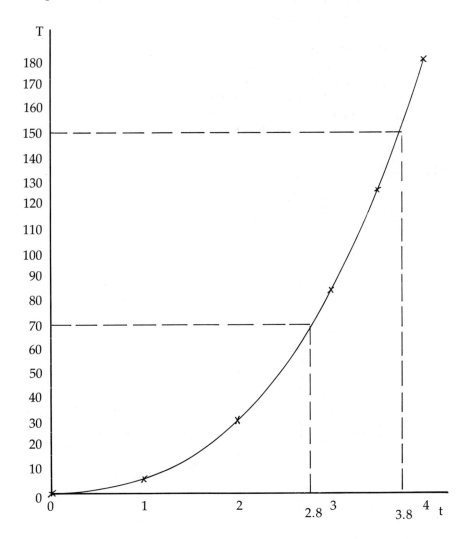

**14.4**  1.  (i)    {3,6,9,12,15,18}
             (ii)   {7,14}
             (iii)  {3,6,7,9,12,14,15,18}
             (iv)   {}
             (v)    {4,5,7,8,10,11,13,14,16,17,19}
             (vi)   {3,4,5,6,8,9,10,11,12,13,15,16,17,18,19}
             (vii)  {4,5,8,10,11,13,16,17,19}
             (viii) $\mathscr{E}$

        2.  (i)    Set of squared numbers.
             (ii)   {5,10,15,20,25}

(iii)     {5,7,11,13,17,19,23}
(iv)     {25}
(v)      {5}
(vi)     {}
(vii)    {5,7,10,11,13,15,17,19,20,23,25}
(viii)   {5,6,7,8,9,10,11,12,13,14,15,16,17,18,19,20,
         21,22,23,24,26}
(ix)     {6,8,9,12,14,16,18,21,22,24,26}
(x)      {6,8,10,12,14,15,18,20,21,22,24,26}
(xi)     ℰ
(xii)    {6,7,8,9,11,12,13,14,16,17,18,19,21,22,23,24,26}
(xiii)   {6,8,9,10,12,14,15,16,18,20,21,22,24,25,26}
(xiv)    {5,6,7,8,10,11,12,13,14,15,17,18,19,20,21,22
         23,24,26}
(xv)     {6,8,9,12,14,16,18,21,22,24,26}
(xvi)    ℰ
(xvii)   {6,8,12,14,18,21,22,24,26}

**14.5**  1.   $P \cap Q = \{12\}$
              $(P \cup Q)' = \{1,2,5,7,10,11,13,14\}$
       2.   (i)     6
            (ii)    {Beryl, Desmond, Leo}
            (iii)   {Chandrakant, Elaine, Fearon, Henrietta}
            (iv)    2
            (v)     3
            (vi)    {Adam, Beryl, Desmond, Guy, Idris, Jacquetta,
                    Kathryn, Leo}
       3.   (i)     {14,18,21,24,28}
            (ii)    {} or ○
            (iii)   {} or ○
            (iv)    ℰ or {13,14,15,16,17,18,19,20,21,22,23,24,25,
                         26,27,28}
            (v)     {13,15,17,19,22,23,25,26,27}
            (vi)    {28}
            (vii)   {24}
            (viii)  {13,15,17,18,19,22,23,25,26,27}

## CHAPTER 15

**15.4**  1.

| A | B | A and B | A or B | (A or B) and (A and B) |
|---|---|---------|--------|------------------------|
| 0 | 0 | 0 | 0 | 0 |
| 0 | 1 | 0 | 1 | 0 |
| 1 | 0 | 0 | 1 | 0 |
| 1 | 1 | 1 | 1 | 1 |

2.

| A | B | A and B | (A and B)′ | B or (A and B)′ |
|---|---|---|---|---|
| 0 | 0 | 0 | 1 | 1 |
| 0 | 1 | 0 | 1 | 1 |
| 1 | 0 | 0 | 1 | 1 |
| 1 | 1 | 1 | 0 | 1 |

3.  C is A′
    D is A or B
    E is (A or B)′
    F is A′ and (A or B)′

| A | B | A′ | A or B | (A or B)′ | F = A′ and (A or B)′ |
|---|---|----|--------|-----------|----------------------|
| 0 | 0 | 1  | 0      | 1         | 1                    |
| 0 | 1 | 1  | 1      | 0         | 0                    |
| 1 | 0 | 0  | 1      | 0         | 0                    |
| 1 | 1 | 0  | 1      | 0         | 0                    |

4.  D is A and B
    E is B or C
    F is (A and B)′
    G is (B or C)′
    H is $\overline{(A.B)}.\overline{(B+C)}$ (A and B)′ and (B or C)′

| A | B | C | A and B | B or C | (A and B)′ | (B or C)′ | H |
|---|---|---|---------|--------|------------|-----------|---|
| 0 | 0 | 0 | 0 | 0 | 1 | 1 | 1 |
| 0 | 0 | 1 | 0 | 1 | 1 | 0 | 0 |
| 0 | 1 | 0 | 0 | 1 | 1 | 0 | 0 |
| 0 | 1 | 1 | 0 | 1 | 1 | 0 | 0 |
| 1 | 0 | 0 | 0 | 0 | 1 | 1 | 1 |
| 1 | 0 | 1 | 0 | 1 | 1 | 0 | 0 |
| 1 | 1 | 0 | 1 | 1 | 0 | 0 | 0 |
| 1 | 1 | 1 | 1 | 1 | 0 | 0 | 0 |

5.  (i)   (A and B and C)′
    (ii)  ((A and B) or (B and C))′
    (iii) ((A or B) and (B or C))′
    (iv)  ((A or B) and (B or C) and (A or C))′

6.  (i)   A or B′
    (ii)  B
    (iii) B
    (iv)  BC′ or A′B′
    (v)   A or B′C

**CHAPTER 16**

**16.4** 1. If the manager is A and the assistants are B and C, the solution is A(B or C).

2. ABC

3. AB or AC or BC

4. D' or DB'C'

5. C−1' and C−2 or C−3

**CHAPTER 17**

**17.2** 1. (i) 6.8   (ii) 5.3   (iii) not defined

2. (i) Jan   (ii) Harriet   (iii) Liang   (iv) Philip
(v) t(4,2)   (vi) t(4,5)

**17.4**   (a) $\begin{pmatrix} 6 & 7 & 8 \\ 9 & 4 & 13 \end{pmatrix}$   (b) $\begin{pmatrix} 6 & 21 & 9 \\ 24 & 3 & 18 \end{pmatrix}$

(c) $\begin{pmatrix} 0 & 14 & 1 \\ 15 & -1 & 5 \end{pmatrix}$   (d) $\begin{pmatrix} 6 & -7 & 7 \\ -6 & 5 & 8 \end{pmatrix}$

(e) $\begin{pmatrix} 50 & 45 \\ 98 & 21 \end{pmatrix}$   (f) $\begin{pmatrix} 4 & 41 & 12 \\ 44 & 19 & 36 \\ 48 & 60 & 48 \end{pmatrix}$

**CHAPTER 18**

**18.3** 1. "Accounting" is at the root, with no modes left of it.

2. The first three columns of the next answer

3.

| −1 | 2 | accounting | −1 | 8 |
|----|----|----|----|----|
| 3 | 6 | packages | 1 | 7 |
| 8 | 4 | include | 2 | 4 |
| −1 | 5 | not | 3 | 5 |
| −1 | −1 | only | 4 | 2 |
| 7 | 10 | the | 2 | 10 |
| −1 | −1 | software | 6 | 6 |
| −1 | 9 | developed | 3 | 9 |
| −1 | −1 | for | 8 | 3 |
| −1 | −1 | users | 6 | −1 |

## CHAPTER 19

**19.10**  1.  (a)  loss of a digit
            (b)  single transposition
            (c)  inclusion of an extra digit
            (d)  double transposition
            (e)  random

  2.  (a)  6147
      (b)  7438
      (c)  21.0%

  3.  (a)    4.38       4      4.3      4.37
      (b)    3.93       4      3.9      3.92
      (c)    8.01       8      8.0      8.00
      (d)    7.10       7      7.0      7.10

  4.  (a)  374
      (b)  729
      (c)  147
      (d)  916

  5.  (a)  0.101101
      (b)  0.703125
      (c)  0.446%

## CHAPTER 20
**Answers to Exercise 20.9**

**20.9**  1.  (a)  invalid
            (b)  invalid
            (c)  valid
            (d)  invalid

  2.  (a)  valid
      (b)  invalid
      (c)  invalid
      (d)  valid

  3.  (a)  6
      (b)  4

  4.  P    is invalid
      Q    is invalid
      R    is valid
      S    is invalid

5.  (a) 0.0011
    (b) 1.0111
    (c) 0.0110
    (d) 1.0001

6.  0.9637

7.  (a) x(8x − 7) + 5
    (b) ((4x − 3)x + 7)x + 2
    (c) (4x² + 7)x + 2

8.  ((5x − 7)x + 3)x − 6;  49.485


**Answers to Further Exercises D**

1.  (i) Matrix Q is

|        | X | Y | Z |
|--------|---|---|---|
| Solar  | 3 | 2 | 0 |
| Gem    | 2 | 0 | 3 |

(ii) Matrix P is

|        | Solar | Gem |
|--------|-------|-----|
| Order  | (100  | 50) |

(iii) PQ is

|        | X    | Y   | Z    |
|--------|------|-----|------|
| Order  | (400 | 200 | 150) |

This means that the order requires 400 of X, 200 of Y and 150 of Z.

(iv) R is

|   | hours-to-produce |
|---|------------------|
| X | 2                |
| Y | 1                |
| Z | 3                |

(v) PQR is

|        | hours-to-produce |
|--------|------------------|
| Order  | (1450)           |

This means that the order will require 1450 hours to produce.

(vi) A second order requires

$$(50 \quad 100) \begin{pmatrix} 3 & 2 & 0 \\ 2 & 0 & 3 \end{pmatrix} = (350 \quad 100 \quad 300)$$

That means 350 of X, 100 of Y and 300 of Z.

(vii) The number of hours to produce the second order is

$$(350 \quad 100 \quad 300) \begin{pmatrix} 1.6 \\ 1 \\ 2 \end{pmatrix}$$

ie 560 + 100 + 600 = 1260
(viii) Labour costs for first order = 3*1450 = 4350
Labour costs for second order = 3.3*1260 = 4158

So the labour costs for the second order are <u>smaller.</u>

2. (a) (i) 0.75*0.50*0.80 = 0.3
(ii) 0.75*0.50*0.20 = 0.075
(iii) 0.75*0.50*0.20 + 0.75*0.50*0.80 + 0.25*0.50*0.80 = 0.475

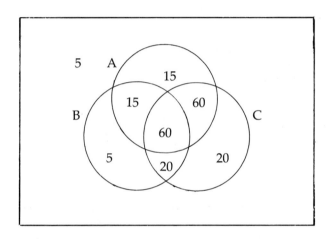

Don't forget to check the total: in this case it should be (and is) 200.

3. (a)      Missing lines are
            1 1 0, 1 0 1, 1 0 0, 0 1 1, 0 1 0, 0 0 1.

(b)/(c)  $X = \bar{A}.C + \bar{A}.B + A.\bar{B}.\bar{C}$.

Y = $\bar{B}.C + B.\bar{C}$

Z = C

4. (a) (i) 2a + b = 200 and 4a + 3b = 460
(ii) $\begin{pmatrix} 2 & 1 \\ 4 & 3 \end{pmatrix}$ $\begin{pmatrix} a \\ b \end{pmatrix}$ $= \begin{pmatrix} 200 \\ 460 \end{pmatrix}$
(iii) $\begin{pmatrix} 1 & 0 \\ 0 & 1 \end{pmatrix}$ $\begin{pmatrix} a \\ b \end{pmatrix}$ $= \begin{pmatrix} 70 \\ 60 \end{pmatrix}$

(iv) That a = 70 and b = 60 is the solution.
(b) 95 of A and 42 of B.

5.  (a) (i) 824 9     (ii) 509 6
    (b) Use 589 6 rather than 509 6 for instance. Then we have
        $5*4 + 8*3 + 9*2 + 6*1 = 68$, not a multiple of 11.
    (c) Change the correct 824 9 to 842 9 (for instance), leading to
        $8*4 + 4*3 + 2*2 + 9*1 = 32 + 12 + 4 + 9 = 57$, not a
        multiple of 11.
    (d) (i) $8*9 + 5*8 + 1*6 + 2*5 + 6*4 + 6*3 + 1*2 + 4*1 = 176 -$
        exactly divisible by 11, hence valid
        (ii) 0 85012 685 1
    (e) (i) 14.08 and 10.08     (ii) 2.8 and 1.2

6.  (i) $X = \bar{A}.\bar{B}.\bar{C} + \bar{A}.B.\bar{C} + \bar{A}.B.C + A.\bar{B}.\bar{C} + A.B.\bar{C}$
    (ii) $X = \bar{A}.B + \bar{C}$
    (iii)

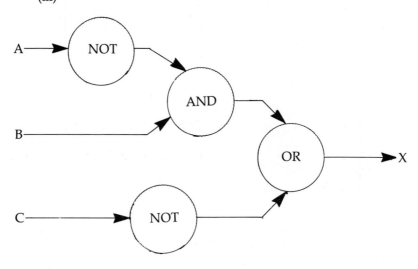

    (iv)

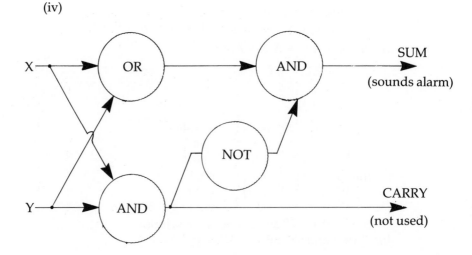

7.  (a)  (i)

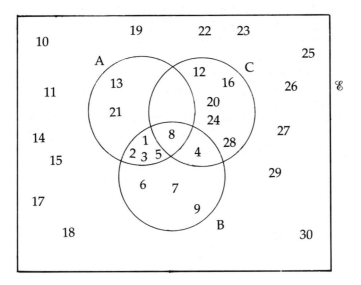

(ii)  The complement is the set of elements in the universal
      set not in the set itself.
(iii)  {10 11 14 15 17 12 16 20 24 28 18 19 22 23 25 26 27 29 30}
(iv)  If x = 8 it is TRUE.
      If x = 5 it is FALSE.

    (b)   (i) x≤3  and  x>−1
          (ii)  −1<x≤3


8.   (a)  X ≡ (A.B.C + (A + $\bar{B}$).$\bar{C}$).($\bar{A}$.$\bar{B}$) which is equivalent to X ≡
          Y.Z in which Y ≡ (A.B.C. + (A + $\bar{B}$).$\bar{C}$) and Z ≡ $\bar{A}$.$\bar{B}$

     (b)

| A | B | C | A.B.C | (A+$\bar{B}$).$\bar{C}$ | Y | Z | X |
|---|---|---|-------|-----------|---|---|---|
| 0 | 0 | 0 | 0 | 1 | 1 | 1 | 0 |
| 0 | 0 | 1 | 0 | 0 | 0 | 1 | 1 |
| 0 | 1 | 0 | 0 | 0 | 0 | 0 | 1 |
| 0 | 1 | 1 | 0 | 0 | 0 | 0 | 1 |
| 1 | 0 | 0 | 0 | 1 | 1 | 0 | 1 |
| 1 | 0 | 1 | 0 | 0 | 0 | 0 | 1 |
| 1 | 1 | 0 | 0 | 1 | 1 | 0 | 1 |
| 1 | 1 | 1 | 1 | 0 | 1 | 0 | 1 |

     (c)  Hence   X ≡ $\bar{A}$.$\bar{B}$.$\bar{C}$   ≡ (A + B + C)

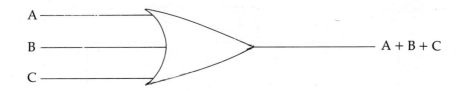

$$A + B + C$$

9.    (a)   (i)

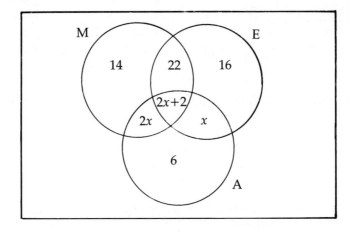

(ii)  $x = 8$, hence 18 had all three faults.

(b)    (i)  0.15
       (ii)  0.02
       (iii) 0.13

(c)

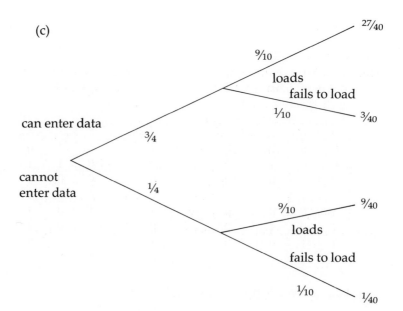

10. (a) (i)

|  | single | triplicate | adhesive |
|---|---|---|---|
| X≡ small | 8 | 5 | 1 |
| large | 18 | 12 | 2 |

(as a matrix $\begin{pmatrix} 8 & 5 & 1 \\ 18 & 12 & 2 \end{pmatrix}$)

(ii) Y≡

|  | $ |
|---|---|
| single | 3 |
| triplicate | 10 |
| adhesive | 15 |

(as column vector $\begin{pmatrix} 3 \\ 10 \\ 15 \end{pmatrix}$)

(iii) $XY = \begin{pmatrix} 8 & 5 & 1 \\ 18 & 12 & 2 \end{pmatrix} \begin{pmatrix} 3 \\ 10 \\ 15 \end{pmatrix} = \begin{pmatrix} 89 \\ 204 \end{pmatrix}$

A small pack costs $89 and a large pack is $204.

(iv) $764

(b) (i)

$$Z \equiv \begin{array}{c} s \\ t \\ a \end{array} \begin{pmatrix} 3.36 \\ 10.8 \\ 14.25 \end{pmatrix}$$

ii) $XZ = \begin{pmatrix} 8 & 5 & 1 \\ 18 & 12 & 2 \end{pmatrix} \begin{pmatrix} 3.36 \\ 10.8 \\ 14.25 \end{pmatrix} = \begin{pmatrix} 95.13 \\ 218.58 \end{pmatrix}$

(iii) $817.62

(iv) 107.0%

11. (a) See Chapter 19.
   (b) (i)   $105x + 100y = 310$
           $100x + 95y = 295$
       leads to $y = 1$ and $x = 2$
      (ii)  Substitute $x = 30$ and $y = -28.4$ into both equations – giving $A = 99.77$, within the margin of error specified for $A$; so the values do yield a correct solution.
      (iii)  The equations are ill-conditioned – the graphs are two very close lines that are almost parallel. Thus a small change in $A$ can make the point of intersection almost anywhere on $105\underline{x} + 100\underline{y} = 310$.
   (c)  Add the numbers in order of size from smallest to largest.

12. (a) (i)

| A | B | C | M |
|---|---|---|---|
| 0 | 0 | 0 | 1 |
| 0 | 0 | 1 | 0 |
| 0 | 1 | 0 | 0 |
| 0 | 1 | 1 | 0 |
| 1 | 0 | 0 | 1 |
| 1 | 0 | 1 | 1 |
| 1 | 1 | 0 | 1 |
| 1 | 1 | 1 | 1 |

(ii) $M = \bar{A}.\bar{B}.\bar{C} + A.\bar{B}.\bar{C} + A.B.\bar{C} + A.B.C$
    $= \bar{B}.\bar{C} + A.B$

(iii)

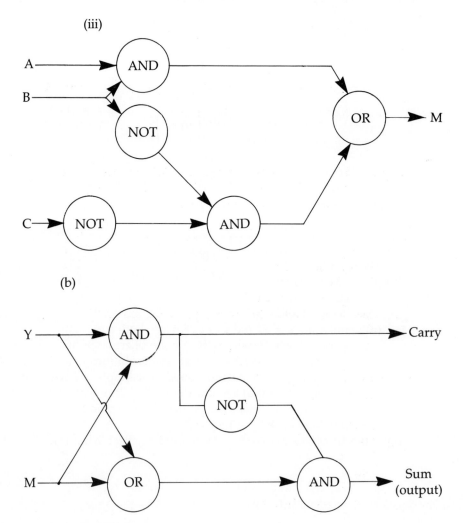

(b)

13. (a)

| A | B | C | M |
|---|---|---|---|
| 0 | 0 | 0 | 0 |
| 0 | 0 | 1 | 1 |
| 0 | 1 | 0 | 0 |
| 0 | 1 | 1 | 1 |
| 1 | 0 | 0 | 0 |
| 1 | 0 | 1 | 1 |
| 1 | 0 | 1 | 1 |
| 1 | 1 | 1 | 1 |

$M = \bar{A}.\bar{B}C + \bar{A}.B.C. + A.\bar{B}.C + A.B.\bar{C}. + A.B.C. \equiv C + A.B$

(b)

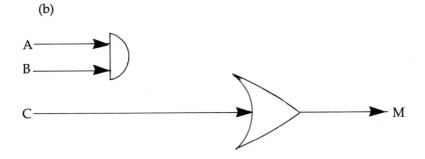

(c) Since $\bar{X}.\bar{Y} - \bar{X} + \bar{Y}$ it follows that $C + A.B. = \bar{C}.(\bar{A}.\bar{B})$

(d) E is the equivalent expression only using NAND logic; NAND is a universal (primitive) gate.

14. (a)

$$\begin{pmatrix} 6 & 10 & 4 & 10 & 8 \\ 6 & 4 & 12 & 8 & 10 \\ 4 & 10 & 4 & 8 & 8 \\ 0 & 0 & 4 & 6 & 4 \end{pmatrix}$$

(b) The breakdown of the order from manufacturer 2

(c)

$$P = \begin{pmatrix} 8.5 \\ 9 \\ 9.5 \\ 10 \\ 10.5 \end{pmatrix}$$

$$NP = \begin{pmatrix} 363 \\ 386 \\ 326 \\ 140 \end{pmatrix}$$

(d) (i) $435.55      (ii) 13%

15. (a)   (i) $x = 0.05/(1-A)$      $y = (4.95 - 5A)/(1-A)$
        (ii) The substitutions each satisfy both equations.
        (iii) The maximum relative errors in both x and y are very
              high – so the solution of the equations is totally
              unreliable.
        (iv) Ill-conditioned
    (b)   (i) The finite length of a stored number means that
              numbers can be held correct to only a fixed number of
              binary digits. When numbers are used in calculations
              that need more than this fixed number of bits, we
              have rounding or truncation. When such numbers
              appear in later calculations, the errors spread.
        (ii) (maximum absolute error true value) * 100%
        (iii) Maximum absolute error is 2e, hence maximum
              relative error is $2e/(X-Y)$* 100%.

# Index